First World War
and Army of Occupation
War Diary
France, Belgium and Germany

29 DIVISION
Divisional Troops
Divisional Signal Company
1 July 1916 - 7 September 1919

WO95/2294/1

The Naval & Military Press Ltd
www.nmarchive.com
Published in association with The National Archives

Published by

The Naval & Military Press Ltd

Unit 10 Ridgewood Industrial Park,
Uckfield, East Sussex,
TN22 5QE England
Tel: +44 (0) 1825 749494

www.naval-military-press.com

www.nmarchive.com

This diary has been reprinted in facsimile from the original. Any imperfections are inevitably reproduced and the quality may fall short of modern type and cartographic standards.

© Crown Copyright
Images reproduced by permission of The National Archives, London, England, 2015.

Contents

Document type	Place/Title	Date From	Date To
Heading	WO95/2294 29 Div Divisional Signal Coy July 1916-Sept 1919		
Heading	29th Division Divl Engineers 29th Divl Signal Coy R.E. Jly 1916-Aug 1919		
Heading	29th Divisional Signal Company R.E. July 1916		
Heading	War Diary Of 29th Divl. Signal Co. R.E. From 1st July 1916 To 31st July 1916 (Volume)		
War Diary		01/07/1916	31/07/1916
Miscellaneous	Divisional Signal Communications		
Miscellaneous	Artillery Communications.		
Diagram etc	Route Diagram 29th Divisional Signal Co July 15th		
Heading	War Diary Of 29th Divisional Signal Co R.E. (T) From 1st August 1916 To 31st August 1916 (Volume 2)		
Miscellaneous	147 Bde. H.Q. Artillery 4th July		
Heading	29th Divisional Signal Company R.E. August 1916		
Heading	War Diary Of 29th Divisional Signal Co. R.E. (T) From 1st August 1916 To 31st August 1916 (Volume 2)		
War Diary		01/08/1916	31/08/1916
Diagram etc	Route Diagram 6th Division Communications		
Miscellaneous	G.S. 29th Division	12/08/1916	12/08/1916
Diagram etc	Route Diagram 29th Divisional Signal Coy August 1st To 31st		
Heading	29th Divisional Signal Company R.E. September 1916		
Heading	War Diary Of 29th Divisional Signal Co. R.E. From 1st September 1916 To 31st Sept. 1916 (Volume 3)		
War Diary		01/09/1916	30/09/1916
Diagram etc	Route Diagram 29th Divisional Communications September 30th		
Diagram etc	Circuit Diagram 29th Divl		
Diagram etc	Divisional Communications		
Heading	29th Divisional Signal Company R.E. October 1916		
Heading	War Diary Of 29th Divisional Signal Co. R.E. T From 1st Oct. 1916 To 31st Oct 1916 (Volume 4)		
War Diary		01/10/1916	31/10/1916
Miscellaneous	Summary Of Work Done In Left Bde Area By 87th Bde Signal Section		
Diagram etc	Diagram Of Communications		
Miscellaneous	Report On Communication During Operation Of 13th October 16		
Heading	29th Divisional Engineers 29th Divisional Signal Company R.E. November 1916		
Heading	War Diary Of 29th Divisional Signal Co. R.E. From 1st November 1916 To 30th November 1916 (Volume 5)		
War Diary	Corbie	01/11/1916	14/11/1916
War Diary	Treux	15/11/1916	17/11/1916
War Diary	A 4033	18/11/1916	30/11/1916
Diagram etc	Diagram (A) Communications taken over by 29. Sig. Co		
Heading	29th Divisional Engineers 29th Divisional Signal Company R.E. December 1916		

Heading	War Diary Of 29th Divisional Signal Co. R.E. From 1st December 1916 To 31st December 1916 (Volume 6)		
War Diary		01/12/1916	31/12/1916
Diagram etc	Route Diagram 29th Signal Co. R.E. (T) 25.11.16		
Heading	War Diary Of 29th Divisional Signal Co. R.E. From 1st January 1917 To 31st January 1917 (Volume VII)		
War Diary		01/01/1917	31/01/1917
Miscellaneous	29th Div. G.	25/01/1917	25/01/1917
Miscellaneous	29th Divisional Signal R.E.	13/01/1917	13/01/1917
Diagram etc	Circuit Diagram 29th Signal Co. R.E. 30/1/17		
Diagram etc	Cavillon Area 3		
Heading	War Diary Of 29th Divisional Signal Co. R.E. From 1st February 1917 To 28th February (Volume 8)		
War Diary	Briqueterie A 4 D 5.4	01/02/1917	07/02/1917
War Diary	Heilly	08/02/1917	21/02/1917
War Diary	Arrow Head Copse	21/02/1917	28/02/1917
Diagram etc	Circuit Diagram Of Communications 29th Signal Co. R.E. 28.2.17		
Heading	War Diary Of 29th Divisional Signal Co. R.E. From 1st March 1917 To 31st March 1917 (Volume 9)		
War Diary	Arrow Head Copse	01/03/1917	31/03/1917
Heading	War Diary Of 29th (1st London) Signal Co., R.E. From 1st April, 1917 To 30th April, 1917 Volume X		
War Diary		01/04/1917	30/04/1917
Miscellaneous	Communication To And From Monchy	18/04/1917	18/04/1917
Miscellaneous	29th Division Instruction No. 4	20/04/1917	20/04/1917
Miscellaneous	86th Brigade	01/05/1917	01/05/1917
Diagram etc	Circuit Diagram 29th Signal Co. R.E. 20/4/17		
Heading	War Diary Of 29th Divisional Signal Company R.E. From 1st May 1917 To 31st May 1917 Volume II		
Heading	War Diary Of 29th Divisional Signal Co. R.E. From 1st May 1917 To 31st May 1917 (Volume II)		
War Diary		01/05/1917	31/05/1917
Miscellaneous	86th Brigade	18/05/1917	18/05/1917
Miscellaneous	86th Brigade	16/05/1917	16/05/1917
Miscellaneous	86th Brigade	19/05/1917	19/05/1917
Miscellaneous	From Lt. I.G. faurett R E	25/05/1917	25/05/1917
Diagram etc	Circuit Diagram Of Communications 29th Signal Co R.E. 17.5.17		
Miscellaneous	D		
Heading	War Diary Of 29th (1st London) Divisional Signal Co., R.E. From 1st June, 1917 To 30th June, 1917 Volume XII		
War Diary	Arras	01/06/1917	03/06/1917
War Diary	Bernaville	04/06/1917	26/06/1917
War Diary	Proven	27/06/1917	28/06/1917
War Diary	Voxvrie Fm	29/06/1917	30/06/1917
Heading	War Diary Of 29th Divisional Signal Co. R.E. From 1st July 1917 To 31st July 1917 (Volume 13)		
War Diary	Voxvrie Fm	01/07/1917	20/07/1917
War Diary	Proven	21/07/1917	31/07/1917
Miscellaneous	Work To Be Done In Order Of Urgency	27/06/1917	27/06/1917
Miscellaneous	The following work has been don while we have been in this order.	20/07/1917	20/07/1917
Miscellaneous	Connections of O.P's to "O" Exchange	19/07/1917	19/07/1917
Diagram etc	Circuit Diagram-Rt. Gap		

Diagram etc	Buried System FWD From "O" Exch.-Right Group		
Diagram etc	Buried System-Rt. Grp. Arty.		
Miscellaneous	29th Division Operations. Instruction No. 4	18/07/1917	18/07/1917
Miscellaneous	XIV Corps Instruction No. 6	02/07/1917	02/07/1917
Heading	War Diary Of 29th Divisional Signal Company R.E. From 1st August, 1917 To 31st August 1917 Volume XIV		
War Diary	Proven	01/08/1917	07/08/1917
War Diary	J Camp	08/08/1917	15/08/1917
War Diary	Zommerbloom Cabaret	15/08/1917	31/08/1917
Miscellaneous	Communication Instructions No 4 Are Cancelled And The Following Substituted	10/08/1917	10/08/1917
Miscellaneous	Communications		
Miscellaneous	29th Divisional Artillery Instructions No. 9	13/08/1917	13/08/1917
Miscellaneous		12/08/1917	12/08/1917
Diagram etc	Communications-Left Arty		
Miscellaneous	D Forward Artillery Communications On Night Of 16th	16/08/1917	16/08/1917
War Diary	War Diary Of 29th (1st London) Divl. Signal Co., R.E. From 1st September, 1917, To 30th September 1917 Volume XV		
War Diary	Proven	01/09/1917	21/09/1917
War Diary	J Camp	22/09/1917	30/09/1917
Heading	War Diary Of 29th Divisional Signal Co. R.E. From 1st Oct 1917 To 31st Oct 1917 (Volume 16)		
War Diary	J Camp	01/10/1917	02/10/1917
War Diary	Elverdinghe Chateau	03/10/1917	03/10/1917
War Diary	F.C.	04/10/1917	10/10/1917
War Diary	Proven	11/10/1917	31/10/1917
Diagram etc	Diagram Of Communications 29th Signal Co. R.E. 9.10.17		
Diagram etc	Circuit Diagram Communications 29th Div. Signal Co. R.E. 9.10.17		
Heading	War Diary Of 29th Divisional Signal Coy. R.E. Volume 17		
War Diary	Basseux	01/11/1917	17/11/1917
War Diary	Moislains	18/11/1917	18/11/1917
War Diary	Quentin Mill	19/11/1917	30/11/1917
Heading	War Diary Of 29th Divisional Signal Co R.E. 1/12/17 To 31/12/17		
War Diary		01/12/1917	31/12/1917
Heading	War Diary Of 29th Divisional Signal Company R.E. From 1.1.1918 To 31.1.1918		
War Diary	Hucqueliers	01/01/1918	03/01/1918
War Diary	Wizernes	04/01/1918	18/01/1918
War Diary	Dead End Ypres	19/01/1918	31/01/1918
Diagram etc	Circuit Diagram 29th Divisional Signal Coy. 9th Jan 18		
Diagram etc	29th Divn. & Column HQ & Brigades		
Diagram etc	29th Divn. Communications Of Brigades In Line		
Map	Wireless and Power Buzzer Communication		
Heading	War Diary Of 29th Divisional Signal Coy R.E. From 1/2/16 To 28/2/18 Volume No		
War Diary	Ypres 28/I1f8065 Canal Bank	01/02/1918	11/02/1918
War Diary	Canal Bank Ypres Steenvoorde	12/02/1918	26/02/1918
Miscellaneous	Lines-Left Divisional And Artillery VIII Corps Appendix I	31/01/1918	31/01/1918
Miscellaneous	Appendix 2		

Diagram etc	Proposed Circuits For Bde HQs At Waterloo And Kronprinz		
Miscellaneous	8th Inf Bde 88th Inf. Bde Appendix 3		
Miscellaneous	86th Inf Bde. Appendix 4	19/02/1918	19/02/1918
Miscellaneous	Caled Packets Appendix 5	00/02/1918	00/02/1918
Miscellaneous	Telegrams Appendix 6	00/02/1918	00/02/1918
Heading	War Diary Of 29th Divl Signal Co. RE From 1/3/18 To 31/3/18 Volume No		
War Diary	Steenvoorde	01/03/1918	07/03/1918
War Diary	Dead End Canal Bank Ypres	08/03/1918	19/03/1918
War Diary	Ypres (Dead End Canal Bank)	20/03/1918	31/03/1918
Miscellaneous	Summary Of Appendices		
Miscellaneous	Signal Communication-29th Division Left Sector-VIII Corps	22/03/1918	22/03/1918
Miscellaneous	War Diary (B1)		
Diagram etc	Diagram Of Circuits At Div. Report Centre. EN 13		
Diagram etc			
Diagram etc	Circuit Diagram Of Forward Communications		
Diagram etc	Diagram Of Battn. Communications		
Miscellaneous	Appendix E Summary Of Messages Dealt With-March 1918		
Miscellaneous	Appendices E Summary Of Spr for March 18		
Miscellaneous	Signal Service Despatch Rider Letter Service		
Heading	29th Divisional Engineers 29th Divisional Signal Company R.E. April 1918		
Heading	War Diary Of 29th Divisional Signal Co. RE. From 1st May 1918 To 31 May 1918 Volume No		
Heading	War Diary Of 29 Div Signal Coy From 1/4/18 To 30/4/18 Volume No		
War Diary	Ypres	01/04/1918	09/04/1918
War Diary	Les Lauriers N.W. Of Merville	10/04/1918	10/04/1918
War Diary	Les Lauriers N.W. Of Merville (about 2 1/2 Miles)	11/04/1918	11/04/1918
War Diary	La Motte	11/04/1918	11/04/1918
War Diary	Caestre	12/04/1918	13/04/1918
War Diary	St Sylvestre Cappel	14/04/1918	19/04/1918
War Diary	Hondeghem	19/04/1918	27/04/1918
War Diary	Wallon Cappel	28/04/1918	30/04/1918
Miscellaneous	Appendix A		
War Diary	Wallon-Cappel	01/05/1918	31/05/1918
Diagram etc	Circuit Diagram Of Communications 29th Divisions		
Diagram etc	Circuit Diagram Of Communications 29th Division		
War Diary	Wallon Cappel		
Heading	War Diary Of 29th Divisional Signal Coy RE From 1st To 30th June 1918 Inclusive Volume No		
War Diary	Wallon Cappel	01/06/1918	21/06/1918
War Diary	Wardrecques	22/06/1918	30/06/1918
Heading	War Diary Of 29th Divisional Signal Co. R.E. From 1/7/18 To 31/7/18 Volume No		
War Diary	Wardrecques	01/07/1918	21/07/1918
War Diary	Bavinchove	22/07/1918	31/07/1918
Heading	War Diary Of 29th Divisional Signal Coy R.E. From 1st To 31st August 1918 (Inclusive) Volume No		
War Diary	Bavinchove	01/08/1918	02/08/1918
War Diary	St Sylvestre Cappel	03/08/1918	28/08/1918
War Diary	Borre	29/08/1918	31/08/1918
Miscellaneous	Appendix A		

Heading	War Diary Of 29th Dv. Sig. Coy For September 1918 Is Missing		
Miscellaneous			
Heading	War Diary Of 29th Divisional Signal Company. R.E. From 1st Oct To 31st Oct 1918 Volume No		
War Diary	Gheluvelt	01/10/1918	03/10/1918
War Diary	Brake Camp	04/10/1918	07/10/1918
War Diary	Ramparts Ypres	08/10/1918	14/10/1918
War Diary	Becelaere	15/10/1918	15/10/1918
War Diary	Ledeghem Station	16/10/1918	21/10/1918
War Diary	Courtrai	22/10/1918	26/10/1918
War Diary	Mouveaux	27/10/1918	31/10/1918
Miscellaneous	Appendix A		
War Diary	Mouveaux	01/11/1918	07/11/1918
War Diary	Rolleghem	08/11/1918	09/11/1918
War Diary	Bossuyt Chatean	10/10/1918	10/11/1918
War Diary	Celles	10/11/1918	11/11/1918
War Diary	St Sauveur	11/11/1918	14/11/1918
War Diary	Flobecq	15/11/1918	18/11/1918
War Diary	Enghien	19/11/1918	30/11/1918
War Diary	Tubize	21/11/1918	21/11/1918
War Diary	Brain L'Alleud	23/11/1918	23/11/1918
War Diary	Ottignies	24/11/1918	24/11/1918
War Diary	Nil Abbesse	25/11/1918	26/11/1918
War Diary	Gd Rosiere	27/11/1918	27/11/1918
War Diary	Huy	28/11/1918	29/11/1918
War Diary	Anthisnes	30/11/1918	30/11/1918
Heading	29 Div Signal Co Dec 1918 Vol 30		
War Diary	Sprimont	01/12/1918	31/12/1918
War Diary	Niveze	01/12/1918	03/12/1918
War Diary	Malmedy	04/12/1918	04/12/1918
War Diary	Kalterherberg	05/12/1918	05/12/1918
War Diary	Kesternich	06/12/1918	06/12/1918
War Diary	Zulpich	07/12/1918	08/12/1918
War Diary	Hermulheim	09/12/1918	09/12/1918
War Diary	Sulz	10/12/1918	12/12/1918
War Diary	Bensberg	13/12/1918	20/12/1918
War Diary	Sand	21/12/1918	31/12/1918
Miscellaneous			
Heading	Rhine Army Southern Division Late 29th Division Divl Signal Coy R.E. Jan-Aug 1919		
Heading	War Diary Of 29th Div Signal Coy. R.E. From 1/1/19 To 31/1/19 Volume No 5		
War Diary	Sand	01/01/1919	31/01/1919
Heading	War Diary Of 29th Div Signal Coy. R.E. From 1/2/19 To 28/2/19 Volume No		
War Diary	Sand	01/02/1919	28/02/1919
Heading	War Diary Of Southern Div Signal Coy RE From 1/5/19 To 31/5/19 Volume No		
War Diary	Sand	01/05/1919	31/05/1919
Miscellaneous	Return Of Messages Registered And Special Packets Dealt With At Sand Signal Office During The Month Of May 1919		
War Diary	Sand	01/06/1919	30/06/1919
War Diary	Sand	20/06/1919	20/06/1919
War Diary	Sand	01/06/1919	30/06/1919

War Diary	Sand	01/07/1919	21/07/1919
War Diary	Sand	01/07/1919	16/07/1919
War Diary	Sand	01/08/1919	31/08/1919
War Diary	Sand	20/08/1919	23/08/1919
Miscellaneous	Sand Appendix A		
War Diary	Sand	01/09/1919	30/09/1919
War Diary	Sand	07/09/1919	07/09/1919
Miscellaneous	Sand Appendix A		

WO 95/2294
2a DIV
Divisional Signal Coy   July 1916 – Sept 1919

29TH DIVISION
DIVL ENGINEERS

29TH DIVL. SIGNAL COY R.E.
JLY 1916 —
AUG 1919

29th Division

29th DIVISIONAL SIGNAL COMPANY R. E.

J U L Y 1 9 1 6

Army Form C. 2118.

WAR DIARY
or
INTELLIGENCE SUMMARY.
(Erase heading not required.)

Confidential.

War Diary
of
29th Divl. Signal Co. R.E.

From 1st July 1916 to 31st July 1916.

(Volume I)

WAR DIARY
or
INTELLIGENCE SUMMARY.
(Erase heading not required.)

Army Form C. 2118.

Signal Coy

Place	Date	Hour	Summary of Events and Information	Remarks and references to Appendices
	1-7-16	6 a.m.	All communication established 10 p.m. the night before were again tested and everything was found to be working well - one telephone line however was found to be weak due no doubt to the length of the line and to the fact that just over a mile consisted of D3 wire with several joints. About 7.30 the exchange at Mailly and Acheux became congested and a second switchboard operator assisted with the Mailly Exchange. About the same hour there was a considerable decrease in the number of messages handed in for telegraph transmission about noon both exchanges were relieved of congestion this due to the fact that operations were more or less at a standstill. During the rear of the day telephone and telegraphic communications were only just about normal. The Dispatch Rider Service except to the Corps hardly existed until about four p.m. and the normal services were continued. Throughout the day artillery communications were excellent. One fault only was recorded and that between the Mailly Exchange and the Left.	"A" "B"

WAR DIARY
or
INTELLIGENCE SUMMARY.

Army Form C. 2118.

Place	Date	Hour	Summary of Events and Information	Remarks and references to Appendices
	1-7-16		Great R.A. This fault was due to a faulty spring in the buzzer board at the Right Group. After six minutes fault was located and rectified. The fault although slight gave me anxious as the C.R.A. most the time was giving orders to his Group Commander to shorten the barrage. The results of the day bring forward the following points. 1. Telephone and telegraph lines must be buried to a depth of at least 6 feet to ensure good communication. A few instances of lines laid in trenches that held out have come to notice. These lines were laid low down on the enemy side of the trench. Lines to battalions from brigades proved satisfactory. One battalion advancing their headquarters into no-mans land never failed to keep in touch with the Brigade, the line however was never exposed to fire as it was laid through a tunnel which opened out in no-mans land close to the battalion headquarters.	

Army Form C. 2118.

WAR DIARY
or
INTELLIGENCE SUMMARY.
(Erase heading not required.)

Instructions regarding War Diaries and Intelligence Summaries are contained in F. S. Regs., Part II. and the Staff Manual respectively. Title pages will be prepared in manuscript.

Place	Date	Hour	Summary of Events and Information	Remarks and references to Appendices
	1.7.16		Another line to a battalion headquarters in Fonmere Land was twice cut during the forty minutes that the said headquarters were there. Other battalions advanced from our own front line but returned before a line had been laid out, a considerable amount of signalling equipment was lost. For instance seven E.O.O's each with one mile of wire and a telephone and aeroplane returned with the telephone only, seven miles of new D1 wire being left behind. Battalions took forward too many telephones with their headquarters with the result that each attacking battalion lost on an average four telephones. It should never be necessary for battalions to take into action more than four instruments, the remainder should be left with the ⟨or⟩ Brigade Transport to be brought up if required to replace casualties	

WAR DIARY
or
INTELLIGENCE SUMMARY.
(Erase heading not required.)

Army Form C. 2118.

Place	Date	Hour	Summary of Events and Information	Remarks and references to Appendices
	1.7.16		2. Two reading posts were established. These posts however were not used on account of the attacking force being held up. Had progress been made they would have proved invaluable as the ground was most suitable for visual.	
			3. Dispatch Riders. Two dispatch rider posts were not used as they were only established in case other means of communication failed.	
			4. Pigeons. Prior to the attack each battalion was provided with four pigeons. These were not used for messages and I regret to report that watertight birds are missing and believed killed.	
			5. Wireless. One station was erected fifty yards from the front line. The other station was packed up ready to move forward, but did not do so. In the case of the station which erected the aerial was broken seven times during the day. In spite of this signals were exchanged hourly with the Corps Directing Set.	

WAR DIARY
or
INTELLIGENCE SUMMARY.

(Erase heading not required.)

Place	Date	Hour	Summary of Events and Information	Remarks and references to Appendices
	1.7.16		5. Contact Patrol Aeroplane. No messages were sent by H^{F} battalions or brigades to aeroplanes. Messages from aeroplanes were received by the 1st Division and transmitted by wire to 29th Div. however effected this latter division.	
			6. General: It was found that a wiretaken event to each artillery group should be established for any future of operation. One telephone for the General Staff Office exclusive of one for the G.O.C did not prove capable of meeting the demand made upon it. A second telephone therefore should be provided for the G.S. this would greatly relieve the pressure on the telephone exchanges. Messages dealt with during the day were as follows:- Telegrams: 386. Sealed Packets (Registered only) 33.	

Army Form C. 2118.

WAR DIARY
or
INTELLIGENCE SUMMARY.
(Erase heading not required.)

Place	Date	Hour	Summary of Events and Information	Remarks and references to Appendices
	27.16		Received notice that headquarters 87th Bde would move their headquarters into the 36th Div Area. Office etc was taken over complete from 10 pt Bde. Communication was established by laying a temporary line to the 36th Div Report Centre from Engelbelmer. Between Engelbelmer and Mailly an existing earth circuit was used. This line proved very unsatisfactory, buzzer signals were very weak and speech was impossible. About 4 pm in the afternoon this line was replaced by a twin D5 signals were much improved and speech was possible. During the day all other communications worked well. The following were dealt with:— Messages 398. Registered sealed packets 58.	

Army Form C. 2118.

WAR DIARY
or
INTELLIGENCE SUMMARY.
(Erase heading not required.)

Instructions regarding War Diaries and Intelligence Summaries are contained in F. S. Regs., Part II. and the Staff Manual respectively. Title pages will be prepared in manuscript.

Place	Date	Hour	Summary of Events and Information	Remarks and references to Appendices
	3.7.16		48th Division who had established their headquarters at Cafe Jourdan finally was increasing our work, this division however were under orders to move which they did about 5.30 p.m. The temporary lines they laid out from headquarters to exchange etc were not picked up, thus leaving the place in a tangle of wires. Every assistance possible from this company was given to the H.Q. of Signal Coy. No further incident occurred during the day	
			Messages dealt with	
			Telegrams 402. Registered Sealed Packets 33.	

Army Form C. 2118.

WAR DIARY
or
INTELLIGENCE SUMMARY.
(Erase heading not required.)

Place	Date	Hour	Summary of Events and Information	Remarks and references to Appendices
	4.7.16		New line laid to 87th Bde from trunk. New line laid to 87th Bde completed (distance about seven miles) this line however proved unsatisfactory as it was used and cut in numerous places shortly after it was completed. Buried line to 88th Bde in their Battle headquarters gave out. This was apparently due to faulty insulation in the multicore cable. They were given another route and communication was established after ½ hour delay. 88th Bde moved their headquarters to Englebelmer. Telegraph and telephone line to them working O.K. 10.30pm. When the brigade moved they kept the vibrator line working at the old office some five hours after they informed the division of the change of their headquarters. This matter was brought to the notice of the general staff. Messages dealt with during the day. Telegrams 437. Sealed Packets registered 54.	

Army Form C. 2118.

WAR DIARY
or
INTELLIGENCE SUMMARY.
(Erase heading not required.)

Place	Date	Hour	Summary of Events and Information	Remarks and references to Appendices
	6/1/16		Thielly taken out of our area. A new route had to be built. An existing route as far as Forceville-Thielly road was extended to the outskirts of Englebelmer where an exchange dug out was built and local circuits connected to it at 88th Brigade moved their headquarters to Vitermont. Only half an hours notice was given, consequently a telephone line as all that could be put in by the time they arrived this matter was brought to the notice of the General Staff. Messages dealt with during the day. Telegrams 394. Registered sealed Packets. 53	

Army Form C. 2118.

WAR DIARY
or
INTELLIGENCE SUMMARY.
(Erase heading not required.)

Instructions regarding War Diaries and Intelligence Summaries are contained in F. S. Regs., Part II. and the Staff Manual respectively. Title pages will be prepared in manuscript.

Place	Date	Hour	Summary of Events and Information	Remarks and references to Appendices
	6/7/16		All available men were employed on connecting local circuits to Exchange and to completing exchange dug out. At 7.30 pm work on Single Current set to 86 st and 88 st on new route. At same hour one trunk line through. Messages dealt with. Telegrams 421. Registered Sealed Packets 35.	
	7/7/16		Work continued on new Exchange and local lines. W T station from trenches with drawn at 4 pm. Both the trench sets and operators handed over to wireless VIII Corps for further training at Reserve Army Hdqrs. These wireless sets have been of little value up to date. Messages dealt with. Telegrams 357 Registered Sealed Pkts 55	

1577 Wt. W10791/1773 500,000 1/15 D. D. & L. A.D.S.S./Forms/C. 2118.

Army Form C. 2118.

WAR DIARY
or
INTELLIGENCE SUMMARY.
(Erase heading not required.)

Instructions regarding War Diaries and Intelligence Summaries are contained in F. S. Regs., Part II. and the Staff Manual respectively. Title pages will be prepared in manuscript.

Place	Date	Hour	Summary of Events and Information	Remarks and references to Appendices
	8/7/16		Bad contact on circuit to VIII Corps lineman constantly on the fault but unable to locate. 87th Bde moved to Achurge and are connected by telephone only. 86th Bde opened up a new office at Mesnil at 8.15 pm through on telephone and Fullerphone signals good. Messages dealt with. Telegrams 321	Registered Sealed Pkts. 32
	9/7/16		Sounder Set working to 86th Bde gives trouble fault due to instruments faulty instruments substituted temporarily for D3. During the day several faults occurred and were found to be in nearly every case due to slack legs. Messages dealt with. Telegram 308	Registered Sealed Pkts. 25

WAR DIARY
or
INTELLIGENCE SUMMARY.

Army Form C. 2118.

Place	Date	Hour	Summary of Events and Information	Remarks and references to Appendices
	10.7.16		Charles Avenue cleared of telephone wires by a working party. This work was no means of satisfactory for every wire was tampered with and to make a satisfactory job every wire was tampered with two actually wanting to batteries. This necessitated the temporary cutting off of the batteries from their OP's. These two lines being the only ones in use. Another officer's fatig[ue] cleared Jacob's Ladder trench and the vicinity. Wire recovered was of very little value - certain portion however can be used again. A discrepancy of two minutes in the daily time During the course of the day trouble was experienced with the fullephon circuit working to Shothole fault due entirely to bad adjustment and a damaged fuller arrest Messages dealt with- Telegrams 268 Registered Sealed Plots 28	

WAR DIARY
or
INTELLIGENCE SUMMARY.

Army Form C. 2118.

Place	Date	Hour	Summary of Events and Information	Remarks and references to Appendices
	11/7/16		Naval party of one officer and seven men cleared trenches of mine in the 8th Bn area than went to Englebelmer fatigued and stayed in several places D5 used for stays no stay were obtainable.	
			Messages dealt with — Sealed Pkts (Registered)	
			962 — 25	
	12/7/16		Party sent out to replace cable between Englebelmer Exchange and 109th Divnl report centre with airline (enemic) distance about 2000 yards time taken 10 hours	
			Messages dealt with — Registered SPs	
			240 — 24	
	13/7/16		Civilian farmer cart laden with hay breaks 4 lines on main trunk route to Englebelmer. French mission informed and asked to stake along to prevent the re-occurence.	
			86th Brigade move headqrs to Archie Corner. An existing phone pair is used & a D3 earth return is laid out from Englebelmer for S.C. Sgt. after replacing a faulty pair of cable	

WAR DIARY or INTELLIGENCE SUMMARY

Army Form C. 2118.

Place	Date	Hour	Summary of Events and Information	Remarks and references to Appendices
	14.7.16		everything works satisfactorily. The usual trench clearing party of an officer and 7 O.R. continue to remove a large amount of derelict wire. Message dealt with 278. Registered SPs 44. 3 Light Draught, 3 Riders and 1 Pack horse arrive to complete establishment. L.D. are too heavy to stand to call for cable wagon work. The horses have been brought up for cable wagon work. The 2 trench W.T. sets with operators return from notice before. Reserve Army. One set erected under a semi permanent aerial. This station to receive press news & men construct their own coil. One message sent daily to Corps H'drs Set + acknowledged. F.O.C. instructs that all wires (derelict + badly laid) in use trenches to be cut + relaid at Artillery of lines a source of great trouble. Their units lay lines indiscriminately & without obtaining the necessary authority from the area officer. Usual maintenance of lines + clearing of trenches. Message dealt with 268. Registered SPs 28.	

WAR DIARY
or
INTELLIGENCE SUMMARY.
(Erase heading not required.)

Army Form C. 2118.

Place	Date	Hour	Summary of Events and Information	Remarks and references to Appendices
	15.7.16		Usual maintenance of lines. Usual parties proceeded to the trenches to recover derelict wire. Message dealt with 237	Reg^n. lied SP's 34
	16.7.16		Usual maintenance of lines. No trench clearing parties sent out. Lt Smith S.E. reports for duty, no warning having been received. Message dealt with 345	Reg^n. lied SP's 135
	17.7.16		Two parties sent out to clear wire. Lt Fawcett + party reel up a metallic line from the rail Station to Passuelle de Magenta via Eveley Road. ADAS 8th Corps orders Lt Braswell to report 12th Div. Lph Bolton + Pearce reduced to the ranks as being unfitted for their duties in the field. Message dealt with 319	Reg^n. lied SP's 53

WAR DIARY
or
INTELLIGENCE SUMMARY.

Place	Date	Hour	Summary of Events and Information	Remarks and references to Appendices
	18-7-16		Lt Pranell proceeds to join 12th Divn on Lt Pook joins 38th Divn. Lt Pries from Hare to No 3 Section vice Lt Pook. A daily test went for each as all lines commenced. All lines previously tested each morning but no record kept.	
	19-7-16		Messages dealt with 313. Registered SPs 28. A crew twice commenced from Englebelmer to 86th Brigade to replace a poled cable line. The new route takes a wider sweep to avoid shelled area. Pole to carry 5 pr. obtained from 28th Airline Section & prepared with X arms. Bow & stay wire also obtained from Airline Section. Stay wire has been asked for but not given; consequently D 5 has to be used which is scarcely wakeful. Test 86th Brigade + forward area with ADAS 8th Corps, new area taken over from 10th Corps unsatisfactory. Messages dealt with 227. Reg'd SPs 25.	38th

Army Form C. 2118.

WAR DIARY
or
INTELLIGENCE SUMMARY.
(Erase heading not required.)

Instructions regarding War Diaries and Intelligence Summaries are contained in F. S. Regs., Part II. and the Staff Manual respectively. Title pages will be prepared in manuscript.

Place	Date	Hour	Summary of Events and Information	Remarks and references to Appendices
	20-7-16		New 10 line route from Englebelmer to F. Dug out commenced. Comic pair from Englebelmer by to 86th Brigade completed. This line about 2100 yds took 6 men 14 hrs to build. No operator report hearing faint clearly a conversation in his receiver. This is reported to O/C wireless 8th Corps. Message dealt with 215. Regrated SPs 38	
	21-7-16		Signals 8th Corps undertake to extend civil train line to new position. This unit situated in Corps Signal Area. Both entrained on new 10 line route. 87th Bde H'qrs move at 2 pm. Message notifying move received at 1.54 pm. Bde section entered telephone pair + wounden line temporarily. Distance moved about 500 yds and only then notice given. A telephone exchange operators arrive to complete establishment. No alternative however in existing personnel on exchange. Message dealt with 276. Regrated SPs 29	

WAR DIARY or INTELLIGENCE SUMMARY

Army Form C. 2118.

Place	Date	Hour	Summary of Events and Information	Remarks and references to Appendices
	22.7.16		New entrance from Eng. debelour completed. All lines working well. Speech greatly improved. Receive orders though A.D.A.S. to commence handing over to deli Sgnals 25th Division. All diagrams at units up to date. Labelling in places not completed. RA run on lines for order St Andrews to stay behind. Attend conference at A.D.A.S's. Arrangements dealt with 291. Reg. letters S.P's. 44.	
	23.7.16		Switchboard changed at 4.30 a.m. Inspect Divis. Capt. Impson + self spend all morning with relieving officers. Left Japon as 2nd in Command of greatest value for handing over lines. A + B section parade on Completh turn out. Certain small deficiencies noted. Arrangements dealt with 228. Registered S.P's 38	
	24.7.16		25th Divnl. do not take over as arranged, but Brigade head qrs. are taken over. Each Brigade section have 1 NCO + 4 linesmen with relieving Brigade for 24 hrs. to difficulties. Lines being kept up - Arrangements dealt with 383. Registered S.P's 51	

Army Form C. 2118.

WAR DIARY
or
INTELLIGENCE SUMMARY.
(Erase heading not required.)

Instructions regarding War Diaries and Intelligence Summaries are contained in F. S. Regs., Part II. and the Staff Manual respectively. Title pages will be prepared in manuscript.

Place	Date	Hour	Summary of Events and Information	Remarks and references to Appendices
	25.7.16		Major & Col Liston move to Beauval. Departure delayed 18 mins due to lack of moving from place to place. Captain Simpson proceeds in advance in car to fix up new office & arrange billets	
	26.7.16	9am	Office closes. New office opens up at Beauval. C.S. to prove to exchange, all other communications by D.R. It seemed moves to new Area to arrange billets. Captain Simpson proceeds to new area to take over from 6th Division. Reserve movement order and fed Signal Coy to army. The last units to move to new Area. Suggest Signal Coy should always move first to new area especially when it is only necessary to leave 5 men to run office.	
	27.7.16	9pm	Office closes down. Company parades 9.30. am marches to Souillans to entrain. B.C. Signals proceeds by car to new area to see O.C. Signals 6th Div.	

1577 Wt. W10791/1773 500,000 1/15 D. D. & L. A.D.S.S./Forms/C. 2118.

Army Form C. 2118.

WAR DIARY
or
INTELLIGENCE SUMMARY.
(Erase heading not required.)

Instructions regarding War Diaries and Intelligence Summaries are contained in F.S. Regs., Part II and the Staff Manual respectively. Title pages will be prepared in manuscript.

Place	Date	Hour	Summary of Events and Information	Remarks and references to Appendices
	28.7.16		S.O.'s arrive by road, & then are distributed to G.S. & Q. who resume communication but Coy does not arrive until 6.30 p.m. A Section proceed direct to 115 R to take over & learn lines in vicinity of this. Returned but Report trunk telephone to Corps & other Bdes. offices 7pm. Local to Q, no other communications. Difficulty in delivering owing to S.O. not knowing country & having to large scale maps. Also Staff	
		10pm	split up. 86th & 87th Bdes. had exchanged & was in touch by phone.	
	29.7.16		To round new area + pst in touch with route etc.	
	30.7.16			
	31.7.16		Lent advance parties to Bn HQrs to work in new offices preparatory to taking over.	

B. Little Capt.
O/C Signals 29th Division
1-8-16.

DIVISIONAL SIGNAL COMMUNICATIONS.

During the forthcoming operations the following systems of communications will be employed.

(a) Telephone.
(b) Telegraph.
(c) Visual.
(d) Despatch Riders.
(e) Pigeons.
(f) Wireless.
(g) Contact Patrol Aeroplanes.
(h) Kite Balloons.

General arrangements in detail.

(a) **Telephone circuits.**

(1) Each Infantry Brigade in its forward battle headquarters will be connected to an advanced exchange in MAILLY WOOD. In addition the 86th Brigade will be in direct touch with a Divisional O.P. at Q.2.b.6.9 and the 88th Brigade in direct touch with another Divisional O.P. at Q.23.a.2.4. Further each of the above named Brigades will have direct lines to the Brigades of 4th and 36th Divisions respectively. The 86th and 87th Brigades will be in direct communication.

(2) Observation posts at Q.2.b.6.9 and Q.23.a.2.4 are both connected direct to the MAILLY WOOD Exchange as well as to the Left and Right Artillery Group Exchanges (C.R.A. communications) communication also exists as per (1).
   The Cyclist O.P. at Q.9.d.1.9 will be connected direct to MAILLY WOOD Exchange.

(3) Divisional Dump situated at Q.9.c.5.4 will be connected to MAILLY WOOD Exchange.

(4) Telephone exchanges are established at MAILLY WOOD, ACHEUX Signal Office and ACHEUX Chateau. There are three trunk lines between the first two named exchanges; one of these trunks is for the exclusive use of the C.R.A. A direct trunk runs from MAILLY WOOD Exchange to ACHEUX Chateau. The Chateau Exchange is for emergency only, and independant of the ACHEUX Exchange. From both ACHEUX and the Chateau Exchanges the following calls may be effected - 4th Division, 36th Division, VIIIth Corps, Fourth Army and BELLE EGLISE.

(5) The Main Divisional Report Centre will be at Q.8.d.45.05. Subsidiary Report Centres will be at Q.19.b.1.3 and Q.14.d.95.25. From these report centres it will be possible to send written messages only.

(b) **Telegraph Circuits.**

In addition to the telephone line, each Infantry Brigade will be connected direct by telegraph from its battle headquarters to Divisional Headquarters. A telegraph circuit will also work direct to VIIIth Corps from Divisional Headquarters. There will be no other telegraphic communications.

(c) Visual reading stations will be established at the Northern (Q.2.b.6.9.) and Southern (Q.23.a.2.4.) Divisional O.P.'s. These stations can receive, but cannot send or acknowledge. Battalion and Company signallers, also F.O.O.'s can send back messages to these stations, which when received will be sent by wire to their destination. Sending and receiving stations will be established at the Main Divisional Report Centre (Q.8.d.45.05) and near the Cafe Jourdain, MAILLY (P.12.d.2.7.). Both these stations will work to a sending and receiving station at ACHEUX WOOD (P.15.a.1.1)

- 2 -

(d) Dispatch Riders.

Motor Cyclist Dispatch Rider posts will be established at AUCHONVILLERS Station (Q.8.b.5.0) and at the Subsidiary Report Centre (Q.19.b.1.3). These Motor Cyclists will convey messages back to the ACHEUX Signal Office.

(e) Pigeons.

Each Brigade will be issued with six baskets of pigeons, each basket containing two birds. Baskets will be issued to Battalions by Brigades as required.
Each Brigade will detail ten men to work the Pigeon Service. Pigeons must be used sparingly and not liberated except in daylight. Empty baskets should be returned immediately to AUCHONVILLERS Railway Station (Q.8.b.5.0), where they will be refilled, and the full baskets returned by bearers to his units.

(f) Wireless.

A Parent Trench Wireless Set with a range of 2½ miles will be installed in the trenches about 87th Brigade Battle Headquarters (Q.16.a.9.9). This set will work to the Corps Directing Set at COLINCAMPS. Attention is drawn to "Notes on employment of wireless" and to "Code for short range wireless during operations". A spare Trench Set will be stationed at Q.16.a.9.9 and will accompany 28th Brigade Headquarters when they advance. This set will work to the Corps Directing Set, and to the Parent Set at Q.16.a.9.9.

(g) Contact Patrol Aeroplanes.

Two aeroplanes will be employed continuously as Contact Patrols. Signals to them by means of lamp and flares will be made in accordance with the arrangements practised.

(h) Kite Balloons.

Signals to Kite Balloons will be made by lamp, but this method of communication should only be resorted to when other means fail.

(j) Stores.

A certain amount of Signal Stores will be dumped close to MAILLY Exchange. These stores will consist of cable, telephones and hop poles. The quantity of stores however is very limited and demands will only be met for pressing requirements.

(k) Burying Cables.

All lines both telephone and telegraph have been buried in trenches about six feet deep. Test dug-outs have been made at certain points. Information just received from YPRES shows that cable buried six feet deep has given good results.

ARTILLERY COMMUNICATIONS.

C.R.A. C.R.A. has communication with :-

(1) ACHEUX Exchange.
(2) G.S. direct.
(3) MAILLY Exchange (direct) - for Group Headquarters.

GROUP HEADQUARTERS. Normal Headquarters are connected direct to MAILLY Exchange.

(a) Left Group - Left Group battle headquarters exchange is alongside the Main Divisional Report Centre (Q.8.d.45.05). To this exchange are connected :-

1. Left Group Battle Headquarters.
2. Left Group Normal Headquarters.
3. C.R.A. via MAILLY Exchange.
4. Batteries of the Group.
5. Group O.P.'s at K.33.d.20.80 and Q.10.a.80.20.
6. 86th Infantry Brigade Battle Headquarters (Advanced)
7. All battery O.P.'s.
8. 4th Division Right Group Exchange.
9. Right Group Exchange (4 lines)
10. Two lines forward to advanced left Brigade Headquarters (86th Brigade Battle Headquarters) to be used by the four batteries advancing into "No Man's Land" and STATION Road. These lines connect back to Group Commanders.
11. Visual O.P. in Cemetry, AUCHONVILLERS.
12. Divisional O.P. at Q.2.b.6.9.

(b) Right Group forward exchange is at Q.22.c.50.70.
To it are connected :-

1. C.R.A. via MAILLY Exchange.
2. Batteries of the group including two 48th Division Batteries.
3. Group Headquarters.
4. Group O.P. at Q.22.d.90.50.
5. Right Infantry Brigade Headquarters (87th Brigade Battle Headquarters.)
6. 36th Division "Centre" Group Exchange.
7. Left Group Exchange.
8. Battery O.P.'s.
9. Divisional O.P.' at Q.23.a.20.40.

All lines forward from MAILLY Exchange are buried in trenches six feet deep.

Divisional visual station back to ACHEUX is within a few yards of the Main Divisional Report Centre and of the Left Group Exchange.

The Dispatch Rider assembly point is at AUCHONVILLERS Station some 500 yards North of the Divisional Report Centre.

Visual in Groups.

Whenever it is possible to get visual between Batteries and Group Exchanges without a transmitting station, this has been done.

All batteries have visual between O.P. and battery.

Visual messages from F.O.O.'s will be picked up and transmitted not only by the Left Group Observation Post, but also by the Divisional Visual Stations at the Northern (Q.2.b.6.9.) and Southern (Q.23.a.2.4.) Divisional O.P.'s.

Criticisms on Communications

"B"

(i) "General scheme of connecting up."
The method employed during the past operations has been highly satisfactory. No faults of any kind whatsoever could be found. There was a certain amount of "overhearing," but this was to be expected & it did not interfere to any extent with communications.

(ii) "Exchange Working":
The "Field Exchange" worked well. The plugs & leads were the only trouble. These were continually breaking. This, I think, is largely due to the fact that the leads are made of copper wire in small strands. These strands frayed where they joined the plug. The result of this was, that, if the lead did not actually break, a short-circuit was set up with the result that no sound passed through the instrument receiver.

The D III instruments are getting worn out. So much so, that different receivers must be held in different positions to enable a conversation to be carried on. This is highly inconvenient as everyone cannot be taught the exact way to work his particular instrument. Many of the 15th instruments now circulating between brigades & Signals H.Q. are old "Gallipoli" instruments &, as such, have seen a great deal of use. If I might, I should like to suggest that, at the earliest opportunity, new instruments should be issued in place of the old.

III "Visual arrangements." No opportunity of visual signalling back to O.P's from the F.O.Os, presented itself. We had no reading station to which we could have sent back messages from O.Ps. if the wires had broken. I refer to messages to D.A.

IV But for these few points, communication were excellent. Batteries had no difficulty in communicating with O.Ps.. O.Ps. had no difficulty in communicating with the central O.P. The D.A., except on two occasions, were in touch with us although rather faintly at times.

T. C. Ratty 2/L.

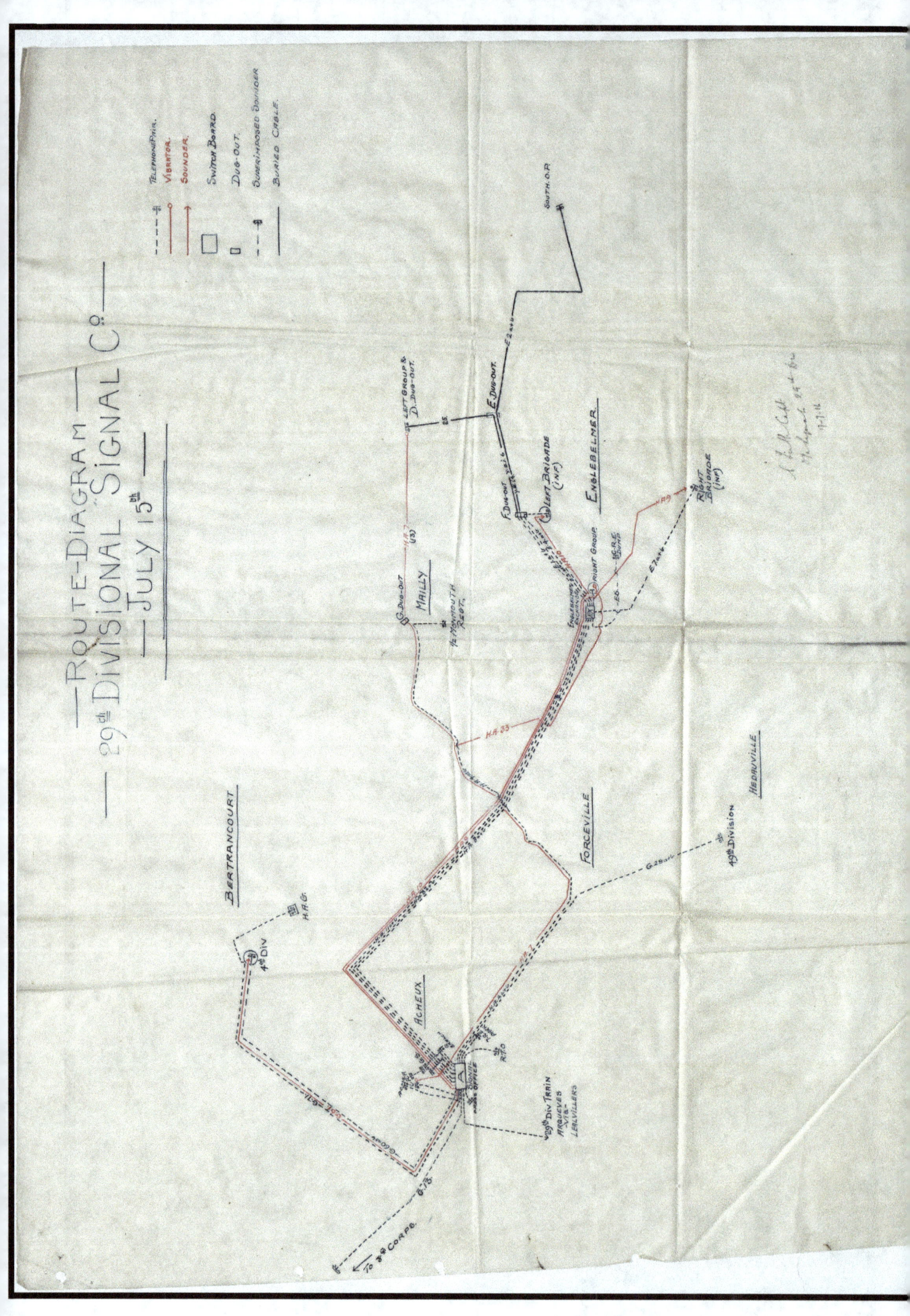

Army Form C. 2118.

WAR DIARY
or
INTELLIGENCE SUMMARY.

(Erase heading not required.)

Vol 2

Confidential.

War Diary
of
29th Divisional Signal Co. R.E. (T)
From 1st August 1916 to 31st August 1916.

(Volume 2.)

147 Bde. H.Q. Hdqrs.

4th July.

Dear Hodgson,

As I was at the Roma Road O.P. for three days and two nights of the "strafe", I am afraid I cannot give you much in the way of criticism.
There is one hitch in the working of the Exchange — if a Battery is in communication with its O.P. via the Exchange (such as L. 97th), you cannot speak to the B.C. without cutting the [...] from the O.P. On several occasions it was necessary to send a message to one of these Batteries while firing in conjunction with the O.P. — if in these cases, a separate line for Battery to Group could be connected up it would be a decided advantage.
The Chatham Street line was badly cut about during Z day — it is quite evident that if a forward O.P. is to be used during such a battle, the line should be dug in all the way.
Apparently most of the D₃ wire for lines in France is not _____

in the trenches. I imagine therefore that in most cases the liaison officer would not succeed in establishing telephonic communication, and since the dawn would have been of much value had the objective been gained. Was any provision made for visual signalling at night? I saw the 42d troops leaving the "Quadrilateral" on the night signalling with a small lamp — a code was being used.

Do you think that the exchange was possibly understaffed for busy hours? I suppose more than 1400 could not work the switchboard if they sign with names.

The whole system of communication seems to have proved very successful, thanks to your unceasing labour.

W.J. Norwood Lt.

29th Division.

29th DIVISIONAL SIGNAL COMPANY R. E.

AUGUST 1 9 1 6

Army Form C. 2118.

WAR DIARY
or
INTELLIGENCE SUMMARY.

(Erase heading not required.)

Vol 2

Confidential.

War Diary
of
29th Divisional Signal Co. R.E.(T)

From 1st August 1916 to 31st August 1916.

(Volume 2.)

WAR DIARY
or
INTELLIGENCE SUMMARY.
(Erase heading not required.)

Army Form C. 2118.

Place	Date	Hour	Summary of Events and Information	Remarks and references to Appendices
	1.5.16	10am	Took over hut offices from 6th Division Lines to the Brigades holding front line both faulty. Test circuit out shows high earth reading. Large amount of works on bounds sets due to always of division. Route diagram of lines as taken over attached. Mirages dealt with 338.	(A)
		5pm	Regd SP's 66.	
	2.5.16		Linemen employed as keeping lines out enfiladed. Complaints from the following have been received — Lon. Hosp. Ypres. Asylum (Hospital showing station). 88th Field Ambulance. West Riding Field Coy. & A.P.M. This is due to lack of instruments having to supply 29th I.A. (left behind) and 20th I.A. (evening div. front.) for main circuit left both 29th DA Lico with 20th DA & 2 machine casualties cause this extra work. Setting up the Electric light takes Offices + 2 hrs work but not yet complete. Mirages dealt with 299. Regd SP's 24	

1577 Wt. W10791/1773 500,000 1/15 D. D. & L.   A.D.S.S./Forms/C. 2118.

Army Form C. 2118.

WAR DIARY
or
INTELLIGENCE SUMMARY.
(Erase heading not required.)

Instructions regarding War Diaries and Intelligence Summaries are contained in F. S. Regs., Part II. and the Staff Manual respectively. Title pages will be prepared in manuscript.

Place	Date	Hour	Summary of Events and Information	Remarks and references to Appendices
	3/8/16		A 30 line in bad condition, working party sent out to replace portions of it with DE also to stay & finally make good the line. Electric light now fitted up complete. Q Branch require telephones installed at 3rd french store and attack brigade transport camp. No telephones for this purpose no referred to G.S. B.dr Sigs take on the payment of the hired features attached. This greatly relieves the work. Message dealt with - 272. Registered SPs - 13	
	4.8.16.		Telephone installed in G.O.C.'s private rooms also in A.P.M's office. Work in A 30 continued. Visit lines of the right brigade. Lines only buried about 1 foot consequently not satisfactory. Attend conference at 8th Corps. Buried scheme discussed. Messages dealt with 273 Registered SPs 24	

Army Form C. 2118.

WAR DIARY
or
INTELLIGENCE SUMMARY.
(Erase heading not required.)

Instructions regarding War Diaries and Intelligence Summaries are contained in F. S. Regs., Part II. and the Staff Manual respectively. Title pages will be prepared in manuscript.

Place	Date	Hour	Summary of Events and Information	Remarks and references to Appendices
	5-8-16		Usual maintenance & patrolling of lines. Message dealt with 320. Reported SPs 22.	
	6-8-16		A.S.A.S. Corps taken over the back portion of the divisional area as far as construction & maintenance of lines is concerned. The scheme greatly relieves the pressure of work on this Coy. Message dealt with 213. Reported SPs 17.	
	7-8-16		Survey new route from here to advanced hqrs. to be by inde take construction. Message dealt with 256. Reported SPs 27.	

Army Form C. 2118.

WAR DIARY
or
INTELLIGENCE SUMMARY.
(Erase heading not required.)

Instructions regarding War Diaries and Intelligence Summaries are contained in F. S. Regs., Part II. and the Staff Manual respectively. Title pages will be prepared in manuscript.

Place	Date	Hour	Summary of Events and Information	Remarks and references to Appendices
	8.8.16		Proceeded to site trenches for trench scheme. Ground very difficult & in places water logged.	
		10.05pm	Step being discharged & messages dispatched at once by wire & by S.R. C at about 11pm while still under pressure of work tops went on accepting & delivering two priority telegrams. Each case the addresses was only about ½ mile further from tops than from hx. Shortage of S.Rs only 5 available at hqrs - 4 men each in area. No reinforcements yet received to replace casualties of July 1st 1916 -	
			Messages dis:d with - 276	
			Replied O.P.s - 37	

1577 Wt.W10791/1773 500,000 1/15 D. D. & L. A.D.S.S./Forms/C. 2118.

WAR DIARY
or
INTELLIGENCE SUMMARY.

(Erase heading not required.)

Army Form C. 2118.

Place	Date	Hour	Summary of Events and Information	Remarks and references to Appendices
	9-8-16		Applied this A branch for reinforcements. Signal dept has note of 1 noto cyclist. G.S. provide 6 men for orderly work to replace trained men. Available men employed on improving lines. One Brigade relief to 2 section. 3 section employed on clearing up the forward area.	
	10-8-16		In the line. Message dealt with 344. Registered S.P.O. 27. One 20 pioneers sent to Army school (signal) for training as a lineman. Usual maintenance & improving of lines. Message dealt with 305. Registered S.P.O. 28.	
	11-8-16		1 bttn battalion placed at disposal of signals to dig trenches for the cups buried scheme. Necessary arrangements made for work the next night. Message dealt with 318. Registered S.P.O. 38.	

WAR DIARY or INTELLIGENCE SUMMARY

Army Form C. 2118.

Place	Date	Hour	Summary of Events and Information	Remarks and references to Appendices
	12.5.16		G.S. asked to regulate the despatch of "special" D.R's. Unauthorised people such as Staff Captains, Intelligence officers fine direct orders for message to be sent by D.R. in contravention of F.S.R. & G.R.O's. 14th Welsh Regt. about 320 strong commence digging trenches for cable.	B
	13.8.16		Message dealt with 299. Registered S.Ps. 40. Four men sent to 8th Corps Visual school for training in Visual. Corps W.T. officer installs an amplifier in dug out. Other instrument allotted by Corps are. Scanning buzzers & earth induction & power buzzer set. Suitable places selected & submit to S.S. for approval. Approval given as per attached.	

WAR DIARY or INTELLIGENCE SUMMARY

Army Form C. 2118.

Place	Date	Hour	Summary of Events and Information	Remarks and references to Appendices
	4.8.16		Party 350 strong continue to dig cable trench. 715 pairs were laid in trench. One 300' long cable was laid in 3 ropes each rope 5 pairs. Two to lay 5 pair rope 25 min. This should improve with practise. Trench could not be filled in as working party had to leave to catch the train. Some 15 men of Coy laid the cable. There men were assisted by armed Coy H.Q. hurryposhall with 248 Regiment SP. 42. Line repaired by working party which was broken by a farmer cart laden with crops. Wire picked up since arrival in area 26 mls. 29.6. 2nd Army pack, the Coy line laid in all trenches dug. Total completed 600 yds. Working party reduced to 181 men. Application made for a large party. Message dealt with 241. Regulated SPs. 56	

1577 Wt.W10791/1773 500,000 1/15 D.D. & L. A.D.S.S./Forms/C. 2118.

Army Form C. 2118.

WAR DIARY
or
INTELLIGENCE SUMMARY.
(Erase heading not required.)

Place	Date	Hour	Summary of Events and Information	Remarks and references to Appendices
	15.8.16		Frontage of trench from the nose daily increase so first sample of arches in position. Working party to A.O.M.S. Working party on twice to dig trench. Arrival completed 190 yards trench overhall taken back to a H.G. Emplacement and an artillery O.P. The cases coming now to height concerned to section in two telephones as covered to battalion Hqs and to batteries (a second. Let down to gallery owing to large amount of fall moisture message hall with 321. Reported G.P.c 32	
	16.8.16		Two eiwes lines stayed & informed generally but commenced on tunnel shafting for lower than to send labour & material message sent with 296. Replied G.P.c 36	

WAR DIARY or INTELLIGENCE SUMMARY

Army Form C. 2118.

(Erase heading not required.)

Place	Date	Hour	Summary of Events and Information	Remarks and references to Appendices
	17-8-16		Usual patrolling & maintenance of wire. No active shelling but enemy buried during night. Message sheet with 440. Reynwid Sos. 33	
	18-8-16		Usual patrolling & maintenance of wire. Enemy's trenches increased to 600, and trenched program made. Packed (Reg inked) containing 500 trans held by S.R. Message dispatched 304. Reynwid Sos. 32	
	19-8-16		Owing to use of telephone forward of Bn. H.Q. halts having an enemy to-day stab. French digging party retired to 200 supposedly experienced in crossing the far road. No change in enemy. Message dispatched with 383. Reynwid Sos. 32	

WAR DIARY
or
INTELLIGENCE SUMMARY.
(Erase heading not required.)

Army Form C. 2118.

Place	Date	Hour	Summary of Events and Information	Remarks and references to Appendices
	20.8.16		Audit closed. Return forms collected once August sent into G.S. The Siemens 68 miles out sandbags of earth. Reserve tele section collected on an average 5 miles per day. Party of 200 continue to dig in cable trench in spite of inclement weather. Average beat with 400 Registered SPs — 29	
	21.8.16		Difficult to proceed as trenches have made work on cable trench hampered. Issued 2 receiving buzzers to each brigade holding front line. Average beat with 398 Registered SPs 33	
	22.8.16		Owing to different rest being detailed to work on cable trench very little progress was made. Average dealt with 365 Registered SPs 34	

WAR DIARY
or
INTELLIGENCE SUMMARY.

(Erase heading not required.)

Army Form C. 2118.

Place	Date	Hour	Summary of Events and Information	Remarks and references to Appendices
	23.8.16		Usual maintenance & patrolling of lines. Work carried on cable trenches. Tonnage dealt with 411.	Reg'd. tel. S.P.'s 39
	24.8.16		Usual maintenance & patrolling of lines. Work continued on cable trenches. Tonnage dealt with 445.	Reg'd. tel. S.P's 34
	25.8.16		Usual maintenance & patrolling of lines. Work continued on cable trenches. Tonnage dealt with 398.	Reg'd. tel. S.P's 38
	26.8.16		Lines "worked" contact during the day. The high wind & dust haring on men permanent route to advanced Hd Qrs. tee 800 men on cable trenches. Tonnage dealt with 374.	Reg'd. tel. S.P's 36

WAR DIARY
or
INTELLIGENCE SUMMARY.
(Erase heading not required.)

Place	Date	Hour	Summary of Events and Information	Remarks and references to Appendices
	27.8.16		Usual patrolling & maintenance of lines. Reinforcements arrived consisting of 3 motor cyclists & other linesmen & 8 Colonial pioneers. No work done on cable trunks. Through check with 364. Registered SP's 44	
	28.8.16		Usual patrolling & maintenance of lines. Very little work done on cable trunks. Through dial test 368. Registered SP's 44. Total SP's for 24 hrs 516.	
	29.8.16		Usual patrolling & maintenance of lines. No work on cable trunks owing to probable discharge of gas. Through dial test with 372. Reg. & line'd SPs: 37	
	30.8.16		Construction party made constructional alterations outside office. Two terminal poles substituted for the two existing ones. Heavy rain causes faults on all lines.	

Place	Date	Hour	Summary of Events and Information	Remarks and references to Appendices

3.9.16

Line trying to test line being installed evidently YD + time take to clear fault. In trying every such as the test boxes on N Kelo found that are useless, they fill up with water causing a complete short. The test boxes being probably abolished but cause contact in low wires also trenches after cause intermittent earthing.

Message dealt with 396 Registered SPs 50

To change of circuit. Total amount of circuit & unused time received up during month 85 miles. Message dealt with 447 Registered SPs 27

Route diagram 1st — 3rd attached

G. St. K. Capt.
O.C. Reynolds 29th Div

31-8-16.

"C"

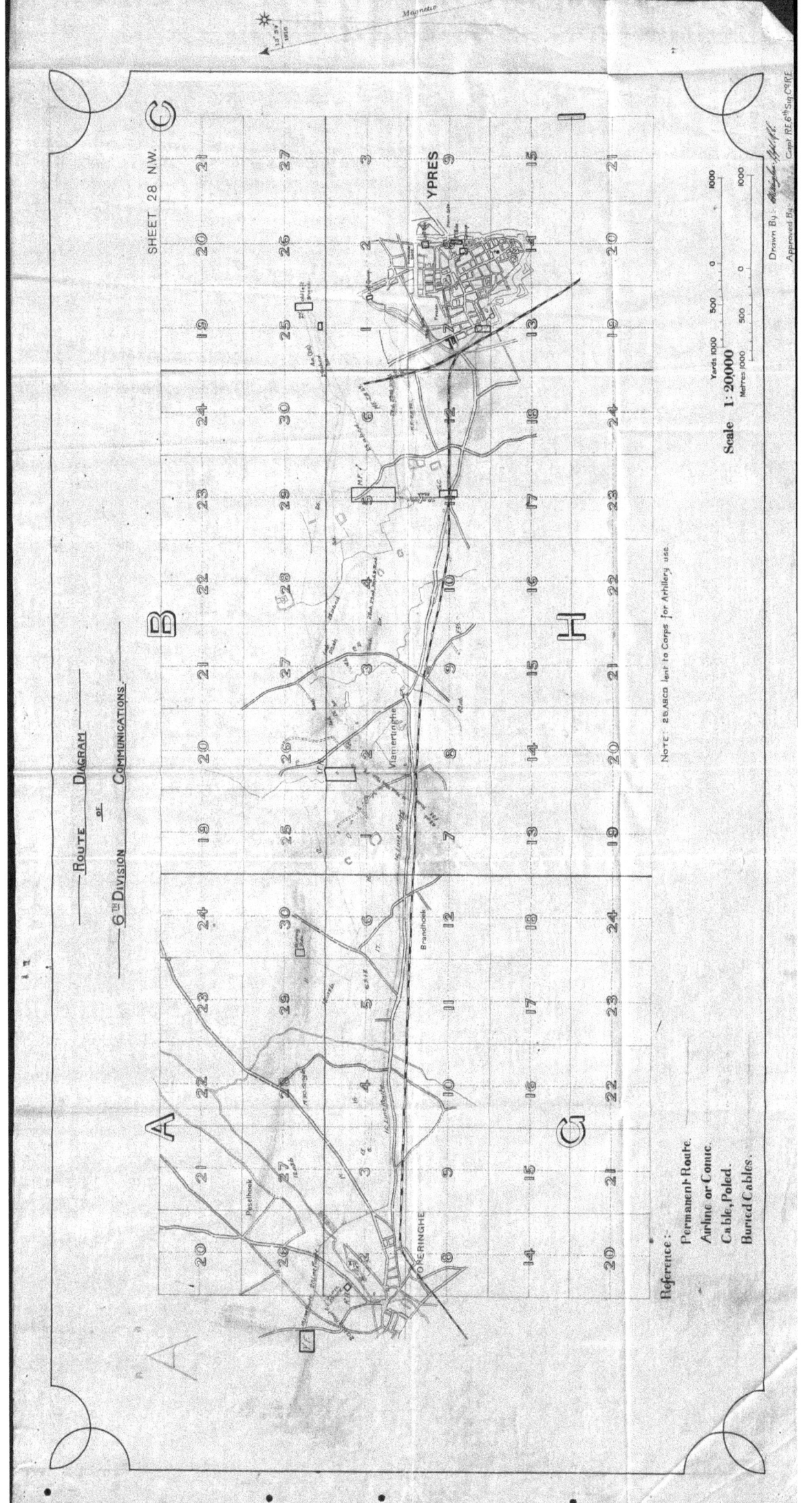

SECRET "B"

1.

G.S.
29th Division.

Will you please confirm the following proposals:-

a.) The two trench W.T. sets to be employed for communication between the two battalion hqrs near Chateau POTIJZE I.4.a 7.4. and the Right Group Artillery I 8 d 1.9.

b.) An Amplifier or overhearing set to be installed at POTIJZE and to work from the vicinity of DUKE ST. The primary duty of this instrument will be to intercept German messages & if possible conversations. It can also be used to check any indiscriminate speaking over the telephone within our own lines.

c.) The installation of a "power buzzer" for the right sector & one in the left, (suitable positions yet to be selected) These instruments to work back to POTIJZE. Later a code book will be issued; in the meantime these sets can be used for S.O.S. purposes.

C. Sink Capt.
O/C Signals 29th Div.

2.

O.C Divl Signals.

The G.O.C concurs in your suggestions.

12/8/16.

C.J. Fuller
Lt.Col.

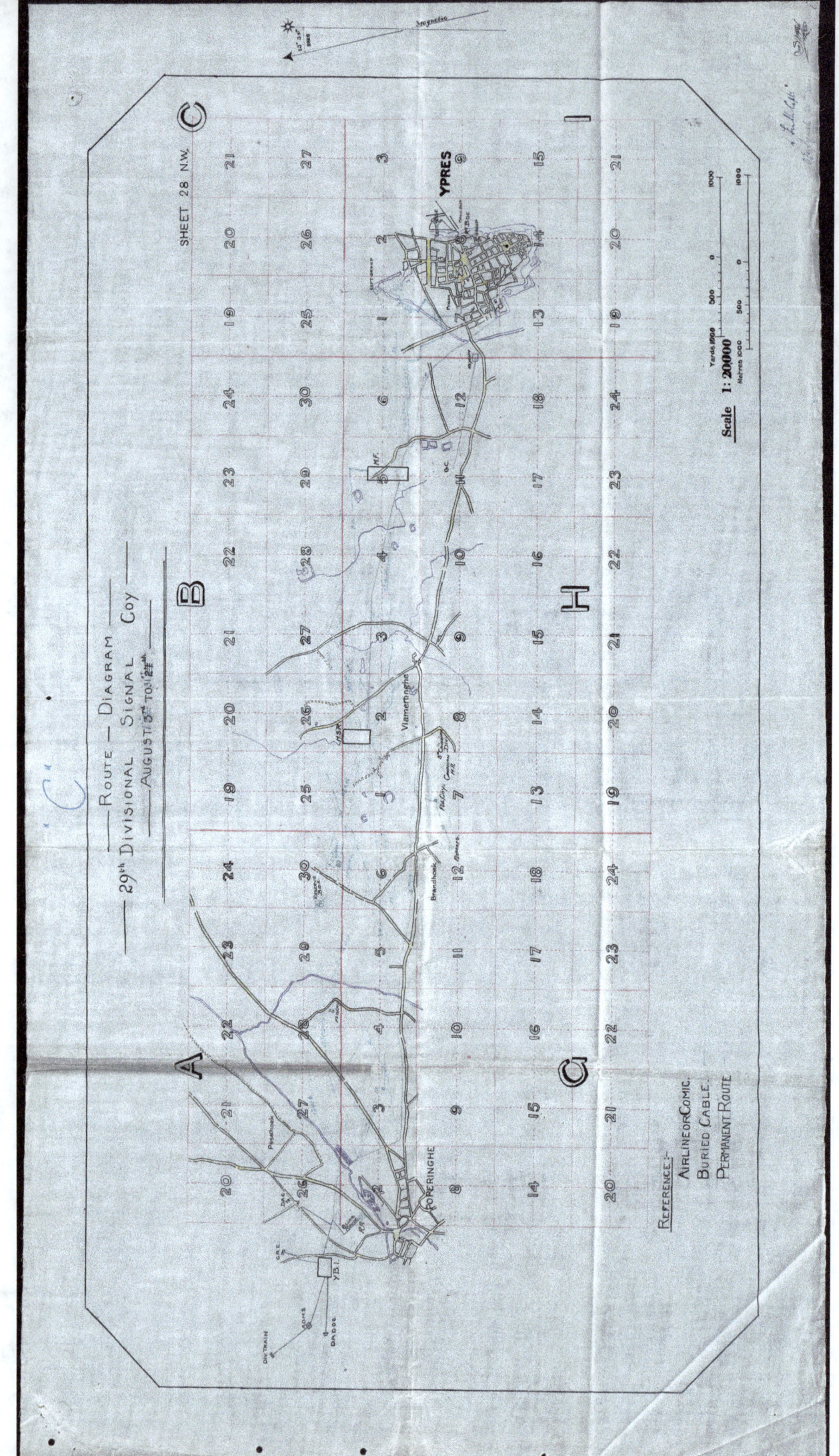

29th Divisional Engineers

29th DIVISIONAL SIGNAL COMPANY R. E.

SEPTEMBER 1 9 1 6

Army Form C. 2118.

WAR DIARY
or
INTELLIGENCE SUMMARY.
(Erase heading not required.)

Vol 3

Confidential

War Diary

of

29th Divisional Signal Co. R.E.

From 1st September 1916 to 31st Sept. 1916.

(Volume 3)

Army Form C. 2118.

WAR DIARY
or
INTELLIGENCE SUMMARY.
(Erase heading not required.)

Place	Date	Hour	Summary of Events and Information	Remarks and references to Appendices
	1.9.16		Usual Maintenance & patrolling of lines. Conference with section officers & orderly officers. The question of magneto and buzzer exchanges was discussed & it was agreed that 6 or 7 line buzzer exchanges for battalions and batteries & 12 or 15 line ditto for group & brigade were necessary. This would save instruments & help to keep the offices tidy. Further it was agreed that battery & company lines were useless as the lines in question were never relied upon for S.O.S. The northern group weekly communication obtained this battalion keep to which the artillery battery is connected. The having of officers (battery officers) & artillery personnel was also discussed. Left group orderly officer has no knowledge of brigade lists to subject to undergo a course at 2nd Army School. Huisages Died will. 456 Regained S.P.s 23	

Army Form C. 2118.

WAR DIARY
or
INTELLIGENCE SUMMARY.
(Erase heading not required.)

Instructions regarding War Diaries and Intelligence Summaries are contained in F. S. Regs., Part II. and the Staff Manual respectively. Title pages will be prepared in manuscript.

Place	Date	Hour	Summary of Events and Information	Remarks and references to Appendices
	2.9.16		Usual patrolling & maintenance of lines. Message dealt with 446. Registered SPs - 31	
	3.9.16		Heavy rain has little effect on buried cable, but lines have been arranged to look on cable trenches. Message dealt with 444. Registered SPs - 28	
	4.9.16		Usual patrolling & maintenance of lines. Message dealt with 432. Registered SPs - 35	
	5.9.16		Sentry heard lines from Brigade forward faulty for the use of the Fullerphone. Bat. faults located & attention given. Message dealt with 389. Registered SPs - 22	

1577 Wt. W10791/1773 500,000 1/15 D. D. & L. A.D.S.S./Forms/C. 2118.

WAR DIARY
or
INTELLIGENCE SUMMARY
(Erase heading not required.)

Army Form C. 2118.

Place	Date	Hour	Summary of Events and Information	Remarks and references to Appendices
	6.9.16		Naval maintenance & patrolling of lines. Work continued on burial scheme. Messages dealt with 385. Registered SP's. 37	
	7.9.16		Naval maintenance & patrolling of lines. Trench dug for cable abandoned for 300 yds owing to water & trench falling in. Trench continued along road - St Jean - Ypres. Messages dealt with 367. Registered SP's. 39	
	8.9.16		Capt Anderson arrives from attachment to 29th Div Cly. Naval party of 400 in cable trenches. Messages dealt with 372. Registered SP's. 22	
	9.9.16		Lt Yeaker arrives as reinforcement (Sn/Lt). As extra 600 men work in area to forward the work during	

WAR DIARY
or
INTELLIGENCE SUMMARY.

(Erase heading not required.)

Army Form C. 2118.

Place	Date	Hour	Summary of Events and Information	Remarks and references to Appendices
	10.9.16		Moonlight. Message dealt with 371. Registered SP's 30. Party of 1000 men work on Cable trench scheme. Morgue Road. Message dealt with 351. Registered SP's 29.	
	11.9.16		Division Hqrs (advanced) shelled by a small HE HV firm. To trench broken. No casualties. Visual class of 16 men from brigade in reserve started training. Message dealt with 291. Registered SP's 21.	
	12.9.16		One man of class not found satisfactory returns to unit. Visual maintenance & patrolling of lines. Message dealt with 308. Registered SP's 18.	

Army Form C. 2118.

WAR DIARY
or
INTELLIGENCE SUMMARY.
(Erase heading not required.)

Place	Date	Hour	Summary of Events and Information	Remarks and references to Appendices
	13.9.16.		General patrolling & maintenance of lines. Messages dealt with 274	Registered SPs 26
	14.9.16		Lees line to A&MS & DIVL TRAIN taken over. Ypres-Foid Old Corrie Aveluno reeled up. to tops & flank divisions working satisfactorily. Lees line Messages dealt with 364	Regd lined SPs 33 Regs lined SPs 33
	15.9.16.		No work on cable trenches by working party owing to fear of retaliation by enemy. Later num be of messages due to circulation of official news telegrams. Messages dealt with 487	Registered SPs 58
	16.9.16.		General patrolling & maintenance of lines. Messages dealt with 452	Registered SPs 38

WAR DIARY
or
INTELLIGENCE SUMMARY.
(Erase heading not required.)

Army Form C. 2118.

Instructions regarding War Diaries and Intelligence Summaries are contained in F. S. Regs., Part II. and the Staff Manual respectively. Title pages will be prepared in manuscript.

Place	Date	Hour	Summary of Events and Information	Remarks and references to Appendices
	17.9.16		Infantry looking on cable trench. On a dark night in average soil complete Infantry do not dig more than 3 ft though in this with the aid of the moon the full depth can be obtained. Timetable laid. Message dealt with 415 Reynolds	SPs. 35
	18.9.16		Area party consisting of 1 Officer & 8 OR arrive for duty in the area. Message dealt with 347 Reynolds	SPs. 52
	19.9.16		Lecture at Army School. Area party proceed to Ypres no rooms available elsewhere. Area party arrive with practically no equipment - only 2 D3's & 4 holders. Message dealt with 318 Reynolds	SPs. 97

Army Form C. 2118.

WAR DIARY
or
INTELLIGENCE SUMMARY.
(Erase heading not required.)

Instructions regarding War Diaries and Intelligence Summaries are contained in F. S. Regs., Part II. and the Staff Manual respectively. Title pages will be prepared in manuscript.

Place	Date	Hour	Summary of Events and Information	Remarks and references to Appendices
	20.9.16		Usual patrolling & maintenance of lines. Messages dealt with 332	Registered SPs. 112.
	21.9.16		Usual patrolling & maintenance of lines. Messages dealt with 304	Registered SPs. 129
	22.9.16		New rules for DRLS increase clerical work owing to large number of registered packets handed in for delivery. Orders intended to cause clerical work but does not do so. Messages dealt with 229	Registered SPs. 132.
	23.9.16		Make further efforts to obtain a lorry. Lighting out. Usual patrolling & maintenance of lines. Messages dealt with 265	Registered SPs. 97

1577 Wt.W10791/1773 500,000 1/15 D. D. & L. A.D.S.S./Forms/C. 2118.

WAR DIARY
or
INTELLIGENCE SUMMARY.
(Erase heading not required.)

Army Form C. 2118.

Place	Date	Hour	Summary of Events and Information	Remarks and references to Appendices
	24/8/16		Capt Andrew on transferred on promotion to 9th Corps H.A. Messages dealt with 281. Registered SPs. 99	
	25/8/16		New line laid to SAA ciary to change of latter hedqrs. Messages dealt with 321. Registered SPs. 107	
	26/8/16		Usual patrolling & maintenance of lines. Wire picked up. 1/4 mile steel airline line recovered. Wire picked up. Messages dealt with 281. Registered SPs. 123	
	27/8/16		Circuit on new route taken into use. Old Ts from main route picked up. Cable recovered 3/4 mile. Messages dealt with 359. Registered SPs. 148	

WAR DIARY
INTELLIGENCE SUMMARY

Place	Date	Hour	Summary of Events and Information	Remarks and references to Appendices
	29.k		The total number of S.C. sets allowed for divis[ional] (two) is not sufficient. In any warfare where permanent routes are built there only is satisfactory. Each divisional Coy should have 6 & 8c sets of these. I should be allotted to each brigade with a repeating coil & battery. I would be better if this formed part of a section equipment. Could not all supernumerary officers joining a signal unit be punished with stunts from the base. Infantry unfit for the trenches could be employed for the purpose. The supply of spare parts for motor cycles is very inadequate. At present 4 machines are idle due to inability of Supply Column being unable to obtain small items. Message Statholith 322. Repeated SPs 109	

WAR DIARY
or
INTELLIGENCE SUMMARY.
(Erase heading not required.)

Army Form C. 2118.

Place	Date	Hour	Summary of Events and Information	Remarks and references to Appendices
	29.9.16		Usual maintenance & patrolling of lines. Messages dealt with 354. Reported SPs 118.	
	30.9.16		Calcium lines changed over from old route to AX. Exchange usual patrolling of lines. 25 units of old route picked up. Total wire collected since August 1st:- 86 miles D5 D3 & D1 26 " Curie, Antice & iron wire. 35 Sandbags of scrap wire. Route diagram for divisional lines marked (A) Circuit " " of lines working from ди.Hqrs (B) Messages dealt with 327. Reported SPs 119.	A B

L. Tickleft.
O/C. Depot. 25th Div.
30.9.16

ROUTE DIAGRAM.
29TH DIVISIONAL COMMUNICATIONS.
SEPTEMBER 30TH.

SHEET 28 N.W.

Scale 1:20000

LINE REFERENCE
— AIR LINE OR COMIC
— BURIED CABLE

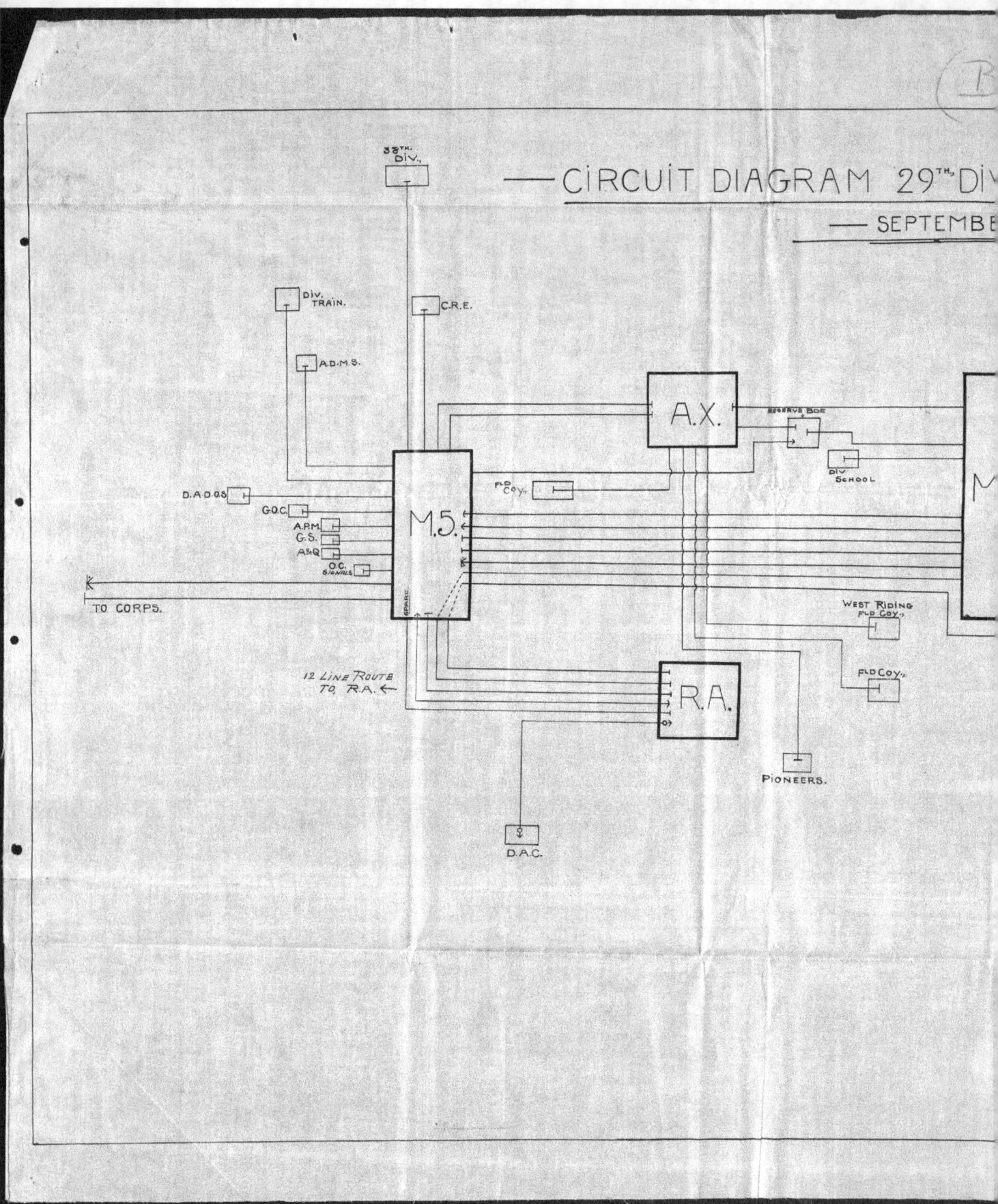

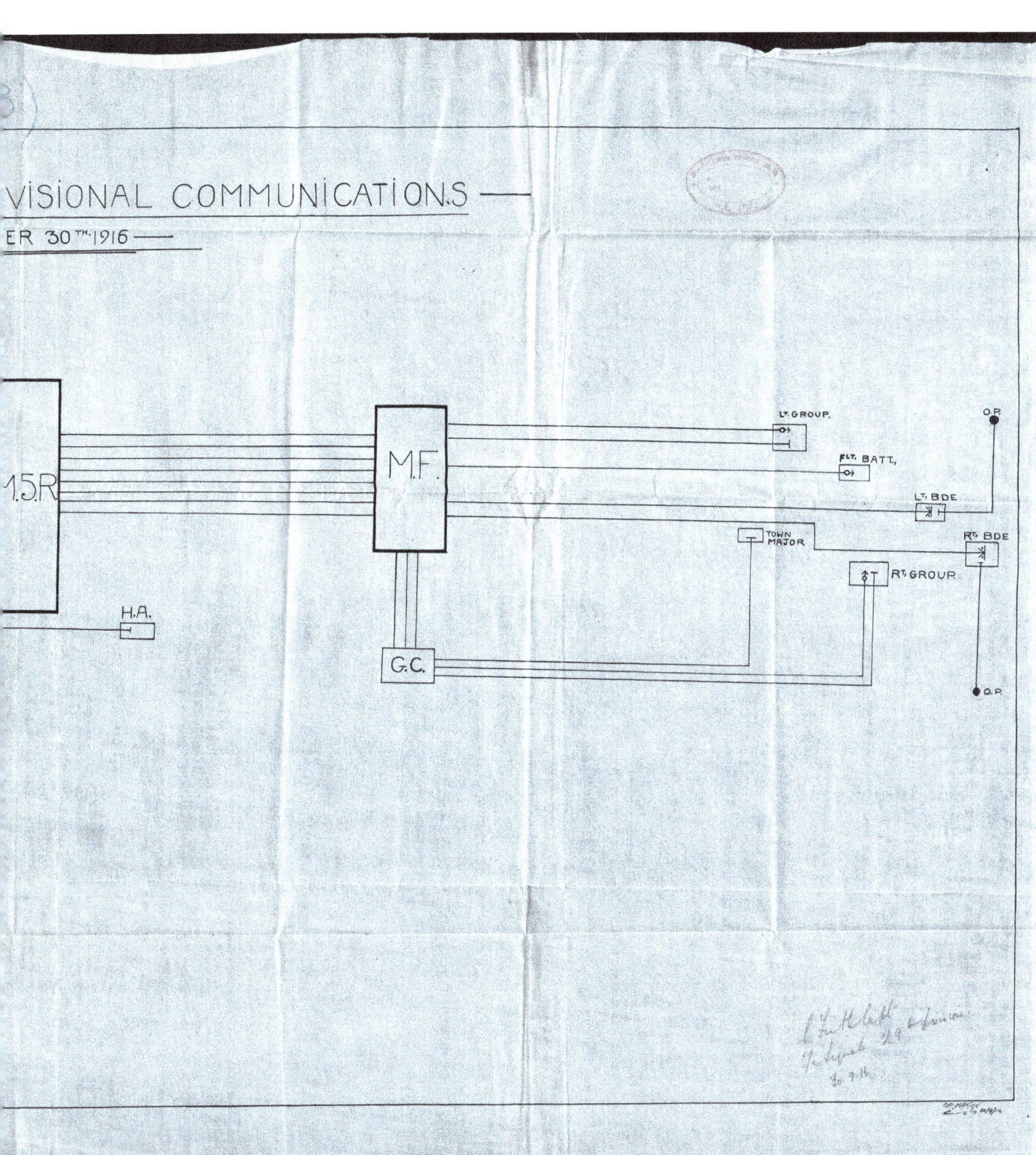

29th Divisional Engineers

$\tfrac{3}{4}$------

29th DIVISIONAL SIGNAL COMPANY R. E.

OCTOBER 1 9 1 6

Army Form C. 2118.

WAR DIARY
or
INTELLIGENCE SUMMARY.
(Erase heading not required.)

Vol 4

Confidential

War Diary
of
29th Divisional Signal Co. R.E.
From 1st Oct 1916 to 31st Oct 1916.
(Volume 4)

Army Form C. 2118.

WAR DIARY
or
INTELLIGENCE SUMMARY.
(Erase heading not required.)

Place	Date	Hour	Summary of Events and Information	Remarks and references to Appendices
	1.10.16		Usual patrolling & maintenance of lines. Messages dealt with 290. Registered SPs. 148.	
	2.10.16		Informed of probable relief by 56th Division. Reconnaissance was to be cut as in advance in the line, 5 men for advanced died here also 1 officer for advanced died here. Used AZAS lines for each file 4 men to died here & 3 to died here. Messages dealt with 354. Registered SPs. 124.	
	3.10.16		Preparation made for handing over. Messages dealt with 328. Registered SPs. 160.	
	4.10.16		Advance parties for one brigade arrived also O.C. Coy. Later men for here & advanced hqrs arrive. Two days guide insufficient for handing over satisfactorily, especially as line is a good deal we must see	

WAR DIARY
or
INTELLIGENCE SUMMARY.

Army Form C. 2118.

Place	Date	Hour	Summary of Events and Information	Remarks and references to Appendices
			previously used as the buried system in course of construction, new open route to exchange shall in R 381. Reported pp 135	
	5.10.16		All preparations for landing our including poles, completed except electric light. Owing to the set not being thorough no exchange could be made. 53rd Div have a largest own a ballot set with a borrowed 8hp Douglas Engine. Office staff hand over at 8 p.m. A signal was to remain with new staff the exchange of two minutes present. Bde sections have left with no batteries to their PC set attached report done in area by action to 2 month in the time "A" message dealt with 425. Reported pp 164	
	6.10.16		Handed over responsibility to OC 53rd Hund by at	

WAR DIARY or INTELLIGENCE SUMMARY

Army Form C. 2118.

Place	Date	Hour	Summary of Events and Information	Remarks and references to Appendices
	7.10.16		I am at which how 5°C 35th assumes command.	
	8.10.16		Company entrain at PROVEN at 6.54 p.m. No trouble experienced. Halted long with a 30-cwt lorry with 2nd Army to convey electric light (cut by road) to CORBIE. But hqrs arrive & open at CORBIE. Exchange at it with a junction to Office at CORBIE. All boards connected by phone, also usual locals including G, A+Q, Town x. Reported tho dent with 13	
	9.10.16		No change. Circuit remains unaltered. Reported tho dent with 60	
	10.10.16		Hqrs move to RIBEMONT. Hqrs close at CORBIE, and open at RIBEMONT at same hour.	

Army Form C. 2118.

WAR DIARY
or
INTELLIGENCE SUMMARY.
(Erase heading not required.)

Instructions regarding War Diaries and Intelligence Summaries are contained in F. S. Regs., Part II. and the Staff Manual respectively. Title pages will be prepared in manuscript.

Place	Date	Hour	Summary of Events and Information	Remarks and references to Appendices
	11.10.16		Rear details 88th moved to 12th Division area. Section accompanied by 2 dr's (not to cyclist) & 2 others too. 86th Bde. to DERNANCOURT & 87th to BUIRE. Both letter in exchange of 3rd Corps & 4th Army respectively. In addition usual trunks on exchange. Messages dealt with — Registered Sps. 444. No changes in situation.	
	12.10.16		Messages dealt with 206. Registered Sps. 95. Rear Bdy. also move to forward positions. Commits by telephone to 30th Div. Exchange & Corps exchange. Messages sent to nearest office. Messages dealt with 201 Registered Sps. 89	
	13.10.16		Everywhere everyone gave every assistance both Corps (15th) Division in the line & out. Company (except Sole section) together for the first	

1577 Wt. W10791/1773 500,000 1/15 D. D. & L. A.D.S.S./Forms/C. 2118.

Army Form C. 2118.

WAR DIARY
or
INTELLIGENCE SUMMARY.
(Erase heading not required.)

Instructions regarding War Diaries and Intelligence Summaries are contained in F. S. Regs., Part II. and the Staff Manual respectively. Title pages will be prepared in manuscript.

Place	Date	Hour	Summary of Events and Information	Remarks and references to Appendices
	14.10.15		Time since leaving England is back to useful work done in getting cable sections together & having no such classes of map reading & joining various cables, held to first advantage. Messages dealt with 192. Regulated SP's 68	
			Attached report from No 2 Section att'd 12th Division on communication during the attack of previous day. Cable detachment work under section officers. Messages dealt with 201. Regulated SP's 58	"B"
	15.10.15		All officers visit forward areas with a view to taking over from right to left division at present holding the line. Cable stations continue having as per previous days. Mounted SP's forward with map & compass reading.	

1577 Wt.W10791/1773 500,000 1/15 D.D.&L. A.D.S.S./Forms/C. 2118. Messages dealt with 298. Regulated SP's 28

WAR DIARY or INTELLIGENCE SUMMARY

Army Form C. 2118.

Place	Date	Hour	Summary of Events and Information	Remarks and references to Appendices
	16.10.16		Electric light plant for workshops overhauled then bearing requires renewal. Training programme continued. Message dealt with 245. Reported SPs 38.	
	17.10.16		Bad roads have effect on motor bicycles. One has handle bars & one frame broken. 2 crankcases holed owing to projecting stones on the roads. The practice of Brigades to send motor cyclists for mails to collect same to bad & was & difficult to stop. On taking up the matter receive no satisfaction. Message dealt with 211. Reported SPs. 53.	
	19.10.16		Prepare to move forward but owing to lack of any definite orders nothing can be done except futher	

Army Form C. 2118.

WAR DIARY
or
INTELLIGENCE SUMMARY.
(Erase heading not required.)

Place	Date	Hour	Summary of Events and Information	Remarks and references to Appendices
			reconnaissance by Officers of forward area. Early of 1 NCO & 10 men sent to assist The Divisional artillery who are in front. The above the equivalent of a cable detachment ten cable wagon & team. Message dealt with 228. Registered SPs. 43	
A.I.L.			Orders received to take over from 12th Div. Second in Command and one subaltern officer proceed to make necessary arrangement for taking over at 5 p.m., both Ivry taking up personnel stock in the unit. Lit assistance from Corps Signals. The usual trouble is experienced in changing equipment. Such articles as switchboards, magneto phones & Electric Light equipment should be standardised. Message dealt with 140. Registered SPs. 34.	

WAR DIARY
or
INTELLIGENCE SUMMARY.

(Erase heading not required.)

Army Form C. 2118.

Instructions regarding War Diaries and Intelligence Summaries are contained in F. S. Regs., Part II. and the Staff Manual respectively. Title pages will be prepared in manuscript.

Place	Date	Hour	Summary of Events and Information	Remarks and references to Appendices
	20.10.16		Considerable trouble with lines between forward test points YT and TP. These consist of three pairs in Cop's trench, very earthy and poles at crossings - and three pairs of cable D⁵ partly poles & partly on ground. Our trouble due to uninsulated joints and earth faults, but five or six breaks due to shell fire were also found. Between 2pm & 3.30pm only one line between YT and TP was through. Also at 12 noon buzzer line between HQ and YT broke down, but was repaired at 2pm. Stay wire on ets fault being closest YT and latter had all available linemen out. About 5pm latter 'phoned lines to forward brigades and buzzer line were O.K.	
			Messages dealt with 445	Registered S.P's 64
	21.10.16		About 5.30 am heavy shelling by enemy Jerupts communication on all except one of the lines between YT and TP, but by 10 am three lines were working well and the others showed earth faults only. Office at YT very untidy, no arrangements having been made to change rapidly from one line to another. Sir move DMkIII telephones sent up for incoming use and also brass terminals to improve the office.	
			Messages dealt with 601	Registered S.P's 84

WAR DIARY
or
INTELLIGENCE SUMMARY.

(Erase heading not required.)

Army Form C. 2118.

Place	Date	Hour	Summary of Events and Information	Remarks and references to Appendices
	22.10.16		Linesmen out all day on lines from YT-TP, but nevertheless no casualties. One lineman wounded, otherwise no casualties. YT shelled a little with high velocity gun. Reserve brigate existing lines abandoned and new working superimposed on direct line formed by a TE (at No 7 Test point. Corps trench) on to one pair between HQ and YT. This pair no longer in use to YT, but is a spare available if required. Owing to mud & prohibition of horse traffic on roads, great difficulty experienced in getting necessary stores up. A limbered wagon with light load requires six horse team. Messages dealt with 1/15. Registered S.P's. 81	
	23.10.16		YT shelled more heavily, especially in early morning. Linesmen still hard at work on lines between YT and TP, but owing to arrival of rubber tape, cable faults were reduced greatly. Main faults Ducts shell fire and concussion from our own artillery, but two phone lines to forward brigades and buzzer line kept through all day. Buzzer line between HQ and YT between 12 noon - 1 pm, but worked on spare to YT until it was repaired. YT office now good. Messages dealt with 692. Registered S.P's. 133.	

WAR DIARY
or
INTELLIGENCE SUMMARY.
(Erase heading not required.)

Army Form C. 2118.

Place	Date	Hour	Summary of Events and Information	Remarks and references to Appendices
	24.10.14		Usual difficulties owing to earth faults & shell fire. Newpau partly in lead covered mults, and badly in D3 cable run from YT to TP. Thought at 4pm just as shell outside TP cuts four other pairs. These were repaired quickly though. Hurry of operations demand extra supply of pigeons but none was available. But to postponement this might have been serious. Registered S.P.'s 110	
	25.10.14		Messages dealt with 659. Linemen still hard at work reducing earth on lines, which contained a number of unsoldered joints, either owing to rapid laying or faulty repair work. All now showing improvement. Shelling round TP again considerable but this causes easily repairable faults. NCO's TP wounded at 4pty. Registered S.P.'s 282 Messages dealt with 758	
	26.10.14		All lines handed over to us forward from YT working well with earth faults due to joints cleared. This was effected by letting in sections of D4mm cable in the worst sections. So the first time since taking over, communications to forward brigades satisfactory. Messages dealt with 824 Registered S.P.'s 160	

WAR DIARY
or
INTELLIGENCE SUMMARY.
(Erase heading not required.)

Army Form C. 2118.

Place	Date	Hour	Summary of Events and Information	Remarks and references to Appendices
	27.10.16		Buzzer line rather faint and fault traced to a point between TP and bridges. This portion armoured cable is in mud (about two feet deep). Every bad joint was discovered, and on repairing this great improvement was effected. The joint was made brutally in dry weather but the extreme wet dampness we have experienced soon finds out bad joints, and the importance of good jointing has been very much emphasised since we have been in this sector. Reconnoitre made for new buzzer line, particularly with regard to avoidance of shelled areas. Great difficulty in obtaining armoured cable for use in forward communication trenches. As these are very muddy and a lot of traffic passes through them, this type of cable is the only solution for successful communication. The Corps are wiring it for their buried system, which seems a waste. Messages dealt with 109.	Registered S.P.s 109

WAR DIARY
or
INTELLIGENCE SUMMARY.

(Erase heading not required.)

Army Form C. 2118.

Place	Date	Hour	Summary of Events and Information	Remarks and references to Appendices
	28.10.16		Preparis in Corps trench working well. Special attention to maintenance of air line PA8 & 9. New line (D main) laid over ground from LV (S17 d 1.4) to Right Brigade, and connected to PA 8 & 9 from YT to LV. This makes great improvement for those lines. Large demands of cable for two attached Div¹ Artillery's. Only 10 miles out of 20 miles demanded for 30th Div. Arty. yet obtained from Corps Dump WIERMILL. They refuse to give more. We are now able to put some proper work into the lines as they do not all break down daily. Messages dealt with 440. Registered S.P's. 221	
	29.10.16		Advance party from 1st Australian Division proceed to York Trench to take over YT and TP. Half our personnel withdrawn. Remainder stayed to show over all lines. All instruments exchanged and ours brought back to TOMMIE'S REDOUBT. This is really the most satisfactory method, if time permits. Electric light sets at POPPIERS changed in afternoon and a number of our stores, including all local telephone evacuated to E11 central. Messages dealt with 914. Registered S.P.S. 168	

WAR DIARY
or
INTELLIGENCE SUMMARY.
(Erase heading not required.)

Army Form C. 2118.

Place	Date	Hour	Summary of Events and Information	Remarks and references to Appendices
	30.10.16		1st Australian Dn Sigs. take over at 9am. Our office re-opened CORBIE at 9am. Company moved over from POMMIERS and E.11 central to three parties, viz 1st Party 1 Cable section complete, G.S. wagon, Cooks wagon from E.11 central. 2nd Party, 1 cable section from POMMIERS, picking up cable wagons at E.11 central. 3rd Party. Men from YT and TP and remainder stores at POMMIERS lorry from latter place. All in at CORBIE by 7 pm. Registered S.P's 9. Messages dealt with 6. 86th Brigade MAMETZ Camp - 87th Brigade FRICOURT CAMP. Both connected to exchange at 5th Australian Division. 88th Brigade at POMMIERS Camp connected to 1st Australian Division. HQ connected to Mil'y Exchange CORBIE. Message dealt with 60¾ Registered S.P's 56	
	31.10.16		85th Brigade to VILLE - connected to 8th Divn. Exchange at TREUX, thro XIV Corps. 86th Brigade to CORBIE. Direct line. 87th at FRICOURT, as for. 30 th inst Company cleaning up men, clothes, horses, harness, wagons, etc. Messages dealt with 121. Registered S.P's 33.	On Surface Cable Sig for Sig

"A"

Summary of Work done in Left Bde Area
by 87th Bde Signal Section

(1) Stations.   Re-organised & rewired Bde Signal Office.
Fitted up an office test box for 12 main
lines.
    Rewired left battn. Sig. office & installed a
7 line P.O. type switchboard. Fitted a test
box for 7 lines.
    Rewired right battn Sig. office & installed a
7 line P.O. type switchboard.
    Rewired the Test Station on St Jean Rd.
Installed screening buzzers in two battalion
signal offices & also in the two Coy.
offices of Left battn.

(2) Lines.   Repaired the Canal quads, of which only
one was working satisfactorily upon taking
over. Defective lengths have been replaced &
all faults removed.
    Scrapped lines L1, L3, A1, OB1, & OB3
& removed as far as possible.
    Replaced defective quad across Canal
to Left Group, by a new steel armoured
quad.
    New lines L2 & L4 have been run
to forward battalions & a new buried line
to Prison battalion from tee in 28 a & b spare
(spare quad).
    The buried Lateral & Coy line commenced
by 6th Div. have been completed & are
now working.

(3) Test Boxes   8 Testboxes have been repaired and

fitted with zinc covers, making them as nearly watertight as possible.

In remainder of test-boxes where repair was impracticable, through connections with rubbered joints were made.

(4) Clearing of Area — Collected approx. 15 miles of cable.

E. E. Green 2nd Lt.
R.E (T.)
3/10/16.

DIAGRAM OF COMMUNICATIONS

"B" COMPANIES

"B"

HDQRS. WC WD BTNS.

SPARE

WB ADV BDE HQRS.

BDE VISUAL

WA

W BDE HQRS

Report on Communication During Operations
of 13th October 16

Battalion Lines

The C.O.'s of the attacking battalions, the ... and ..., were on the open ... only with wires ... with them by ... was established between them ... through ... Coy H.Q. ... through them from ... to the ... ...

D.H.Q. Line

The D.H.Q. Line ... ... with ... line to companies during the attack. It was repeatedly cut by shell fire but was repaired by battalion signallers.

The right battalion had no company line ...

On the night of 12/13 Oct., Sole ... reported a buried cable to assist the right of GUEUDECOURT to the front line. This line was cut about 10 a.m. on the 13th by barrage. Then cut in many places and never put right.

Visual

A visual station was established just behind the firing line at the right of the village. They used a "Lucas lamp" but ... was achieving that enemy station could not read the signals.

A pilot lamp was issued to the left battalion the night with 2 ... to advance. It was not found necessary to use it.

Pigeons

Two pairs of birds were issued to each of the attacking battalions.

The left battalion kept its pigeons in the front line during the attack. It was not found necessary to use them and they were liberated next morning.

The right battalion had no pigeon man. One was stwo attached to this battalion but was led quite sick, and one was wounded. The birds were kept at battalion headquarters during the attack, and were liberated next morning.

Orderlies

Runners proved the only means of communication from the attacking troops. The right battalion used runners from the disabling lines to headquarters. The left battalion employed runners while lines were broken.

15/10/16

Lt ───────
OC 61st Bn.

29th Divisional Engineers

29th DIVISIONAL SIGNAL COMPANY R. E.

NOVEMBER 1 9 1 6

WAR DIARY
INTELLIGENCE SUMMARY

Vol 5

Confidential.

War Diary
of
29th Divisional Signal Co. RE
From 1st November 1916 to 30th November 1916.

(Volume 5)

Army Form C. 2118.

WAR DIARY
or
INTELLIGENCE SUMMARY.
(Erase heading not required.)

29 Div. Signal Co. R.E. (7)

Instructions regarding War Diaries and Intelligence Summaries are contained in F. S. Regs., Part II. and the Staff Manual respectively. Title pages will be prepared in manuscript.

Place	Date	Hour	Summary of Events and Information	Remarks and references to Appendices
CORBIE	1/7/16		Division at rest. Company route march in morning in full marching order. Cleaning harness in afternoon. C.R.E. connected to Horse exchange. Also 86th Bde at CORBIE 88th at VILLE via 87th Div. TREUX via XIV Corps. 87th Bde moving back to FRAINES. Inter-Company phone lines changed somewhat during the day. Messages dealt with 84. Registered S.P's 43	
	2nd		Inspection of harness equipment, also R.H.S stores batteries divided into two groups one to dump next time we move — one to take up with us, in order to reduce number of journeys of lorry. Messages dealt with 95. Registered S.P's 42	
	3rd		Cattle wagon drill. One detachment to MERICOURT to lay line for 86th Bde from there to VILLE to connect two battns. to the brigade line. O.K. 5pm. Route — S. of TREUX. Messages dealt with 96. Registered S.P's 24	

WAR DIARY
or
INTELLIGENCE SUMMARY.

Army Form C. 2118.

(Erase heading not required.)

Place	Date	Hour	Summary of Events and Information	Remarks and references to Appendices
ORBIE	4th		Services to 86th Bde from H.Q. Div TREUX fixed up by superimposing on 'phone route. Two DR runs per day to 87th AIRAINES. Phone via ABBEVILLE. Company training - inspection of kit, route march, & lecture on putting to listeners. Messages dealt with 105. Registered S.P.S. 30	
	5th		Company training - cable wagon drill. & Good improvement in condition of horses & harness noted. Also turn-out of men. Clean arms inspection. Messages dealt with 40. Registered S.P.S. 34	
	6th		Sunday. Church parade 9.30 a.m. Otherwise day off for men. 87th Bde AIRAINES connected via ARMY – XV corps – 4th Division, for 'phone messages. Messages dealt with 54. Registered S.P.S. 30	
	7th		Company training. Route march in full marching order. Clean arms inspection. Lecture, map reading to N.C.O.s. Messages dealt with 91. Registered S.P.S. 30	

Army Form C. 2118.

WAR DIARY
or
INTELLIGENCE SUMMARY.
(Erase heading not required.)

Instructions regarding War Diaries and Intelligence Summaries are contained in F. S. Regs., Part II. and the Staff Manual respectively. Title pages will be prepared in manuscript.

Place	Date	Hour	Summary of Events and Information	Remarks and references to Appendices
CAIRO IE	6th		Company training. Cable wagon Drill. Lecture map-reading to DR's, A.P.M. office connected to exchange. Messages dealt with 44. Registered S.P.'s 33	
	9th		Company training. Painting class to Linemen. First instruction in cable wagon for a few men. Kit inspections, and also harness. Messages dealt with 53. Registered S.P.'s 31	
	10th		Company training. Cable wagon Drill. Owing to a certain amount of minor sickness, many of others employed on looking after horses & harness, so only two detachments could turn out for drill. Messages dealt with 94. Registered S.P.'s 52	
	11th		Company training. Route march. Lecture to Linemen on map reading. Messages dealt with 108. Registered S.P.'s 30	

WAR DIARY
INTELLIGENCE SUMMARY.

Army Form C. 2118.

(Erase heading not required.)

Instructions regarding War Diaries and Intelligence Summaries are contained in F. S. Regs., Part II and the Staff Manual respectively. Title pages will be prepared in manuscript.

Place	Date	Hour	Summary of Events and Information	Remarks and references to Appendices
GRBIE.	12th		Company training. Cable wagon drill. D in Signal School connected to D/4 URS exchange. RMS stores further divided. All visual stores set aside for own at Div. Signal School. This leaves only one lorry load to move forward.	
	13th		Messages dealt with 163. Registered S.P's 30. Company training. Lecture on fighting to Lucernen. LIEUT KING, General List, arrives for duty vice LT SMITH, sick to England. LIEUT KING, Billets etc. fixed up for Div. Signal School. Messages dealt with 120. Registered SP's 45.	
	14th		Company training. Cable wagon drill. LIEUT KING goes to Div School in charge of Signal School. Ten men from each brigade, attn. from Div Arty report at D/4 URs for the course of instruction. Stores for buntry sent to D/4 URs under Sgt CHUBB & Pte WRIGHT. Sgt Chubb Senior instructor at school. Messages dealt with 99. Registered SP's 30.	

WAR DIARY
or
INTELLIGENCE SUMMARY.

Army Form C. 2118.

(Erase heading not required.)

Place	Date	Hour	Summary of Events and Information	Remarks and references to Appendices
TREUX	15th		Div HQ move to TREUX. 87 & 86 Bdes CORBIE. 87 Bde BRIQUETERIE via 8th Div. 88th Bde SANDPITS via XIV corps. Move to TREUX complicated by breakdown of lorry, but managed to convey stores required by nightfall. Messages dealt with 162. Registered SP's 150	
	16th		Advance party of linemen with necessary instruments and 12 Sig Div Advanced HQ in G.S. wagon. Two linemen report to 87th & 88th Bdes. G.S. wagon fails to return owing to sticking in a muddy track. 87th Bde front line, right sector. Messages dealt with 264. Registered SP's 241	
	17th		First office relief with instruments sent to 8th Div Advanced Rear HQ in lorry. Also electric light set a party to erect it. Lorry returns 6 p.m. 88th Bde HQ in front line left sector. DHQ GUILLEMONT via 8th Div. Messages dealt with 248. Registered SP's 14	

WAR DIARY
INTELLIGENCE SUMMARY

Army Form C. 2118.

Place	Date	Hour	Summary of Events and Information	Remarks and references to Appendices
A4a33	18th		Company marched from TREUX 4.30am, arrived MEAULTE. Company arrived 12 noon. Office taken over from Bde Dr at 10 am, Party for Rear HQ meanwhile having left at MONTAUBAN. Trouble with line to DADOS – Div Train. No phone at DADOS – phone at Div Train faulty. 86th Bde moves to BRIQUETERIE. Messages dealt with 485. Registered S.P.'s 23.	For diagrams of lines reference see attached (A) attached
	19th		Working parties on lines to AR – Rear HQr – Div Train. DADOS & in trench via MINDEN POST. New trestle route – 4 pair cable complete except for crossing of TRONES WOOD SIDING (railway), leading in at Div Office. Sounders to 85th & 86th brigades substituted for buzzers working OK. Messages dealt with 646. Registered S.P.'s 44.	
	20th		TRONES WOOD siding crossing completed in morning. Also leading in at Div Office, and AR, on new trestle route. Working to forward brigades and AR OK on this route at 4 pm. Three 'phone pairs, three single wire sounder lines in to Rear HQr improved a little, working sounder to Bde at 6 pm. Messages dealt with 658. Registered S.P.'s 40.	

INTELLIGENCE SUMMARY.

(Erase heading not required.)

Place	Date	Hour	Summary of Events and Information	Remarks and references to Appendices
	21st		Change over from old post to Rear HQ (from Aires HQ) to new pair on semi-permanent corps route. Work superimposed sounder on this. Signals improved. Line laid to Div. RE dump. O.K. at 12.30 p.m. Party at HQ on tidying up, and improving lines inside aerodrome Signal Office. Messages dealt with 536. Registered S.P.'s 42	
	22nd		Cables forward from A.T.R. required two days work: routes on the whole very scattered, poles too small; one pair on ground part of the way, trunks for storm to replace. Called by airline route. Bn. to A.T.R. and RE dump faulty; found at crossing under railway, also in office, where parties trenching rendered by predecessors, who used NDB for this. Three men B.N.Co's A.T.R. to get on with work on forward cables. Messages dealt with 489. Registered S.P.'s 46	
	23rd		Work on Signal office and above it continued - also on cables forward from A.T.R. One route completed - two pairs on this Nos 2,4,9,6 Left Brigade. Work on old lines to Rear given good results and three pairs to Rear HQ now O.K. Messages dealt with 625. Registered S.P.'s 41	

1577 Wt.W10791/1773 500,000 1/15 D. D. & L. A.D.S.S./Forms/C. 2118.

WAR DIARY
or
INTELLIGENCE SUMMARY.
(Erase heading not required.)

Army Form C. 2118.

Instructions regarding War Diaries and Intelligence Summaries are contained in F. S. Regs., Part II. and the Staff Manual respectively. Title pages will be prepared in manuscript.

Place	Date	Hour	Summary of Events and Information	Remarks and references to Appendices
	24th		Signal office complaints - great improvement in all ways. Trouble with Div Train Supplies by sending their (French) telephone list; trouble recurred owing to wrong use of letter. All such should have explicit instructions as to use printed on them. Line-work:- cable forward of AR continued, also No 9 post to T8 c cleared of GINCHY. Double entries to Corps & onwards to Rear HR on same route (MT4). Work continues on old DB line, no interruption upset by bad balance on MT4. Messages dealt with 626.	Registered S.P.'s 34
	25th		Line to corps still wrong; also MT4. Work on cable route AR 15 to y20 c 10 completed. Two distinct straight routes made, viz Nos 2, 4, 9 and Nos 1, 5. Six pairs tapped out from correct from T8c to Cow TRENCH (Survey Post) for use of left Brigade which has been having difficulty with its Left Battn, in sunken road north of LES BOEUFS. One shell hole on 6ft buried route was quite 36" deep which is probably reason for all pairs not being through; only 12 out of 30 appear thro'. Messages dealt with 457.	Registered S.P's 49

Army Form C. 2118.

WAR DIARY
or
INTELLIGENCE SUMMARY.
(Erase heading not required.)

Instructions regarding War Diaries and Intelligence Summaries are contained in F. S. Regs., Part II. and the Staff Manual respectively. Title pages will be prepared in manuscript.

Place	Date	Hour	Summary of Events and Information	Remarks and references to Appendices
	26th		Cable lines went underfire on MT & Rear HQ again. Dugout found for between left Bn in TOWTRENCH and one Pair from SURVEY POST to Right Baths laid. The clears left Bde of YYY and AB system for its Right Baths. One more pair tapped onto Railway (RENAD WOOD) crossing trestle route in view of four more pairs being built alongthis. Corps cable detachment promised for this. Work on tangle of wires. Amed HQ proceeding also on building of station. Messages dealt with 596. Registered S.P's 50	
	27th		Pair from SURVEY POST to left Bath. Left Buzzer strong, and YYY AB system now only annoying. Maintenance of other lines heavy owing to rain. Work at Abred HQ as usual. Messages dealt with 590. Registered S.P's 46	
	28th		Commence new route 4 pair AR to GUILLEMONT QUARRIES. Aligning of poles difficult owing to fog. Two pair wired completed to Road 4.30pm, about 500 yds. Maintenance of other lines & work at Abred HQ as usual. Messages dealt with 634 Registered S.P.S. 72	

1577 Wt. W10791/1773 500,000 1/15 D. D. & L. A.D.S.S./Forms/C. 2118.

WAR DIARY
or
INTELLIGENCE SUMMARY.

Army Form C. 2118.

(Erase heading not required.)

Place	Date	Hour	Summary of Events and Information	Remarks and references to Appendices
	29th		Div. Signal school visited. Progressing satisfactorily. Good N.C.O. instructors still required urgently. New route to 6 QUARRIES poles a few letters, wiring completed to north end of rail-crossing. Maintenance as usual. Work at HQrs shews some result but having arrival of telegraph poles for building small route to locals, this result is not very striking. Two and a half pairs to rear HR given up, also three pairs GHQ-DHQ to MR - all waiting for opportunity to trundle in. Party from Corps commenced work adding two pairs to trestle route GAR - Registered S.P.'s ½. Message dealt with 620	
	30th		Route AR to QUARRIES completed, except for leading in and regulating. Should be in use tomorrow and will then release two poles cable routes five pairs in all for this relief. Seven ways about 500 yds. complete on trestle route to APR and existing four ½ pairs on this route strained up. Waste route re-stayed. Three new lead boxcovs. Corps batty to trunk work. Registered S.P.'s 46. Messages dealt with 711	Diagram of Communication taken on 18th Sept. (A) attached. C.R.Sugden Capt. RE for OC 29 Div S.T.Co

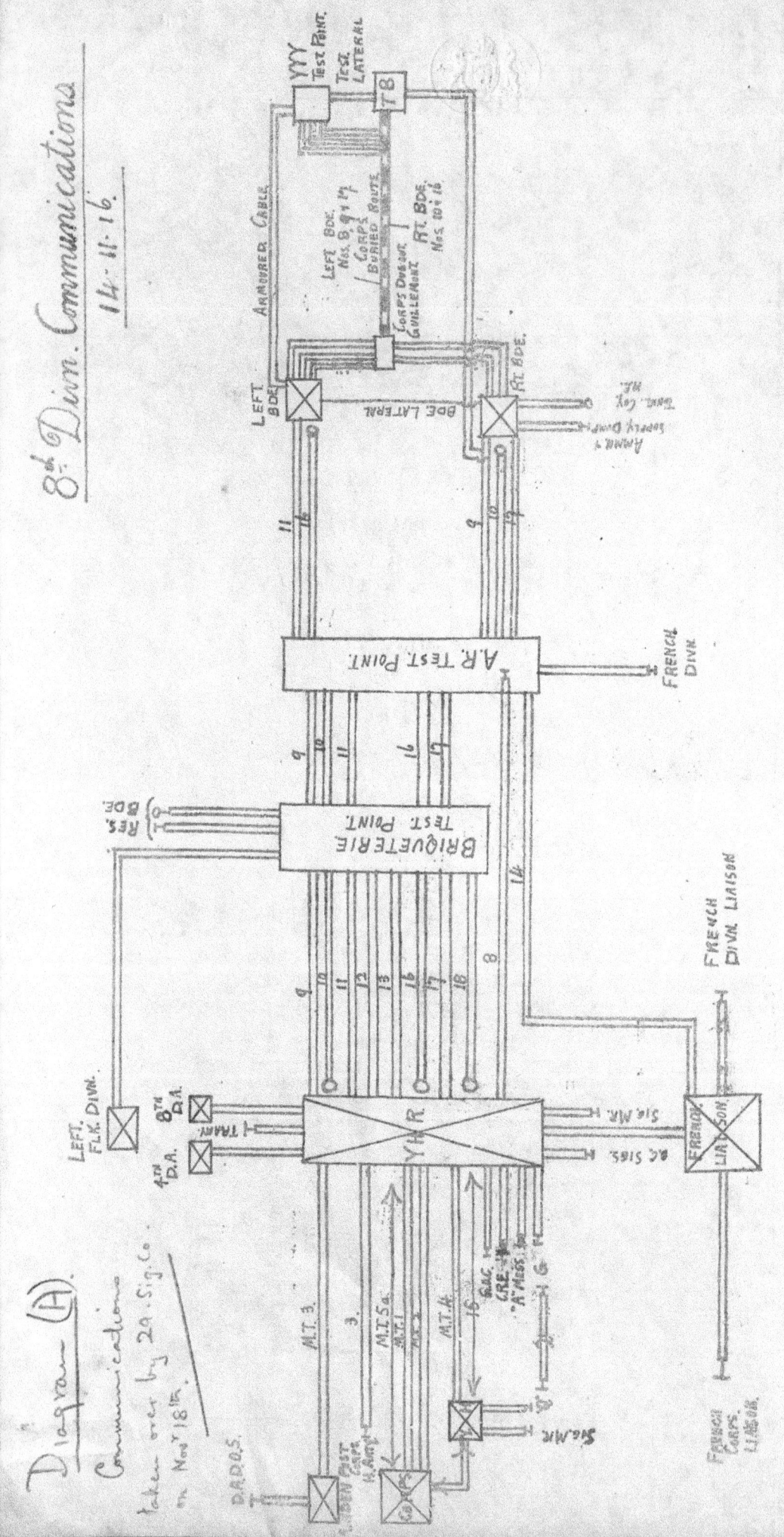

29th Divisional Engineers

29th DIVISIONAL SIGNAL COMPANY R. E.

DECEMBER 1 9 1 6

//
Army Form C. 2118.

WAR DIARY
or
INTELLIGENCE SUMMARY.

(Erase heading not required.)

Vol 6

Confidential

War Diary

of

29th Divisional Signal Co. R.E.

from 1st December 1916 to 31st December 1916.

(Volume 6)

WAR DIARY
or
INTELLIGENCE SUMMARY.
(Erase heading not required.)

Army Form C. 2118.

Place	Date	Hour	Summary of Events and Information	Remarks and references to Appendices
	1.12.16		Route to GUILLEMONT QUARRIES completed. One phone has now one sounder to each brigade, and one phone put to Arty exchange. QUARRIES Commune crusher. Afternoon route to local phones & electric light. Message dealt with 853 Registered S.P.'s 46	
	2.12.16		Test work out, still sew TRONES WOOD siding. Cpl. Batt working on route repaired all wires in about half-an-hour. Sidings still open as Divis. has no wires out. 8 bays of broken trestle work complete. Continuation of work in organizing wiring at NHR. Forward lines all correct. Right brigade taken over from French on its right, putting one more battalion in the communication via hunts again. Ready dug-out message exchange allotted with B.S.C. Messages dealt with 703 Registered S.P's 62	
	3.12.16		Trestle work continued. Also work at A Delta. Tails laid from Corps (BC) route Repair to second four letters. Normal maintenance. All wires correct. Message dealt with 666 Registered S.P.'s 56	

WAR DIARY
or
INTELLIGENCE SUMMARY

Army Form C. 2118.

Place	Date	Hour	Summary of Events and Information	Remarks and references to Appendices
	4.12.16		Line laid by Right Section (Regt Bde) to advance in southern road (T6) of FRANK AVENUE. Traffic route work continues. Local offensive route completed. Second line to Rear HQ on Corps route completed, working well after party had spent day in straining wires on Corps (BG) route. New Corps Sister wire route (Wires Arras Hd) copse much damaged by frost. This shows necessity of having wires fairly slack in cold weather. Acetham degree of slackness also leads to prevent damage by concussion as seen in shelling on 2nd inst. Somme Shea OK. Message dealt with 644. Registered SPi.s 49.	
	5.12.16		Traffic route completed to Railway crossing. Small 9-pair open wire lay commenced to replace all cables radiating from Big Office except pairs to 2nd Div. BRIQUETERIE. O.C. Hqs. 20th Div with officers came up for CORBIE. Took over communications with a view to taking over. Two tongue Section officers with party proceeds to Brigade HQ line for same purpose. Message dealt with 766. Registered SPi.s 52.	

WAR DIARY or INTELLIGENCE SUMMARY

Army Form C. 2118.

Place	Date	Hour	Summary of Events and Information	Remarks and references to Appendices
	6.12.16		Wiring on traffic route completed. Also replacement of cables by the sides of the JKQ. Working parties pair men am & pm. One a phone to Heavy Arty Group via Heavy Arty Exchange T.W. Theatre replaced band SS nearly D.A.A. attached. Mud has damaged considerably Inhabiting (including R.E.) waggons in are to to station at I.O.M. workshops, one Menage (S-85 B2c sector - Sp.Gd.) despatches (I.O.M. as Orderly men to go on with repairing these. New E.L. wagon came 5pm, working at 6.30pm Long running on road. Message dealt with 4/0. Registered S.P.'s ⅙	
	7.12.16		Traffic route staying emptying. All sixteen wires brought into use, and cables on the route raised from poles. Re-wiring & hiring of lines at H.R.(Arco) completed. Stabling for horses very nearly sufficient to hold two all the horses. Break on Copse Buoy causes disorganization. Horse from no. brigade. Each brigade however had one pair left uncut 20 communication not attempted. To pair (Allied) picked up between H.R. + BRIQUETERIE. Messages dealt with 922. Registered S.P.'s. 101	

Place	Date	Hour	Summary of Events and Information	Remarks and references to Appendices
		8.2.8	Since the Corps moved south the still seem slow of their advance yesterday. Too many Germans in the act to try & get them even through. One himself seems on return from 10M but a still slow and another is sent down. Nearly new 3 fell to hasten work. In season was to give measured to 3 to hasten work. In season was to give to bomber brewing but the first pretty accounts of its trying to make El long commences the road but cannot to block or the buffer heavy dust took 911. Reported SPt 83 General help tip around it. 15th by Baalmen but on one Bukthoud. The unit appeared that on advanced party of trusses from 29th Dn were 1st 16 hrs they arrive too late to start work. It paid one to a bad time of night. Elsewhere out with the lot sent unable of the book fell on the statements but a safer son. Reported SPt 95 here died a tools 1031	

WAR DIARY
or
INTELLIGENCE SUMMARY.
(Erase heading not required.)

Army Form C. 2118.

Place	Date	Hour	Summary of Events and Information	Remarks and references to Appendices
	10.12.16		2nd Division advance party to set stations & the personnel of the bay withdrew. Hus harness room completed through Q near hqrs on new route via MONTAUBAN. Message dealt with 1101. Registered SPs 58.	
	11.12.16		All personnel & transport of 29th Sigs. reached for CORBIE with exception of office relief and 10 linemen. Bus time bed 95 ways with broken back stand empty. Sorry to mend & procure new state of found that delay 5 min. 20th Sigs. arrived about 4 p.m. & take over billets. All plans including route diagram, defence scheme re handed over to 20 in command. 20 installed their electric light & make arrangements to carry on from 7am. The next day. Sorry to move & consequently reduced number of messages. Units & CoPs are capacited. Received circuit to sees by superimposing on phone pairs. Messages are also sent to CoPs in rear hqrs. Messages dealt with 629. Registered SPs 65.	

WAR DIARY or INTELLIGENCE SUMMARY

Army Form C. 2118.

Place	Date	Hour	Summary of Events and Information	Remarks and references to Appendices
	12.12.16	8 am	29th relieved in the office by 20th with exception of telegraphs.	
		9 am	20th Div. S.L.Sub works & wires taken out.	
		10 am	20th Div. take over one line to rear hdqrs down owing to shelling of Corps route. Also alternative line to A.R. thro'line & everything in order. Office opened at CORBIE at same hour by advanced party. Dismounted sappers leave for CORBIE by empty 20th E.L. lorry & on S.L. lorry. Message dealt with 463. Reg.n bid 5R. 18	
	13.12.16		Company march at 7.30 am for PICQUIGNY arriving here about 2.30 pm. About 20 men proceed by lorry to CAVILLON & open up office there at 4 pm. CORBIE office closes down at the same hour. Billets very crowded but linen under cover. No place for store which is necessary to all stores & no transport requires an haul. No communication with billets who are still on the move. Message dealt with 441	
	14.12.16		86th & 87th bdes assume that one connected by telm wing lines. Sounds. Reinforced in order to put the necessary Reglind Sty. 12 lines.	

WAR DIARY
or
INTELLIGENCE SUMMARY.

Army Form C. 2118.

Place	Date	Hour	Summary of Events and Information	Remarks and references to Appendices
	15.11.16		Telephone communication. About 9.5 p.m. 88th Bde Hqrs arrive & are temporary in power. Telephone & telegraph communication established with the 3 Bdes. Ammunitions from to Bdes to Bns. Bns in touch with their battalions. Regular run 3 times daily arranged. R.E.R calling at each village in the divisional area. Messages dealt with 690. Registered SP's — 20	
	16.11.16		All lines to Brigades working well but extemporised line to VIENACOURT unsatisfactory, an intermittent fault on line. Corps signals informed. Messages dealt with 582. Registered SP's. 29. 2 detachments seem out to postings line to 87th Bde who move from SOUES to HANGEST and to make the necessary alterations on the 116" Brigade battalion lines. Messages dealt with 740. Registered SP's 35	

WAR DIARY
or
INTELLIGENCE SUMMARY

Army Form C. 2118.

Place	Date	Hour	Summary of Events and Information	Remarks and references to Appendices
	17.12.16		Cable detachments continue their work + furnished the estimation + additions. No programme of having submitted owing to new spending time on Equipment, harness + wagons all of which require time + attention. Messages dealt with 390. Registered SPs. 34	
	18.12.16		No change. Messages dealt with 402. Registered SPs. 19	
	19.12.16		No change. Messages dealt with 398. Registered SPs. 26	
	20.12.16		Airline stores drawn from 4th Army to build 2 circuits from CAVILLON to OISSEY. Construction party not available to build 61 line used to build single line from PLEQUIGNY to AILLY sur BRESLE. This line to replace a line of D1's removed which does not give satisfactory working. Proceeded to 61TQ to interview DAS Sunbeam car broke down – cross wheel trouble. Messages dealt with 416. Registered SPs. 31	

Army Form C. 2118.

WAR DIARY
or
INTELLIGENCE SUMMARY.
(Erase heading not required.)

Instructions regarding War Diaries and Intelligence Summaries are contained in F. S. Regs., Part II. and the Staff Manual respectively. Title pages will be prepared in manuscript.

Place	Date	Hour	Summary of Events and Information	Remarks and references to Appendices
	21.12.16		Examination oral & practical of Signal School. Normally conduct oral exams in instruments. Candidate went in Helio but otherwise food after as that a course. Final exam at the school.	
			Message dealt with 419	Registered S.P's. 31
	22.12.16		School breaks up. No change	
			Message dealt with 431	Registered S.P's. 34
	23.12.16		No change	
			Message dealt with 412	Registered S.P's 40
	24.12.16		No change	
			Message dealt with 428	Registered S.P's. 30
	25.12.16		A quiet day except for an official telegram. After 10 am very few message.	
			Message dealt with 190	Registered S.P's. 35
	26.12.16		No change	
			Message dealt with 435	Registered S.P's 29

Army Form C. 2118.

WAR DIARY
or
INTELLIGENCE SUMMARY.
(Erase heading not required.)

Place	Date	Hour	Summary of Events and Information	Remarks and references to Appendices
	27.12.16		No change hereoges deal- with 343	Registered SPs 26
	28.12.16		No change hereoges deal- with 349	Registered SPs 28
	29.12.16		No change hereoges deal- with 355	Registered SPs 23
			" " 420	31
			" " 313	31
	30.12.16			
	31.12.16		Diagram marked "A" shews positions as handed over on 12-12-16.	6 5in H. left Vedquad 29th Div'n on 31.12.16.

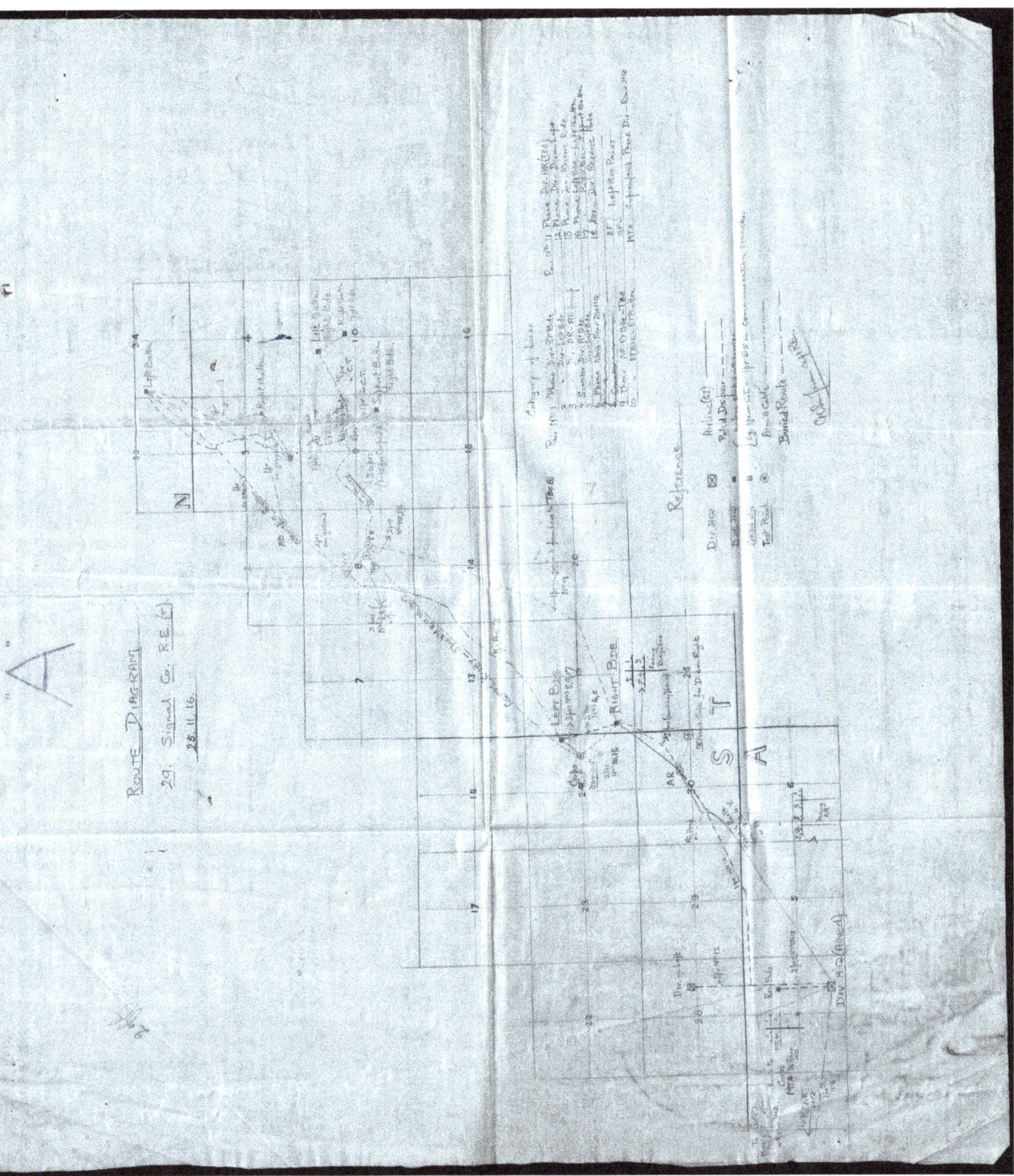

Army Form C. 2118.

WAR DIARY
or
INTELLIGENCE SUMMARY

(Erase heading not required.)

Vol 7

Confidential

War Diary

of

29th Divisional Signal Co. R.E.

from 1st January 1917 to 31st January 1917.

(Volume VII)

WAR DIARY or INTELLIGENCE SUMMARY

Army Form C. 2118.

Place	Date	Hour	Summary of Events and Information	Remarks and references to Appendices
	1.1.17		No change. Message dealt with	313 Registered SP's 41
	2.1.17		" " "	432 " 39
	3.1.17		" " "	214 " 31
	4.1.17		" " "	404 " 32
	5.1.17		Arrangements made for Contact patrol aeroplane to Jan Kerkele. Scheme undertaken by 2 battalions. Panels, strips & ground sheets wanted also a Hucks Electric light lamp. Clouds too low. Aeroplane did not arrive. Clouds about 300 ft. Message dealt with	343 Registered SP's 18
	6.1.17		Lgt & 10 men start to build a 4 wire route to OISSY, distance 2 mls. Lack of party rather handicapped the look of party. Chauvin for 8t wire (60 lb) & bolts for te S-top poles, stores obtained from Army Stores at RIBEMONT & drawn by Halford Lorry. Message dealt with	290 Registered SP 36

Place	Date	Hour	Summary of Events and Information	Remarks and references to Appendices
	7.1.17		Work continued on roads. Cpl Hansfield from 48th Aus Line Section very useful in instructing pioneers as to correct procedure in constructing semi-permanent roads. SA Cable detachment turns out for cable drill. Dismounted number very hazy, due chiefly to being employed in the office. Mounted numbers very fair but detachment commanded breaks change brigade out in stables. Two horses evacuated 1 mt from unit next door. All steps for prevention to laid down in circular memo taken to prevent the disease spreading.	
	8.1.17		Wrote message dispatch 294 reported 8 Pte all works on route to OISSY continued to cable detachment turn out for work. Jack same as for "S.A." Some small articles of equipment missing – section officer informed to take necessary action. Earlt	

WAR DIARY
or
INTELLIGENCE SUMMARY

Army Form C. 2118.

Place	Date	Hour	Summary of Events and Information	Remarks and references to Appendices
	9.1.17		pegs, shells, tent poles & brushes among rubbish mixing. In further cases of mange two isolated & clipped. Mange dealt with 360. Reported SP's 52. Orders received to move to CORBIE on 11th inst. however continues en route & came jemm-led o.c. hoses. Result quite satisfactory as far as he knew, his jour, but took was concerned, but looks was glos, the horses will be improved upon. A detachment turn out for function. The regulation sents sent that this due to old men being in the team. Every man knew this was his job except one no. 4. Suspected mange case evacuated by No. 75 who inspects the stables & puts place was out of Bounds. Num. a glo. dealt with 436. Reported SP's 50.	

1577 Wt. W10791/1773 500,000 1/15 D. D. & L. A.D.S.S./Forms/C. 2118.

WAR DIARY or INTELLIGENCE SUMMARY

Army Form C. 2118.

Place	Date	Hour	Summary of Events and Information	Remarks and references to Appendices
	10-1-17		Contact patrol scheme arranged in the morning for 87th Bde & in the afternoon for 88th Bde. The latter fell through owing to bad weather. "A" Cable Section inspected & found to be satisfactory. Turn out of men could be improved. Put the horses & harness fair. 88th Section carry out a visual scheme with visual signallers in the section. Was daylight lamp tested & reported sent to G.S.	
			Message dealt with 506. Revisited SPs 7	
	11-1-17		by marches to CORBIE arriving 4 p.m. One detachment remain behind to pick up a temporary line from MANGEST to LE QUESNOY via SOUS office at CAYEUX closes at 3 p.m. & replans CORBIE at same hour. Subscribes on the phone me via DAR - me via GCO & the other direct. Put signal school reading lamps for night work required on front line hut quite satisfactory. Shall with 248. Reported SPs 24 messages	

1527 Wt. W10791/1773 500,000 1/15 D.D.&L. A.D.S.S./Forms/C. 2118.

Army Form C. 2118.

WAR DIARY
or
INTELLIGENCE SUMMARY.
(Erase heading not required.)

Instructions regarding War Diaries and Intelligence Summaries are contained in F. S. Regs., Part II. and the Staff Manual respectively. Title pages will be prepared in manuscript.

Place	Date	Hour	Summary of Events and Information	Remarks and references to Appendices
	12.1.17		One suspected mumps case evacuated to M.V.S. General clean up. Electric light installed in officers' Mess Staff to see off to have lights.	
	13.1.17		Kisongo dealt with 268. Reported SPs. 23. "A" Section turned out early drill under Capt Simpson. considerable improvement shown. Noticeable weather but 2/c. 12th Division to find out point on the Lake now. Every thing however came on when we were in. The Tuneholding the same sector. Kisongo dealt with 281. Reported SPs. 3.	
	14.1.17		Greatly handicapped owing to can being to workshops. General Shaw M.T. absent off after leave to England. 2nd in Command proceeds with the advance party to commence Lake new. Halford Long duet Kisongo dealt with 155. Reported SPs. 38	
	15.1.17		All the Company (except 10 men) have to have on the line.	

Place	Date	Hour	Summary of Events and Information	Remarks and references to Appendices
	16.1.17		Coy moves a day early in order to facilitate the take over at 10 a.m. All approaches to here closed between 6 a.m. & 11 a.m. 17th Signal Coy arrive here (Erbie) from the line. Messages dealt with 233. Regd. tel. S.Ps. 29. Take over from 17th Coys at 10 a.m. Office at Erbie above.	
	17.1.17		At the same hour. All amendts working well but signal office not tidy owing to it being moved from a dug out to a Nissen hut. By 4 p.m. nearly all the officers except Signal Office lit by electric light. Lorry runs off the road, this being impossible owing to frost &c. Messages dealt with 208. Regd. tel. S.Ps. 42. Remainder of electric light fittings but two to Brigettine thirty during away Corps route but this to Brigettine thirty during away with a poled cable line. All cables around the can to peeled up. Conference by S.O.C. 3 p.m. Messages dealt with 426. Regd. tel. S.Ps. 26	

WAR DIARY
or
INTELLIGENCE SUMMARY.

(Erase heading not required.)

Army Form C. 2118.

Place	Date	Hour	Summary of Events and Information	Remarks and references to Appendices
	18.1.17		All lines working well. Sappers reel up spare lines to the Rasputine & recover 3000 yds D5 cable & one pole. 29th F.A. take over from 11th J.A. by now R.A. offices to the D of withdrawing their personnel. All R.A. lines put through test panels in office – same took well. Message dealt with 639	
	19.1.17		Repeated SPs 53. Some doubtful lines received. Two limbered wagons for to looks help with broken hooks. Reputed scheme for buried lines by R.E. Signals who submits scheme for buried scheme. G.S. cannot give the necessary labour until a late date. In view of the fact that divisions are only in the line for a short time it appears more practicable for area parties to have all test dugouts on buried routes. This would ensure both reliefs from the bury & would free divisional sappers for other work. Messages dealt with 689. Repeated SPs 49	

WAR DIARY
or
INTELLIGENCE SUMMARY

Army Form C. 2118.

Place	Date	Hour	Summary of Events and Information	Remarks and references to Appendices
	20.1.17		NCO & 4 men sent to a brigade section to help with lines & battalion which are [earthy?] & give trouble. Remaining available men stay [hostile?] route & recover derelict cable. Menagha dealt with 646	
	21.1.17		Information received from GS of forthcoming minor offensive. In consequence reconnoitre work & views carrying divisional line forward to the command put. Menagha dealt with 588. Reported SPs 62	Reported SPs 59
	22.1.17		Unit Signal School to make final arrangements for the assembly of the officers class. Beds & table obtained from the CRE for officers mess tent. Two officers detailed to reconnoitre lays in dugouts with a view to installing an E.L. plant. El-Girha reconnoitred again to find OP which GS wishes to be connected up. Terrace hoot. Dont Corps put on all lines. Menagha dealt with 666.	Reported SPs 49

WAR DIARY
or
INTELLIGENCE SUMMARY.

(Erase heading not required.)

Army Form C. 2118.

Place	Date	Hour	Summary of Events and Information	Remarks and references to Appendices
	23.1.17		Line to Corps from Rear hqrs closed down at 20 all hqrs moved to A.B.H.S moved forward to Staffix. The only vehicles to Coy HQ's sick & handicrafted in consequence.	
	24.1.17		Faulted lines retied out. hq engr dealt with by. Reported S.P. 50. Provisional S.P. at V7 c 7.3 connected by wire to Batt. HQ & put in as Brigade unit. 2½ miles of wire issued. Sgt. Lineman detailed for this O.P. Arrangements made with B.S.O. & wireless officer re power buzzer & wireless. Asked for papers from O/C at Corps HQs. Attached marked Ⓐ sent to G.S.	Ⓐ
	25.1.17		Two D lines laid from 87th hqrs to then command post each line 2½ miles long. Line paid out in the usual way but reliefs were necessary	

WAR DIARY
or
INTELLIGENCE SUMMARY

Army Form C. 2118.

Place	Date	Hour	Summary of Events and Information	Remarks and references to Appendices
	26.1.17		an account of the tops state of the weight of the drums. the tres & the men from resting bde section assisted in carrying out the work. two D turn lines also laid from end of the C/fs being to bde C.P. for the maintenance of these lines 2 men were stationed at bde C.P. + two men at bde H.W. heavy shell work 645. Resistered S.P. 69. Two shot long the of cable laid is the vicinity of bde hqs to complete existing arrangements. Personnel consisting of 1 Sigmr. + 3 Operators + 2 Linesmen sent to the hqs to forward work. th Corps sent up to supervise in charge this office.	Returned S.Ps 55
				Returned S.Ps drall with 644

WAR DIARY or INTELLIGENCE SUMMARY

Army Form C. 2118.

Place	Date	Hour	Summary of Events and Information	Remarks and references to Appendices
	27/11		All lines forwarded personally tested & reported to General Staff. Food supple all round. At 5.30 am an attack hour attack commenced the report all lines through.	
		8.10 am	CRA's command line to Lions Office pes weak. Fault rectified by changing from cable to air line on rear to of line.	
		10.5 am	Intermittent due on G.S. line. Fault on local came replaced by new line.	
		10.30 am	Fault on no 16 telephone switchboard. Traced to broken spring. Another no 16 substituted. Messages by pigeon arrive during afternoon, but take 2 – 3½ hrs, due no doubt to the severe frost. Wireless not used except for a test message which proves satisfactory. Messages dealt with 608. Replies SP, w	

WAR DIARY
or
INTELLIGENCE SUMMARY

Army Form C. 2118.

Place	Date	Hour	Summary of Events and Information	Remarks and references to Appendices
	28/1/17		At 9pm of pigeons sent for the operation 5 are so far missing. All pigeons were released & their failure to arrive is due to either puncture or faulty & slightly misty weather or their arriving at the loft from their line took about 6 hours. Pigeons reached destination. Forwards for cable made biweekly or Corps not met. The want in a temporary shortage to brigade & battalions in new area was larger than the of cable. The shelling is heavy & alternative route an necessary. Base buzzers working to amplifier were not rescued. Sufficient hot-living rations. & small potentials made locally has been food much but owing to difficulty in obtaining necessary stores men have not been made. The attached diagram shows the proposed potentiometer.	

1577 Wt.W.10791/1773 500,000 1/15 D.D.&L. A.D.S.S./Forms/C. 2118.

WAR DIARY
or
INTELLIGENCE SUMMARY.

Army Form C. 2118.

Place	Date	Hour	Summary of Events and Information	Remarks and references to Appendices
Srinagar	29.1.17		Having to cover fort it was found that along the ground became faulty & rarely when a slight tension set in. No thorough examination has as yet been made but it appears that the insulation cracks. Fault has so far appeared on D turn cable. Tested Dr wagon on line to fire trouble which is enclosed by the fort. The hook heads away from the dynamo to the fort. Springs break, & G.S. limbered wagon with lock up box usually capacity of limbered RE would prove satisfactory as per sketch. Registered SPs: 53	

Dealt with SPY

WAR DIARY or INTELLIGENCE SUMMARY

Army Form C. 2118.

Place	Date	Hour	Summary of Events and Information	Remarks and references to Appendices
	30.1.17.		This would give an additional carrying capacity which is required. Message dealt with 541. Reported SP's. 48.	
			Owing to a large quantity of stuff being obtained this trail had to be reduced to the establishment of a clerk or the assist. Corps is needed to cope with the clerical work.	(B)
			Question of stores for Artillery limb submitted to A.D. hyp'h agreed to as for attached marked (B) — note. All DR's found done by motor DR's — motor cyclists thus set free work to effective as DR'S clerk. Message dealt with 544. Registered SP's. 45	(B)

Army Form C. 2118.

WAR DIARY
or
INTELLIGENCE SUMMARY.
(Erase heading not required.)

Place	Date	Hour	Summary of Events and Information	Remarks and references to Appendices
	31.1.17		Proceed to Signal School & give a lecture on:- a.) work of a divisional Signal Coy b.) Liason between Infantry & Aircraft. c.) Carrier pigeon Service. All officers NCOs & men attend. Lecture lasts 1½ hrs. Sunbeam car in very bad condition. 3 wheels loose due to worn hubs. Circuit diagram (C) is attached. Marked (C) is attached. Reported OPs 53 heavy gun dead with 490 attached marked. While in rest - Tilles 6 attached marked. Diagram of lines. L. Littlehof Lt. 29th Signal Coy RE OC 29th Signal Coy RE 31.1.17.	C D

(A)

29th Div G.

The Signal arrangements for the forthcoming offensive are as follows:-

1. <u>Telephone & Telegraph.</u>

In order to give the necessary direct lines between Brigade Commander and the Liaison Officer with brigade and General Staff and G.O.C. R.A., two metallic lines are being laid from Guillemont Quarries to T.9.B.3.3. At Guillemont Quarries these lines are joined to existing lines on the Divisional Trestle Route. Between Division and the Brigade Command Post an intermediate exchange will be put in as the magneto telephone in use will not ring through the whole length of the line. This exchange will be at Guillemont Station. As an alternative a line in the buried system will be attached to this exchange and will be used if the exposed lines fail. All messages by telegraph between the Brigade Command Post and the Division will be sent on another line in the "bury" & same will be transmitted by morse from Guillemont Station

2. <u>Runners.</u>

A runner post will be situated just off the Duck Boards about T.8.D. central. This runner post will work forward to the Brigade Report Centre and backward to a motor cyclist post established just south of Ginchy near the anti-aircraft guns. These motor cyclists will work direct to the division

3. Wireless.

A wireless station will be erected at T.9.B.3.3. and will send to a parent set at Guillemont station whence the messages will be transmitted by morse or in the event of the lines in the back area not working to a similar station situated at these headquarters.

4. Pigeons

9 pairs of birds will be available. Four pairs will be alloted to each battalion and 1 pair will be kept at the Brigade Command Post for cases of emergency.

5. Contact Patrol Aeroplane.

There will be an aeroplane station at the Brigade Report Centre for communication of messages to aircraft.

6. Signal Arrangements in front of Brigade Command Post.

A triplicate "earth" return line will be laid between the Brigade Command Post and Antelope trench (Advanced battalion Hqrs of both battalions). At these Headqrs a power buzzer will be installed which will work to a receiving set in T.10.B.1.8. This receiving station will be in touch by telephone with the Brigade Command Post.

Telephone lines in triplicate will be laid from these Headquarters to Company Headqrs in dug-outs about T.6.B.1½.6½. where a power buzzer will also be installed.

Battalion Headqrs of the Right Brigade in the Sunken Road about T.12.A.6.9 will be connected to the Headquarters in Antelope trench. This will provide an alternative route between the attacking battalions

(3.)

and their brigade

An aeroplane station will be established at the Advanced battalion headquarters in antelope trench

The Divisional "O.P." situated about U.7.c.8.2. will be connected to the exchange at T.17.D.

Capt
OC 29th Div Sig Co
RE

To. O.C. ~~Guards Divisional Signals.R.E.~~
   ~~17th Divisional Signals.R.E.~~
   ~~20th Divisional Signals.R.E.~~
   29th Divisional Signals.R.E.
   ~~Acting Company Quartermaster, XIV Corps Signals.~~

(B)

The following proposals having met with general acceptance, will accordingly be adopted, and Officers Commanding Divisional Signal Companies should advise Divisional Artillery Units accordingly.

(1). All Artillery units covering the Front of a Division will indent for supplies of cable through O.C. Divisional Signal Company actually in the Line.

(2). Brigades and Batteries in the Reserve Area, will indent direct on A.D.Signals.

(3). In the event of a relief of Artillery Units while their Division is holding the Line, outstanding indents will be sent to A.D.Signals for adjustment.

Lieut Colonel,
Somerset.L.I.,
A.D.Signals XIV Corps.

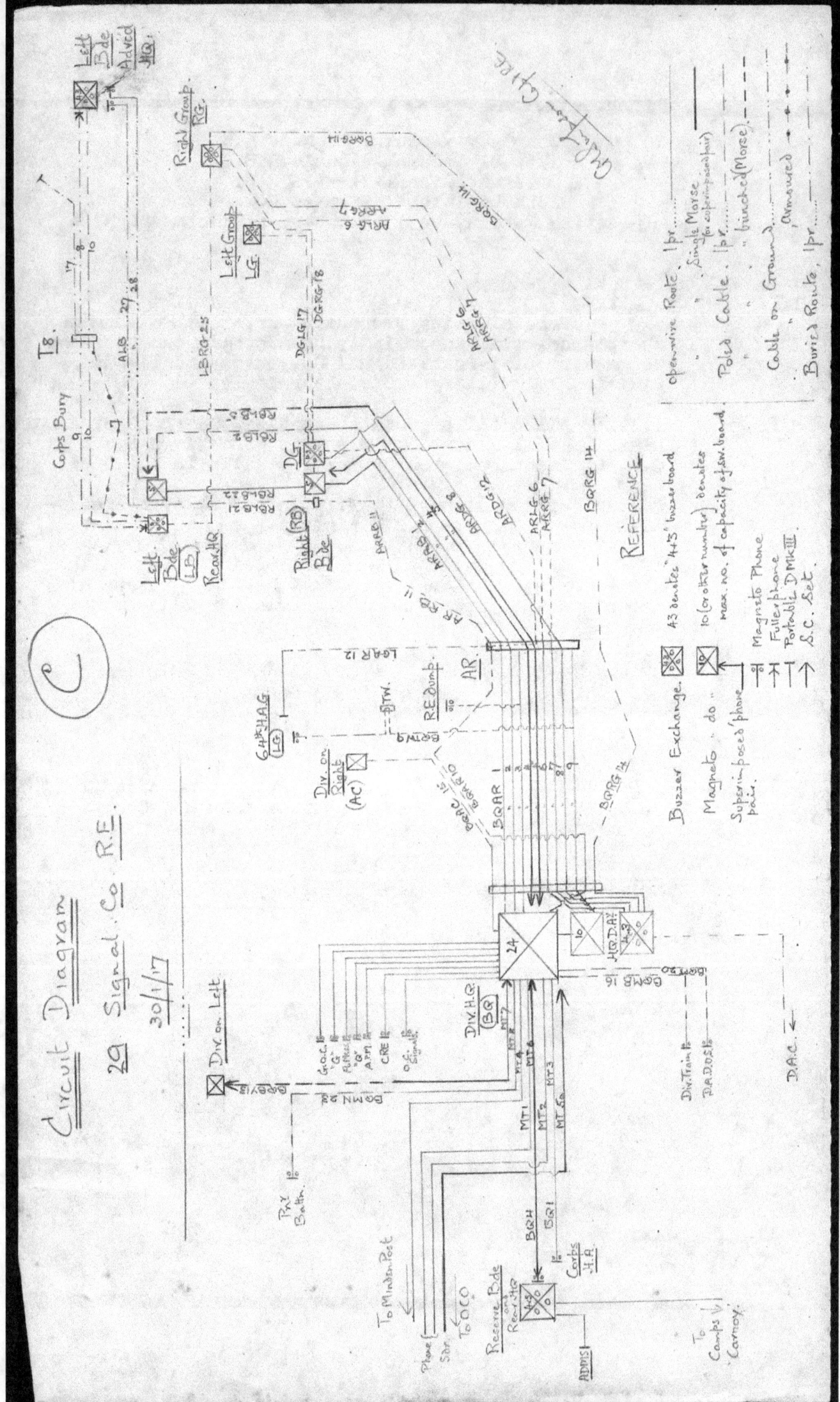

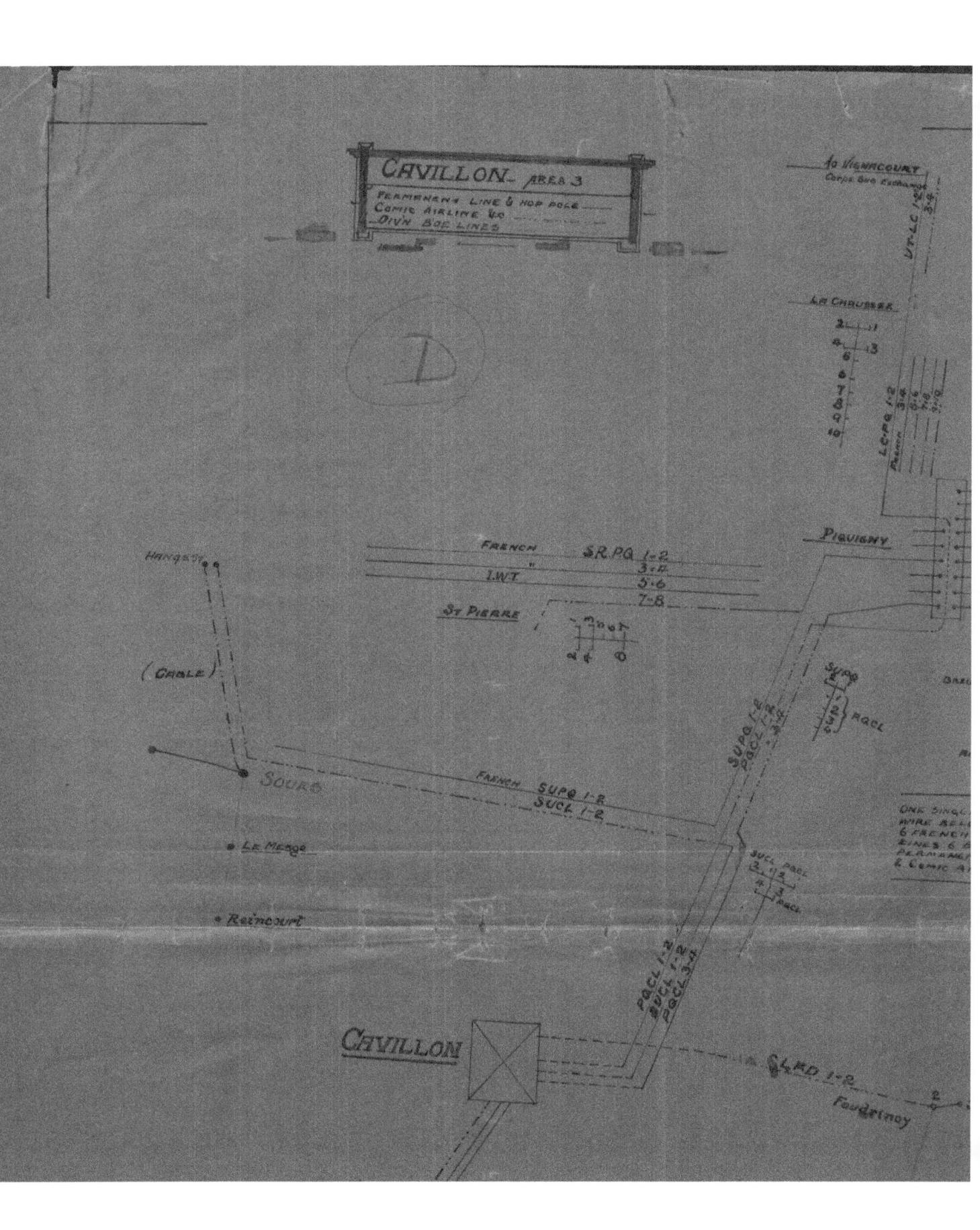

Army Form C. 2118.

WAR DIARY
or
INTELLIGENCE SUMMARY.

(Erase heading not required.)

Vol 8

Confidential.

War Diary

of

29th Divisional Signal Co. R.E.

From 1st February 1917 to 28th February 1917.

(Volume 8).

D.H.Q. Signals.

WAR DIARY
or
INTELLIGENCE SUMMARY.

Army Form C. 2118.

February 1917.

Place	Date	Hour	Summary of Events and Information	Remarks and references to Appendices
BRAYELLE Ads 5.4.	Feby 1st		Owing to frozen ground, impossible to peg the lines, which however work well on ground. Ground lines Left Brigade Rear HQ located stop cut by shell fire behind GINCHY. Also line between Right Brigade & Left Brigade Rear: about 5.0 pm Maintenance of other lines continued. Messages dealt with 607. Registered S.P.S. 60	
	2nd		Frost. Usual maintenance, more especially Trestle route. 40 cars arrowed good send to MAIE wood for burying under C.T. Using big fires from TI8 a 3.9 to front line by Pioneer bath. Messages dealt with 527. Registered S.P.S. 81	
	3rd		Party sent out to TI8 a 3.9 to lay cable in C.T. dug by pioneers. On arrival, reconnoitred trench & found scheme impracticable. Maintenance continued, especially relaying of lines between Right brigade & G.I. (Rear left Bde). Considerable theroupins difficulty experienced in watering horses owing to frozen state of water mains. Only one water a day possible on several days. Messages dealt with 682. Registered S.P.S. 53.	

WAR DIARY
INTELLIGENCE SUMMARY
(Erase heading not required.)

Place	Date	Hour	Summary of Events and Information	Remarks and references to Appendices
	4th		Fault on lines to Reserve Bde & Corps HA, also NoG to Right Group. Linesmen for Coy. Lines sent OUT. Otherwise normal maintenance - ground too hard for any construction or digging. Messages dealt with 600. Registered S.P's 89	
	5th		Same as above. Line No 27 & 28 from G.L. to A Bde Left Brigade cut twice during day by shell fire, but soon repaired, a few linesmen are detailed Div Tran for these two points. Wireless Div Tram gives trouble, but partly due to fault in office of. Registered S.P's 95. Messages dealt with 660	
	6th		Normal maintenance. No faults. Advance party 20th Div Sigs arrive. Messages dealt with 656 Registered S.P's 81	
	7th		Advance Party 20th Div Sigs. sent on to man all out-stations, and men of 29 Sig. Co. at these places come in. Our advance party move to HEILLY to partially man HEILLY Signal Office, & to secure billets. Messages dealt with 714 Registered S.P's 101	

Army Form C. 2118.

WAR DIARY
or
INTELLIGENCE SUMMARY.
(Erase heading not required.)

Place	Date	Hour	Summary of Events and Information	Remarks and references to Appendices
HEILLY.	8th		Company moves to HEILLY, leaving behind 2 office staffs, 2 DR linemen, and instrument repairers. Also O.C. Signals. Remainder arrive HEILLY 3pm. 2nd Lt. C. moved out in morning, proceeding to line & staging at CITADEL. HEILLY Sig. Office taken over at 8pm by our office-relief. Intact officially. Messages dealt with 64. Registered S.P.'s 81	
	9th		General clean-up men, horses, billets. Picket lines reorganized to avoid damaging trees. Ice-broken in stream adjoining to obtain water. Point close at hand. Office in line handed over to 20th at 10am. Messages dealt with 620. Registered S.P.'s 86	
	10th		Long 15 HOURS fatigue supplies kits and CRM's office "A" detachment out under Lt Gerke, with special attention to rapidity & smartness. Improvement shown. Commence overhauling & greasing our cattle wagons, slipping each at a time "SS" wagon started on. Messages dealt with 357. Registered SPS. 36	

Army Form C. 2118.

WAR DIARY
or
INTELLIGENCE SUMMARY.
(Erase heading not required.)

Instructions regarding War Diaries and Intelligence Summaries are contained in F. S. Regs., Part II. and the Staff Manual respectively. Title pages will be prepared in manuscript.

Place	Date	Hour	Summary of Events and Information	Remarks and references to Appendices
	11th		Church parade, clean arms, inspection 10.30 a.m. All round improvement in turn out noted since tour in line in November-December. All rifles passed. Message dealt with 351	Registered S.P.'s 42
	12th		"A" detachment out on cable drill, rifle wagon; S.A. wagon being overhauled. Also B. wagon. Messages dealt with 378	Registered S.P.'s 30
	13th		"B" detachment on drill. Remainder as usual. Messages dealt with 307	Registered S.P.'s 27
	14th		"SB" detachment on drill. Usual work on bikes & stables. Messages dealt with 323	Registered S.P.'s 43
	15th		"A" detachment on drill. Parade strength as usual. Messages dealt with 384	Registered P.'s 48

1577 Wt.W10791/1773 500,000 1/15 D. D. & L. A.D.S.S./Forms/C. 2118.

WAR DIARY
or
INTELLIGENCE SUMMARY.
(Erase heading not required.)

Army Form C. 2118.

Place	Date	Hour	Summary of Events and Information	Remarks and references to Appendices
JEALLY	16th		"SA" detachment on duty. Remainder routine as usual. 3rd Course at Div Sig. School commences. This course for 80 men instead of 40. Sgt Ward from No 3 section is one instructor from 84th Bde. sent as additional instructors. More flags requirement asked for by G.S. 2/Lt GREEN from No 3 Section goes to Command Sig school, 2/Lt KING from signal school to command No 3 Section. Messages dealt with 2/3	Registered S.P.s 63
	17th		"B" detachment out. All round improvement noted in all detachments. Insulation complete, except "rat-sent". R.E. train visits JEALLY, and portion entertained by Fifth Corps Signal Company. Messages dealt with 56	Registered S.P.s 43
	18th		Church parade 11 am. Relief arrangements by no of 17th Division Signals upset by Thaw precaution. Stoppage of lorry traffic. Brigade orders held up at RAINNEVILLE & BUSSY. Messages dealt with 439	Registered S.P.s 60

Army Form C. 2118.

WAR DIARY
or
INTELLIGENCE SUMMARY.
(Erase heading not required.)

Place	Date	Hour	Summary of Events and Information	Remarks and references to Appendices
	19th		Advance party, linemen only, proceed in G.S. wagon to ARROW HEAD COPSE (AC) the H.Q. of 17 Divn. Arrive about 2.30 p.m. L/Cpl Stoke also goes up to see O.C. Signals 17 Div. about points of interest; also to see camp. B de sections to Mamoz LA NEUVILLE to entrain tomorrow, unable to see at advance parties. Their return will be late. That precautions cause great inconvenience as more of the unit would have been by lorry yesterday. Messages dealt with 483. Registered P's 35	
	20th		Advance party, first office relief arrive AC 1pm, having marched to CITADEL yesterday. Advance body, 2nd office relief & linemen arrive CITADEL. Brigade sections detrained PLATEAU 3.30pm & marched straight up. Relief completed 8pm, through lines tk, finished 2pm original operation order. Messages dealt with 402. Registered P's 37	
	21st		Office opened AC at 10 am, office HEILLY taken over by 17 Sigs. at that hour. Remainder of company marched up, bivving at FRICOURT CIRCUS.	

Army Form C. 2118.

WAR DIARY
or
INTELLIGENCE SUMMARY.
(Erase heading not required.)

Instructions regarding War Diaries and Intelligence Summaries are contained in F. S. Regs., Part II. and the Staff Manual respectively. Title pages will be prepared in manuscript.

Place	Date	Hour	Summary of Events and Information	Remarks and references to Appendices
ARROWHEAD COPSE	21st		Horse & driver to CITADEL under CSM. CQMS with GS wagon and two light springs to MINDEN POST. Operators Vokmen, motorcyclists (new 2 at MINDEN POST), two mounted DRs to AC with whitecoat one light spring. Lines OK but line to Left Brigade somewhat precarious. Messages dealt with 434. Registered S.P.3. 51	
	22nd		Normal maintenance, linesmen becoming accustomed to circuits dispositions. One light spring from CITADEL to O'REILLY to get more stores. Messages dealt with 343. Registered S.P.5. 54	
	23rd		Linesleid from ML to Left Bde HQ with twisted D5 in view of operations. Burying (140 new 1/2 Mammoths) commenced between CAP ML. 31.0.4.98. Messages dealt with 5/15. Registered S.P.3. 16	

1577 Wt. W10791/1773 500,000 1/15 D.D.&L. A.D.S.S./Forms/C. 2118.

WAR DIARY
or
INTELLIGENCE SUMMARY.
(Erase heading not required.)

Army Form C. 2118.

Place	Date	Hour	Summary of Events and Information	Remarks and references to Appendices
	24th		Line laid to Grenade Officer near TRONES WOOD SIDING. Burying continued, extensively. Corps Signals personnel. All stores at HEILLY moved, including stores for DAOURS. Flurry except six telephones still in use (by 178th Signals, telephones not yet arrived down). 2/Lt MUIR reports for duty with company). Messages dealt with 526. Registered S.P's 82	See 2/Lt SINGLETON. "Wireless"
	25th		Louder Kloft Bde, informed by cutting out portion of bury from CA to No1 Test box on CAMI route and replacing with D'tain overground. Artillery given old overhead route (line common) for use to MX exchange by 2nd S. Army Brigade. Destroyed by D'wA'ky baby to BD, for temporary use. Telephone from HEILLY brought up to CITADEL, with remainder stores. All other stores go to DAOURS. Messages dealt with 588. Registered S.P's 66	
	26th		"C" bar, howleft Brigade Group HQ At their Advanced Command Post (Ye HERULE) laid by Sgt Lowmark. Party Throughout 1pm. One line on CAMI bury handed over to Heavy artillery, as replaced by D'tain overground (buburg). Burying continued — 280 yards to complete. Messages dealt with 611. Registered S.P's 65	See a/lc Diagram "A"

WAR DIARY or INTELLIGENCE SUMMARY

Army Form C. 2118.

Place	Date	Hour	Summary of Events and Information	Remarks and references to Appendices
	27th		"D" line laid from Left Bde Group HQ to the T.C.P. by L/Cpl Owen's party. Throughout 1pm All lines complete. In preparation of minor offensive. Visual stations and power buzzers arranged between various stations and pigeons sent out to both brigade groups. Newbury CAPTML completed 4-5pm. Some special lines allotted for own use and working by 6pm. Left Bde Group moved to Command Post about 6pm. Also 7pm "A" "B" lines dis, but nothing through via REACH and "C" line Station call HW allotted Left Bde rear HQ. At 9pm. Direct lines from VB1 and Div Arty. to RAKE working well via "A" "B" (passed). Extra personnel, operators & linemen sent out to stn. Messages dealt with 658. Registered S.P.'s 52	See Diagram
	28th		All ways through nothing until 5:15 am; also forward lines from Bde C.P. to Advd. Battn HQs zero at APM 5:25 am At 5:55 am all lines between Brigade and battalions cut by barrage and SALLY-SAILLISEL. Power buzzers and continuous wave wireless from SALLY Church working the whole time. Lines from rear to HEBUTE held, except for two short disconnection on "C", each quickly repaired. No Interruption of telegraphic communication with HEBUTE. Messages dealt with 654. Registered S.P.'s 55	

Cal Superm Capt RE
for O/C signals 29 Div.

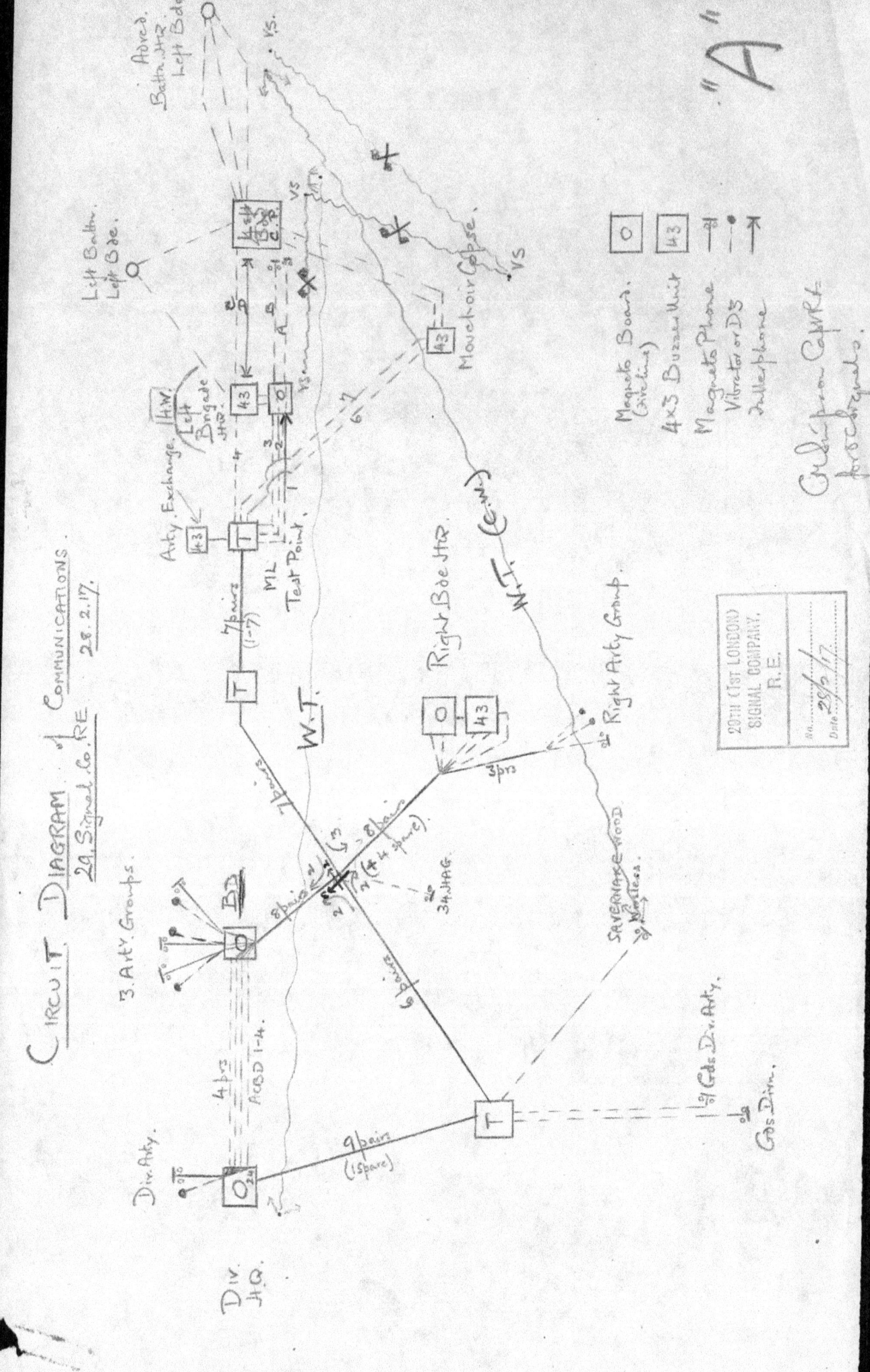

Army Form C. 2118.

Vol 2

WAR DIARY
or
INTELLIGENCE SUMMARY.
(Erase heading not required.)

Confidential

War Diary

of

29th Divisional Signal Co. R.E.

from 1st March 1917 to 31st March 1917.

(Volume 9.)

Army Form C. 2118.

WAR DIARY
or
INTELLIGENCE SUMMARY.

(Erase heading not required.)

29. Div. Signal C. RE

Place	Date	Hour	Summary of Events and Information	Remarks and references to Appendices
Arrowhead Copse.	1st		Left Bde HQ sit'd at HEBUKE. Heavy maintenance required on lines up to this place from Mle owing to mud, traffic, shell fire. All lines on old buried cables to M.L. replaced by lines on new bury. Work on lines becoming very heavy, owing to mud. Messages dealt with 650. Registered S.P's 53.	
	2nd		Party picks up old overground lines between CA MLb, have replaced by bury. 50% between at out stations attend to DHQ in view of relief. Messages dealt with 429. Registered S.P's 95.	
	3rd		(Arrival) Company (less operators at HQ and HW, and 50% linemen not withdrawn yesterday and 1 water cart, 1 light spring wagon) move to HEILLY, picking up transport etc at FRICOURT. Allotment of lines for flank Divisions relieving us arranged, but nothing definite yet known as to their proposed locations. Messages dealt with 67. Registered S.P's 54.	

1577 Wt. W10791/1773 500,000 1/15 D. D. & L. A.D.S.S./Forms/C. 2118.

WAR DIARY
or
INTELLIGENCE SUMMARY.
(Erase heading not required.)

Army Form C. 2118.

Place	Date	Hour	Summary of Events and Information	Remarks and references to Appendices
	4th		Guards division (on right) take over HQR and Right Bde with their left Bde, Such to be they Comes under us Command. GOC 29 Division. 20th Division (on left) takes over at Boesinghy? Rose Villa (HW) at 10 am and make use of all our lines there. We have work on one line to F Bde at COMBLES. Grant's Division making use of the other via Angle Wood. Trench Stores handed over to relieving divisional signal companies concerned. Messages dealt with 349. Registered SP's 49	
	5th	10 am	G.O.C. hands over command of front line to G.O.C. Guards Divn. The necessary re-arrangement of lines completed. Capt Signals arranges for men as each bn office vacated by us. Six linemen left with above for 24 hrs. Certain area stores handed over. Remainder of Coy move to Meilly Zone by road remainder by train. All communication is reserve area arranged by 2nd in command with advance party. Thourgh dealt with 241 Registered SP's. 40	

Army Form C. 2118.

WAR DIARY
or
INTELLIGENCE SUMMARY.
(Erase heading not required.)

Instructions regarding War Diaries and Intelligence Summaries are contained in F. S. Regs., Part II. and the Staff Manual respectively. Title pages will be prepared in manuscript.

Place	Date	Hour	Summary of Events and Information	Remarks and references to Appendices
	6th		General tidy up. Over haul of vehicle and equipment.	
	7th		Two limbered wagons R.E. faulty. Reported SPs. 39. 2 Sappers to 10 M tramels wood for repair. One body condemned & replacement undertaken. Menage dealt with 334.	Gun sent in for repair. One Reported SPs. 36.
	8th		Lecture anywork lecture to men on cattle drill & later detachment out under 2nd in Command. Good progress made with new men. Further over hauling of equipment. Menage dealt with 318.	
	9th		Shot lecture at signal school. The school ordered to England but is to remain on the strength. One detachment at cattle drill. Menage dealt with 292.	Reg-a tured SPs. 35. Kit bag at Reported SPs. 38

WAR DIARY
or
INTELLIGENCE SUMMARY

Army Form C. 2118.

Place	Date	Hour	Summary of Events and Information	Remarks and references to Appendices
	10th		Owing to inclement weather no detachment sent out. 2 cable wagons and water cart painted. Purchased Stewart clipping machine, hand clippers not satisfactory. Visit 8 S Sig. to discuss "final" scheme of instruction. Much useful info-mation obtained.	
	11th		Menagea dealt with 26½ 2 motor cycle frames break in front of tank thus:- [sketch: Tank → Break] to apparent reason for breaks. G.O.C. approves of the appointment of battalion signal officer. Officer posted as above after a satisfactory standard has been attained at the school. Menagea dealt with 333	Reported SPs. 24 Reported SPs. 41

WAR DIARY
or
INTELLIGENCE SUMMARY.

(Erase heading not required.)

Army Form C. 2118.

Place	Date	Hour	Summary of Events and Information	Remarks and references to Appendices
	12th		Eleven remount drawn. Stamp of hides rather small except for lioneses. No horses up to the weight of officers requiring them. Owing to wet weather no instruction is being carried out. Cable drill carried out.	
	13th		Cable wagon cleaned & painting same started. Menage dealt with 2½. Repainted S.P.s 31. Lg cable wagon drill owing to bad weather. Wash pump in B&P lighting set gives trouble. Same sent to D.S.E. for returning. New remount develope skin disease. Animal isolated & clipped & washed with sulphur. Two limbered wagons sent to collect. finished & teams dealt with 295. Menages Repainted S.P.s 32.	

WAR DIARY
or
INTELLIGENCE SUMMARY

Army Form C. 2118.

Place	Date	Hour	Summary of Events and Information	Remarks and references to Appendices
	14th		Lecture to NCOs then warfare continues. Painting of wagons continues.	
	15th		Wagons dept with 280. Registered OR 30. Coys Commanders conference CE Signal attend. Capt Simpson lectures to officers & was attending the signal school. Cars fitted with wireless screen. Wagons dept with 326. Repeated SPs 45.	
	16th		Bdg (notes) & sappers instructed to trap making. One of Coy are then class made daily instruction. In the morning packed on the ground to the afternoon a lecture. Painting of wagons continues. Bale cart on loaded & painted.	
	17th	2/am	Wagons dept with 359. Regtd SPs 34. Orders received that divisions will have to find another area on 19th-20th inst. Hqs SNR to find out what communications exist. All those with HQs etc!	

1577 Wt. W10791/1773 500,000 1/15 D. D. & L. A.D.S.S./Forms/C. 2118.

WAR DIARY
or
INTELLIGENCE SUMMARY.
(Erase heading not required.)

Army Form C. 2118.

Place	Date	Hour	Summary of Events and Information	Remarks and references to Appendices
	18th		Marched in tops. RE on off hand + numbers 16.84 on rear fore. Nos 2, 3, 4 platoons to be done later. Troop riding class in times. Transport draft with 409. Registered SPs 41. Church parade for all ranks except those on duty. Local events in chateau grounds. Fault due to rats eating insulation from wire thus bought in from windows. Registered SPs 421. Transport draft with 421.	
	19th	9am	Advance party consisting of 2 officers relief @ took two servants proceed to CAVILLON by motor lorry. 2nd in Command proceeds by car to find out what commission lines exist for brigade purposes other than that already known by DD Sup. Billets are also arranged in village OISSY 2 miles from HQs. Message dealt with 283. Registered SPs 28	
	9am			

1577 Wt. W10791/1773 500,000 1/15 D. D. & L. A.D.S.S./Forms/C. 2118.

Army Form C. 2118.

WAR DIARY
or
INTELLIGENCE SUMMARY.
(Erase heading not required.)

Instructions regarding War Diaries and Intelligence Summaries are contained in F. S. Regs., Part II. and the Staff Manual respectively. Title pages will be prepared in manuscript.

Place	Date	Hour	Summary of Events and Information	Remarks and references to Appendices
	20th	7.15am	Company has office relief & advance party march to OISSY.	
		10am	Office at OFFEUX closes & opens at CAVILLON at the same hour.	
			Line to MOLLIENS VIDAME found to be faulty. Several poles down caused by farmers ploughing land & breaking stays.	
			Line to HANGEST party relld up by our party.	
			To our work 86th Bde at TAILLY.	
			Line to Army extended from PQ - late works interchale Company arrive after 24½ mile march.	
	21st	4.15pm	Two cable wagons sent out to lay line (Earth O) from CAVILLON to TAILLY. (8½ miles) mobile wire used. Right link PPo. 6	
			Field linesmen with cable sent to repair HANGEST line, but return 5pm reporting cable wagons necessary	

WAR DIARY or INTELLIGENCE SUMMARY

Army Form C. 2118.

Place	Date	Hour	Summary of Events and Information	Remarks and references to Appendices
	22nd		Two pairs CAMBON to OISSY extended to O.C. Trans & O.C. Sig. Sounds reported on latter. Hangar draft with 198	
	23rd		Cable wagon completed. HAMBEST line to LE MESSE for use to inspect signal log. on 28th inst. G.O.C. division ran to be inspected. Hangar draft with 218.	Resisted S.P. 23. Stays & rough battalion. Repeated S.P. 23.
	24th		Inspection for inspection – hangar repainted painted inside. Lack of priorities. Hangar draft with 282. Took on wagon hamess etc continued attd. to 26th to be carried out conjunction with divisional scheme. Hangar draft with 282.	Resisted S.P. 14. Stay from poles up to. Repeated S.P. 27.
	25th		Out for inspection on limbers. Hangar draft with 291.	Repeated S.P. 33.

Army Form C. 2118.

WAR DIARY
or
INTELLIGENCE SUMMARY.
(Erase heading not required.)

Place	Date	Hour	Summary of Events and Information	Remarks and references to Appendices
	26th		The following hand for S.O.C. two sections — Hqrs G.S. wagon, H.S. water cart & 6 mounted DRs "A" Cable section less 2 Q. B Cable section less No Q. S.O.C. inspected coy & returns of work — he has remark were condition of heavy 6 horse van only — 76hrs employed on ditum. Turn out good. After the inspection two lines had to be laid from Dun Hqrs to 2 bdes (imaginary.) He also went but took 13 mins from Commues to Ranc Britaine including 3 poles crossings 900 yards. Line to send the tight about h. hr. This line was laid out by a heavy party, also laying about 600 yds. work on this was attacked. Remark by S.O.C. Reginald SR, 50 I marked through dealt with 24th.	

WAR DIARY
or
INTELLIGENCE SUMMARY.
(Erase heading not required.)

Army Form C. 2118.

Place	Date	Hour	Summary of Events and Information	Remarks and references to Appendices
	27th		Party sent to Signal School to collect stores & personal. Infantry instructors & personal returned to unit. Officers return to No 3 Section vice others to No 1 Section.	
	28th		Horses dealt with 328. Received SPs 23. Cable wagon drill by No 1 Section. Remainder on cleaning up after inspection. Horses still kris-taken. hay purchased. Horses dealt with 269. Received SPs 23.	
	29th		Div. Hors. Hosps. inspected by M.V.S. Line CAVILLON - TAILLY reeled up & on exchanged also line HANGEST-SOUS-LEMESGE. Horses dealt with 184. Received SPs 455.	
	30th		Officer at CAVILLON closed down & return vane here at HENACOURT. Call further parties in advance with cell phones & horses. Parties follow by lorry & one detachment leaves columns to reel up HANGEST -	

WAR DIARY
INTELLIGENCE SUMMARY
(Erase heading not required.)

Place	Date	Hour	Summary of Events and Information	Remarks and references to Appendices
			SOOS - Detachment up from YIGNACOURT at 6 p.m. by the above detachment marches from OISSY at 9.30 a.m. arriving 115 NACOURT 2 p.m. The horse (R) very weak, & forwarded to M.Y.S. to commence work late except the one to HENACOURT. a 3 horse[?] wire between 8 a.m. & 2 p.m. arranged to below not to ever. Reported SPs 31, 132.	
	31st		Serious mis[?] has [?]played on dreamy [?] between & wagons. Horse standing very muddy. Reported SPs 2d[?], 131.	

J.L. Haft[?]
Lt. 29th April by R.E.
1-4-17.

29TH (1st LONDON)
SIGNAL COMPANY
R.E.

C O N F I D E N T I A L.

War Diary

of

29th (1st London) Signal Co., R.E.

From 1st April, 1917   To 30th April, 1917.

V O L U M E X.

-o-o-o-o-

WAR DIARY
or
INTELLIGENCE SUMMARY.

Army.

Place	Date	Hour	Summary of Events and Information	Remarks and references to Appendices
	April 1st – 30th 1917.			
	1st		Train marches to BEAUVAL area. Usual advance billeting party sent on advance. Office closed. Return at 10 am as usual. R.E. branch down connection with body of wagon piss way. Lorry sent back to collect stores.	
			One with bde. Beauval hdq. Brigade office transmit for corps & Army.	
	2nd		Troops march to LUCHEUX area. Usual arrangement. 1st Signals 4th of hqs troops consisting of M.V.S. Reserve Cop & S.A.A. tractors. Cmn established with all brigade.	Reported SPs 47 Reported SPs 135
	3rd		Situation unchanged. 3 horses L.D. evacuated to 2LOC suffering from debility. General clean up.	Reported SPs 22 Reported SPs 360 Reported SPs 83

WAR DIARY
or
INTELLIGENCE SUMMARY.
(Erase heading not required.)

Army Form C. 2118.

Place	Date	Hour	Summary of Events and Information	Remarks and references to Appendices
	4th		Situation unchanged	
	5th		3 T.D. horses evacuated to 2 of C debility. Remainder dealt with 483. Division marches to BOUQUEMAISON area. Reported SPs HQs. HQs not touch except by D.R.	
	6th		BAVINCOURT. No touch with the 251. Horses dealt with 251. Division moves to COURTURELLE area. HQs not changing. No touch with HQ except by D.R. Reporting SPs ?	
	7th & 8th		Exchange Horses dealt with 383. Division now in "3 area. Signs upon post to tell in BAVINCOURT ditto to "tele at COURTURELLE. Reported SPs 75. Flying Corps came in contact. 3rd Bde. Complain to DDAS fault cleared by divisional linesman. R.Flame lin sent to A.D.Sigs.	
	9th		Message dealt with 390. Reported SPs 106. Corps circuit busy chiefly with "New lines". Ordered to be prepared to move at 6 hrs. notice.	

WAR DIARY
or
INTELLIGENCE SUMMARY.

Place	Date	Hour	Summary of Events and Information	Remarks and references to Appendices
	10th		Bde Baker had carried over to each brigade sector the complete detachment sent to RA hqrs. Trenage draft with 329. Reported SPs. 78	
			Conference by Corps Commander OC Syrah attends. Lt E Green selected by DAS for appointment to officer ye RA Syrah. His officer takes up his appointment vice Lt T M MacLachlan to no 3 section. 3 days reserve rations issued to Coy to be carried. Two days rations including oats carried on limbered RE & SS wagons. This in addition to 1 days iron rations. Remaining days rations carried on lorry & supply wagon. Col received to be ready to move at 3 hr notice. Trenage draft with 329 Reported SPs 76	
	11th		96th Bde move to SIMENCOURT who commence to establish Qnston ordered to move to ARRAS. Larger ago dealt with us. Reported SPs 162	

Army Form C. 2118.

WAR DIARY
or
INTELLIGENCE SUMMARY.
(Erase heading not required.)

Instructions regarding War Diaries and Intelligence Summaries are contained in F. S. Regs., Part II. and the Staff Manual respectively. Title pages will be prepared in manuscript.

Place	Date	Hour	Summary of Events and Information	Remarks and references to Appendices
	12th		HQrs. move at 8:30am to WAGONLIEU. 3 btns to ARRAS. Latter proceed to line to relieve 12th Div & come under orders of 12th Div. After 4 hrs delay communication established with 1st Corps. At 8 pm more supers in front. Forage dealt with 22B.	
	13th	9am	G.O.C. 29th Div taking over command of front line. Began taking over all lines forward to hole also 2 Corps line faulty. 5 am under 17th Bgy to lay line. Statement starts (ST SAUVEUR) to 86 Bde. This line from cable head. Otley carried by inability to thurst at 11:45 am ARRAS to cable head, to linen have spans now & 2 from 12th Signals being labelled. 2 line men forward also 87 & 88 & finally link on line to forward 2 pm in fitting succeed. About 2 pm in fitting to Cauph Dr.	

1577 Wt.W.10791/1773 500,000 1/15 D.D. & L. A.D.S.S./Forms/C. 2118.

WAR DIARY
or
INTELLIGENCE SUMMARY
(Erase heading not required.)

Army Form C. 2118.

Place	Date	Hour	Summary of Events and Information	Remarks and references to Appendices

Line though that working most uncomfortoy. Our own line was to had got. About 5 pm the omnibus the only one working. Hd 10d by line forward abolished & now concentrated on maintaining omnibus & line to C6th. Final established between 86 A & forward means to manage to divisions much used when line forward.

Broken station erected 88d hrs communicating to the D.S. at BOIS DES BOEUF who transmit trench set at there hqs.

The All trouble with lines due to traffic and the of pers, pun, ammunition wagons, pack animals tanks etc. State of affairs reported to A. & Sigs. but latter unable to do the work, his men being fully occupied. Suggested that thout-poles will

WAR DIARY
or
INTELLIGENCE SUMMARY.
(Erase heading not required.)

Army Form C. 2118.

Place	Date	Hour	Summary of Events and Information	Remarks and references to Appendices
	14th		slab he put up capable of carrying about 20 pairs. Both sides of Cambrai-Arras road shewn w[ith] cable both working + duplicate. H.A. unable to keep two through to O.Ps. Through message dealt w[ith] K.334 Registered SPs. 133. Enemy shelling & bombing traverses to forward b[attalio]n area at 1.30 a.m. Enemy were far too busy to repair too our own lines & came to have to return in work resumed when daylight arrived. Line the 10.30 a.m. During morning 88th attack – no news back via flank b[attalio]n of 17th Div until not clean. Visual thus worked with success. 3 lost men age res? 2 sent. Stay at H.Q.D.S. road on whole quieter. New route to & forward b[atta]ln. Airline to Bois des BOEUF via FRC thence D-tion line fired, telephone wk sounds du prin[cipale] pond.	

Place	Date	Hour	Summary of Events and Information	Remarks and references to Appendices
	15th		Message dealt with 449. Registered SP's 110. 89th Bde attack at 5.30 a.m. and reach objective. Line to Bde & alternative broken by shell fire. Messages sent via flank Bde of 17th Div as for previous day. Mule & L.T. also used to relieve congestion. New route started from cable head to 86th Bde along N side of road + 100 - 150 yds clear of road. Shot poles used with a short iron arm 4" long with slit each end for the twisted cable to drop into. Close hitch on every fourth pole. 2400 yards con Klahel. Co/rs five wire of 1 detachment of BQ cable section. 24 Priority mess sent + 27 received.	
	16th		Messages dealt with 262. Registered SP's. 110. Route (cable) com pleted to 86th Bde except for last	

WAR DIARY or INTELLIGENCE SUMMARY

Army Form C. 2118.

15/9/40

87th Bde move then Bgde & a party sent to lete cable to their new position. Line was filed & found OK.

Lines down to hole as each route. During the time messages sent by broken. 33 men ago sent & received by broken during the day, both most osts facing enemy ft for delay due chiefly to time taken to encipher & decipher.

Frenchy reconnoitred with a view to installing a four buzzer & a lot set. Amplifier installed at lot station but power buzzer for an OP in fool line but officer reconnoitring failed to find location of OP.

Arrangements for S.O.S discussed with E.O.C R.A.
Message dealt with 295. Repeated SP: 135.

WAR DIARY
or
INTELLIGENCE SUMMARY.
(Erase heading not required.)

Army Form C. 2118.

Place	Date	Hour	Summary of Events and Information	Remarks and references to Appendices
	17th		During early hours 3.10am horse pit ran into & broke a pole on airline route began chopping lines will avoid that route was pulled down for 6 days all lines being dis A.T Sigs & APM Corps asked to warn to prevent repetition. Heavy mo sent by B.T but owing to the humber sent confusion occurred at the directing station. Itld route to 86th completed & a turn D5 (place) on poles in addition to D3 pair Route with 86th transferred. Himage deal with 330. Registered SP's 135.	
	18th		Poled route to 86th Bde improved. Poles stayed all along the route. "B" detachment lays an alternate route to 82nd bde via TILLOY. This route to clear of the main ARRAS—CAMBRAI road & thus less liable to be broken. TILLOY however periodically	

WAR DIARY
or
INTELLIGENCE SUMMARY.

(Erase heading not required.)

Army Form C. 2118.

Place	Date	Hour	Summary of Events and Information	Remarks and references to Appendices
			Shelled.	
			Still confusion at the D.S. Average take 2-4 hrs to F.E. through.	
			Visual tested but not used.	
			W.T station installed at MONCHY + found to hyper at dawn + place in accordance with "A" attached.	"A"
			Communication to + from MONCHY. Average delay with 33b Regd SP² 157	
	19ᵃ		"A" section this day line in line to RUE DE LA PAIX	
			No hyp 96ᵗʰ Corps HA. This line for one with 72ⁿᵈ HAG the front supporting division front. Later this HAG move to TILLOY + line used for one with 15ᵗʰ Div in flank division communication complete	
			b detachment line (alternative) to forward bde hadqrs. Last ½ mile armoured turn. One works well + is in a non shelled zone.	

WAR DIARY
or
INTELLIGENCE SUMMARY.
(Erase heading not required.)

Army Form C. 2118.

Place	Date	Hour	Summary of Events and Information	Remarks and references to Appendices
	20th		A letter dealt with 446. Repelled SP: 190 henages made. Kin line secure & some work.	
			B" Section have on a whole earned rest. Effort made to give men a halt but - Manzeers full working our cut up found very heavy work in bad weather.	
	21st		henages dealt with 400. Repelled SP: 222 Both sections out. A hidden layo a span for an alternative route to forward the hgn line commenced armour turn, D turn & further at armour ties. to Leslin layo running from hinely to site selected for advanced exchange N 5 a 7-9. All there lines laid in view of forthcoming operations on large front. whole line typed	

WAR DIARY
INTELLIGENCE SUMMARY

Army Form C. 2118.

Place	Date	Hour	Summary of Events and Information	Remarks and references to Appendices
			convoy being despatched stuck in the mud. Efforts to extricate unsuccessful.	
			Suggestion to A.S. Hqrs to advance the 6 portable D.3.s for immediate use sanctioned.	
			16 mules D.3, 8 mules D.2 & 2 mules armoured drawn from Corps dump.	
			Army Artillery Bde Sigs 29th D.A. sent to signal Batta referred to personnel accompanying same. Major sanctioned by S.O.C. forwarded to M.S. A.S. Signal Hqrs dealt with 399. Reported S.P.s 228.	
	22nd		12th Division Sigs sent 7 men to assist with their artillery communication. These men placed under orders of O/c D.A. Signals.	
			A section (dismounted men) move forward to exchange to see country by daylight with a view to laying lines to 88th Bde during night. "B" section	

WAR DIARY
or
INTELLIGENCE SUMMARY.

(Erase heading not required.)

Army Form C. 2118.

Place	Date	Hour	Summary of Events and Information	Remarks and references to Appendices

Day one advanced and four reserve Coy hqrs to
Found exchange
At 7.30 pm a billion lay out, then to 66th Bde
(1050) from tent line) and lay behind to 87th Bde
in MONCHY. While the B. being done Captain Simpson
was up forward exchange of dug out. While
will returnd at hand make table & bench.
Exchange installed in same dug out that some
distance from Compftrs & & T ----
Two poor diggers had killed but not working.
Tn. M. Coys have Constantly out & see men to return.
All night lines laid by 10 teams at which time
Bde. arrive at then forward hqrs & resume tel.
leaves up

11.30 pm line to Bde Div ---- ---- forward
had by shell fire. Thiepval until with 394 — Reference SP 163.

Army Form C. 2118.

WAR DIARY
or
INTELLIGENCE SUMMARY.
(Erase heading not required.)

Instructions regarding War Diaries and Intelligence Summaries are contained in F.S. Regs., Part II. and the Staff Manual respectively. Title pages will be prepared in manuscript.

Place	Date	Hour	Summary of Events and Information	Remarks and references to Appendices
	23rd		All lines though & working at 2.15 am. Only telephone to forward bde. hqrs to reserve bde.	
		4.45am	Attack commences. Unable to speak to 87th line & front due chiefly to various cables used in building the line.	
			Supply of cable proves difficult, several long journeys having to be made. In future will establish a forward dump. So far as forward as possible. The wire from this dump being controlled by me.	
			Hostile shell fire in back area slackens & turns to converge about this line to MONCHY. This at intervals but hostile fire too heavy to keep & cause maintained & avail being done owing to Jamming & Poor buzzer obs. at MONCHY. Of little value. Poor buzzer of little use. Lines cannot be kept intact.	

WAR DIARY
or
INTELLIGENCE SUMMARY.
(Erase heading not required.)

Army Form C. 2118.

Place	Date	Hour	Summary of Events and Information	Remarks and references to Appendices
	24th		Orders supplied to each attacking Bde that only two Bdes received & those of no tactical importance. Some casualties reported but this to be expected owing to the heavy shell fire in vicinity of trenches. Percentage of "Urgent Operation Priority" msgs large. Attached "B" shows arrangements made for communications. msgs dealt with 529. Registered SPs 123. Information received that 3rd Div will take over line. Hq 3rd Div accordingly and 3 wires to E.C. & to MN to acquaint themselves with lines. 3rd Div open new hqrs & lay 3pm to HQR Sn at this point change is made for all lines running forward. Shrapnel shell fire on back area increases & lines to bde and now frequent. Lt Gibb & Cmsn B Section relieve Lt Kemp & men of A Section at M.N.	B

WAR DIARY
or
INTELLIGENCE SUMMARY.

Army Form C. 2118.

Place	Date	Hour	Summary of Events and Information	Remarks and references to Appendices
	25th		Messages dealt with 456. Registered SPs 151 when below need to handed over to Sys 32nd Div when relief is completed. May be any time at or after 5am to noon. Charges are taken place at 11am. All lines working to satisfaction of Sys YC. Limber sent to lent pounds to collect stores used by lines men all lines men report back by 8pm except one ordered to remain at E.C. At 2 pm Company (less arty det) marched to WARLUS under El-King. Messages dealt with 299. Resumed SPs 159	
	26th		Office closes 10 am and moves to COVIN opening there at the same hour. Coy moves from WARLUS to COVIN arriving there 6.50 pm. Personnel from ARRAS moved by 2 L Coy stores etc from WARLUS by 30 L DSC. Lorry Halford undergoing entensive over haul after 12 mon the running	

WAR DIARY or INTELLIGENCE SUMMARY

Army Form C. 2118.

Place	Date	Hour	Summary of Events and Information	Remarks and references to Appendices
	27th		Things dealt with 154. Registered SP's 81. Bdis forbn move to the COUIN area 86th Bde. SOUASTRE as superimposed from 87th Bde not yet fixed up. 81st Bde on phone then delivered by orderly. General clear up & overhaul of wagons equipment etc.	
	28th		Things dealt with 217. Registered SP's 148. Trains reb lined routine. Lamp sent to XSC for repair. returns test paid for small out office made consisting of - terminals for 6 metallic return lines salvo and 1 hand for men. The whole mounted on one piece of wood.	
	29th		Things dealt with 221. Registered SP's 109. Lamps for telephones from reads show large deficiency. Also number of hand signallers greatly depleted by recent actions. The attached marked "C" was D.G.S. C.	

WAR DIARY
or
INTELLIGENCE SUMMARY.
(Erase heading not required.)

Army Form C. 2118.

Place	Date	Hour	Summary of Events and Information	Remarks and references to Appendices
	30		for circulation to units. Registered SPs. 128	
			Messages dealt with 246	
			Had routine rent brigade. Spr Harvey & Krumbe were	
			submitted for D.C.M. & M.M. respectively to S/O for	
			immediate reward. Both have been shewn great	
			coolness while acting as linesmen with their	
			divisional lines. Spr Tucker awarded Military Medal.	
			Messages dealt with 343. Registered SPs. 161	
			Diagram of lines in use on 23rd attached herewith. D	

J Smith Major
O/C 20th (1st London) Sig Co R.E.
1-5-17

S E C R E T.   29th Division No. C.G.S.44.

86th Brigade.
87th Brigade.
88th Brigade.   "A"
C.R.A.
C.R.E.

Communications to and from MONCHY.

1. Messages from Bn. H.Q. in MONCHY to H.Q. of Bde. at H.34.c.cent. To be sent by runner to the cellar of the house with RED roof at N.6.b.9.5. These messages will then be sent by wireless or Power Buzzer to N.5.a.5.9., thence by telephone or runner to the Brigade.

2. Messages from F.O.Os. to be handed in at the same place N.6.b.9.5. They will then be sent by wireless, and will be received by receiving stations at the H.Q. of the R.F.A. Bdes.

3. A power Buzzer is established at N.12.b.9.5. and will be used almost exclusively by F.O.Os. who will send messages to the receiving amplifier at N.5.a.5.9., thence by wireless to H.Q. of Artillery Bdes.

4. All messages handed in at the 2 Power Buzzers, (1) at N.6.b.9.5. (2) N.12.b.9.5. by F.O.Os. must be in code and the following will be used :-

    All quiet on Right   O K R
     "   "   " Left   O K L
    Counter-preparation Right   C P R
        "   Left   C P L
    S.O.S. Right   S O S R
     "   Left   S O S L

5. At all other Wireless Stations messages can be handed in "in clear", as the operator has the code word, which is changed periodically by O.C. Divisional Signal Coy., and enciphers all messages, and the operator at the receiving end deciphers all messages before handing the message to the addressee.

6. An orderly from each Bn. in MONCHY will be sent to the Wireless and Power Buzzer Station at N.6.b.9.5. MONCHY.

7. All company commanders in MONCHY will render a certificate to their Commanding Officer that they personally know the exact position of the Wireless Station.

8. Frequent use should be made of these means of communication to ensure efficiency at the critical moment.

9. On the 15th Division relieving the Right Brigade, the Wireless Set now working with that Brigade will be sent to MONCHY and will be prepared to advance when opportunity offers.

                                                  Lieut-Colonel, G.S.,
                                                    29th Division.

18th April, 1917.

JRM

"B"

SECRET. 29th Division No.C.G.S.44.

29TH DIVISION INSTRUCTION No. 4.

Copy No. XI

20th April, 1917.

Communications.

The following will be the arrangements for communications during the operations.

(1) <u>Telephones and Telegraph lines.</u> 3 pairs of cable exist between Divisional Headquarters and Estaminet Corner. At this place there is a test point for linemen. There is also a linemen's test point at the cable head (G.30.d.2.2). From Estaminet Corner 3 pairs of lines (all going by different routes) are laid to 86th Brigade Headquarters at H.34.c.7.6. - two pairs poled cable and a third pair armoured twin,

From 86th Brigade Headquarters 2 pairs of armoured twin run by different routes to a forward exchange and linemen's post about N.5.a.7.4. From this exchange the 87th Brigade at MONCHY is connected by armoured twin, also the 88th Brigade at N.12.a.8.1. There is also a direct lateral line between the two Brigades.

The 45th and 51st Brigades on the flanks at N.10.d.3.7. and at H.23.b.4.1. respectively will also be connected to the 88th and 87th Brigades by lateral lines.

(2) <u>Wireless.</u> One set at N.5.a.7.9. working to a Crossley set at Place St. Croix, ARRAS. A second set at N.6.b.8.3. working to the same Crossley set. A third set will be packed up in the cellar at N.6.b.8.3. ready to move forward to a position about O.2.a.7.5. This will depend upon the situation after the attack.

(3) <u>Power Buzzer.</u> There will be a Power Buzzer at N.6.b.8.3.; another one at N.12.b.9.6. and a third at N.12.a.8.1. These three power buzzers work back to an amplifier at N.5.a.7.9.

(4) <u>Pigeons.</u> Pigeons (probably 12 per Brigade) will be supplied to each of the attacking Brigades.

(5) <u>Runners.</u> A runner post will be established at N.5.a.7.4. These runners will work forward to the Brigades and back to a runner post at 86th Brigade Headquarters H.34.c.7.6. where another post will be established. The latter working to mounted despatch riders or motor cyclists (according to the state of the main road) about H.33.c.8.2.

(6) <u>Visual.</u> Visual communication will be established and will be used only in the last resort for getting messages from MONCHY (probably near 87th Brigade Headquarters) to Place St. Croix (Brasserie), ARRAS.

(7) <u>Artillery communications.</u> The arrangements for the artillery are practically the same as for Brigades of Infantry as far as the forward exchange at N.5.a.7.4. From this point lines will be laid to the positions to be occupied by the groups of 29th and 12th Divisional Artilleries, when they advance.

/8.

(8) The utmost caution must be exercised in using the telephone or telegraph prior to the operations, since the enemy are known to be in possession of listening sets.

C.F. Fuller

Lieut-Colonel, G.S.,

29th Division.

```
Copies 1 - 5   General Staff.
        6      86th Brigade.
        7      87th Brigade.
        8      88th Brigade.
        9      C.R.A.
       10      C.R.E.
       11      Officer i/c Signals. ✓
       12      A.A. & Q.M.G.
       13      A.P.M.
       14      A.D.M.S.
       15      3rd Division.
       16      15th Division.
       17      17th Division.
       18      VI Corps.
       19      VI Corps H.A.
       20      1/2nd Monmouth Regt.
       21      12th Squadron R.F.C.
```

SECRET.   C

HEADQUARTERS,
29th DIVISION.
GENERAL STAFF.
No. 6954
Date 1-5-17

86th Brigade.
87th Brigade.
88th Brigade.
1/2nd Monmouths.
Divisional Signaling Officer (for information)

During the recent operations undertaken by the 29th Division there have been many casualties amongst the trained signal personnel of Units, with the result that many Units have no longer their trained establishment of signallers. If the Division continues fighting in the near future, units will very shortly be so depleted in signal personnel that they will be unable to run any internal communications. At present no facilities exist for training and units will therefore have to rely on what personnel they have left.

With regard to instruments there is already a serious shortage of telephones, so much so that it will take a month to meet the demands submitted since the Division came out of the line.

To obviate the above the following precautions will be taken in future :-

(1) While close fighting continues not more than 50% of the establishment of signallers of units will be taken into the fight. Further any Assistant Instructors (other than the N.C.O. acting as Battalion Signalling Sergeant) will be left in rear and not employed in fighting. They will be reserved for training men when opportunity arises.

(2) Not more than 4 out of the establishment of 7 telephones will be taken into the line with the assaulting troops.

/ (3)

(3)   Owing to the shortage of Signalling Officers, Battalion Signalling Officers should only be employed at their own work, save in exceptional circumstances, when the tactical situation imperatively demands their employment in the firing line.

                                                      Lieut-Colonel, G.S.,

1st May, 1917.   29th Division.

JRM

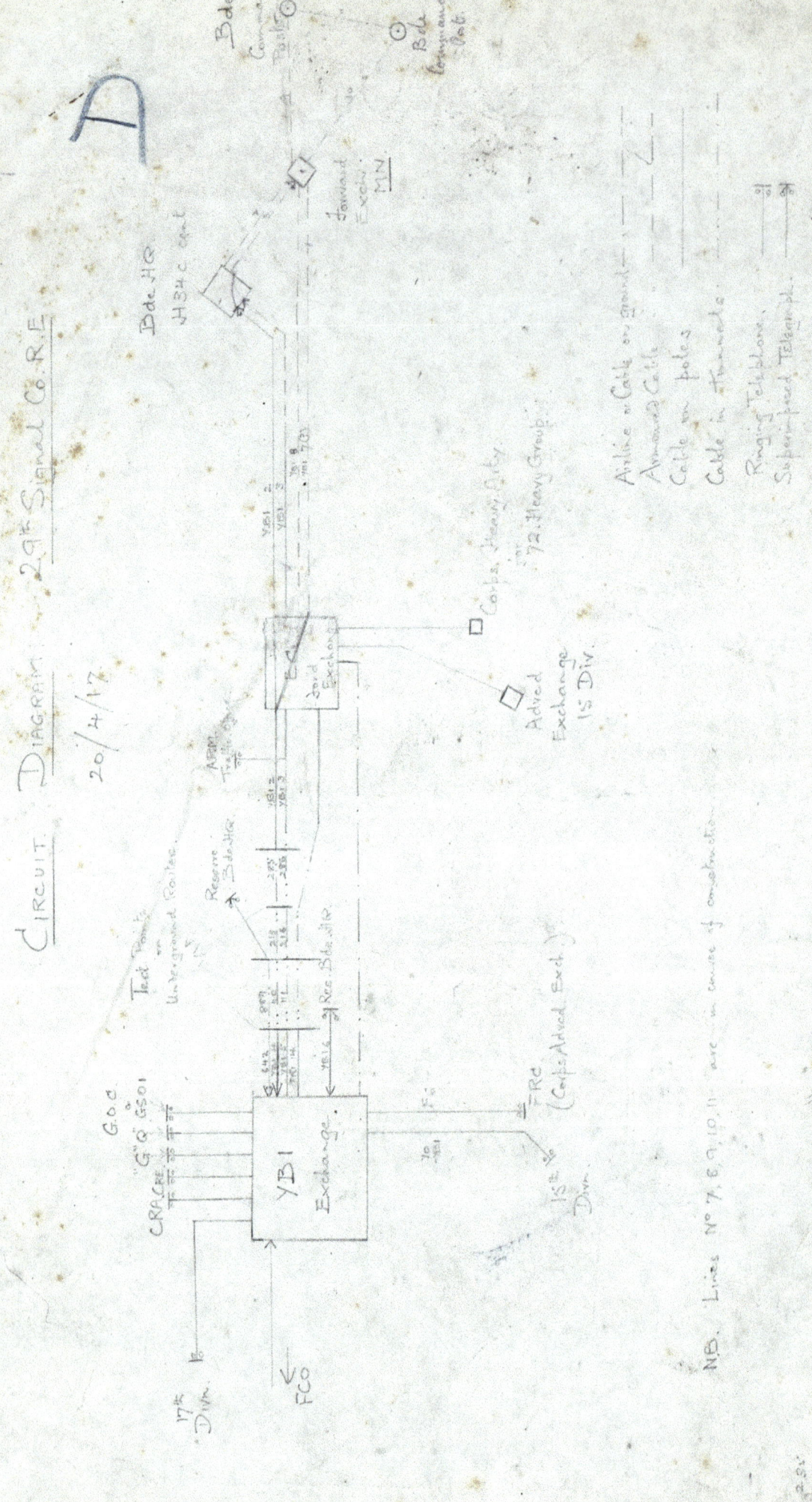

CONFIDENTIAL

War Diary

of

29th DIVISIONAL SIGNAL COMPANY R.E.

From 1st May 1917   to   31st May 1917

VOLUME II

-o-o-o-o-o-o-

CONFIDENTIAL

Army Form C. 2118.

WAR DIARY
or
INTELLIGENCE SUMMARY.
(Erase heading not required.)

Instructions regarding War Diaries and Intelligence Summaries are contained in F.S. Regs., Part II. and the Staff Manual respectively. Title pages will be prepared in manuscript.

Confidential.

War Diary

of

29th Divisional Signal Co. R.E.

from 1st May 1917 to 31st May 1917.

(Volume 11.)

Place	Date	Hour	Summary of Events and Information	Remarks and references to Appendices

WAR DIARY
or
INTELLIGENCE SUMMARY.
(Erase heading not required.)

Army Form C. 2118.

Instructions regarding War Diaries and Intelligence Summaries are contained in F. S. Regs., Part II. and the Staff Manual respectively. Title pages will be prepared in manuscript.

Place	Date	Hour	Summary of Events and Information	Remarks and references to Appendices
	1st		Orders rec'd to move to ARRAS. Advance party of 2 Lieutenants + an officer relief with one to proceed to ARRAS.	
	2nd		Messages dealt with 131. Registered SPs 173. Coy marches at 9am for ARRAS to arrive 6pm. to office to take over billet site + start work + arrange for the remainder to lay local circuits + 2 Lds to ARRAS. Corps line Searches reinforced. British bound. CRA carried led to Int. 3rd 12th + 56th Div with a view to taking over should situation demand. 3rd Lieun test system. Messages dealt with 134. Registered SPs 40.	
	3rd		Lineman in Corps reserve Salvage party reel up derelict wires. Messages dealt with 188. Registered SPs 145.	
	4th		2 Cos + new form draft posted to RA Infantine + a proportion of L/cpls (L/sgt + L/Cpl) posted to HQ RA	

WAR DIARY
or
INTELLIGENCE SUMMARY.

Army Form C. 2118.

Place	Date	Hour	Summary of Events and Information	Remarks and references to Appendices
	5th		Message dealt with 150. Registered SP's 90.	
			No change.	
	6th		Message dealt with 146. Registered SP's 132.	
			No change.	
	7th		Message dealt with 142. Registered SP's 136.	
			No change. 87th & 88th Bdes move to DUISANS and BERNEVILLE. Communication obtained with Coys.	
	8th		Message dealt with 149. Registered SP's 142.	
			Coy moves to WARLUS and takes over lines occupied by 15th Div. All communication handed over by 15th Div.	
			Same working still.	
	9th		Message dealt with 170. Registered SP's 149.	
	12th		Towing of wire suffers pieces continued chiefly in connection of Bdes wires - also made Riding close [illegible] with to [illegible] brig. now in 2nd Division to give further instruction to some of the [illegible] [illegible] numbers 86th, 87th Bdes relieve each other on the 11th	

WAR DIARY
or
INTELLIGENCE SUMMARY.

(Erase heading not required.)

Army Form C. 2118.

Place	Date	Hour	Summary of Events and Information	Remarks and references to Appendices
	9th to 12th cont.		Telephones issued when at D.35. He is a Staff man opened on南? Infantry battalions not batteries of Artillery can see them better will make no attempt to do so. The reducing practicability of true ambush Brave signal inclined by Divnal Cos. Sufoces. They are too bulky to be the commsdt. Infantry should be better comsalways carry Div.s New draft under instruction.	
	9th		Messages dec'd with 235 Registered SP's 174	
	10th		" " 234	86
	11th		" " 234	159
	12th		" " 240	210
	13th		Information received re relief of 3rd Div. Advance party with two runners sent forward to man teol. points. Lines practically the same as they were when in sector last month otherwise more notice desirable. New draft under instruction. Minage dealt with 257 Registered SP's 152	

WAR DIARY
or
INTELLIGENCE SUMMARY
(Erase heading not required.)

Army Form C. 2118.

Place	Date	Hour	Summary of Events and Information	Remarks and references to Appendices
	14th		Office staff with a load of stone proceeded to ARRAS. Lieut Kirk left office at 6:00 to go to main road to 3rd HQrs. All tracks & lines to main road of 3rd Div. laid out by party of surveyors. 7 new head covered cable lengths laid down. Message dealt with 274.	
	15th	11am	Pinned SPs 207. GOC taken on command of fort. All lines forward working well. Sounder to Brigade in alternative system able to test points below as in being worked on from 12th Div in addition to present front. Coy moves from WARLUS to ARRAS. Relieved SPs 142.	
	16th		Lines run out to one line of 12th Div & new test-points test at BLANGY established. Right side sector placed under immediate charge of Lt Kirk & left sector under	

WAR DIARY or INTELLIGENCE SUMMARY

Army Form C. 2118.

(Erase heading not required.)

11 Sigs with B Section
"Y" Cable Section lent from Corps this section
helps to man the RA Tel. pounds fc RA
has 4 divisional Artilleries & 1 Army FAB under
his command. To both the RA Captain has been
of 1 officer & some men now 12th Signal Coy.
RA Exchange & Repeaters - both that of the division
was lost when RA refused assent not by a M line
cable supply of 2 & 3 - there very poor Corps
allot 3 on a demand of 26 supply of cable
meets all requirements with the aid of salvage, harder
owing to 2 artillery lines having come here Rl
personal enough NCO withdrawn to work under the RA
Signals. this party provide a small working party for the
Improvement of lines to pigeon and an account of bad weather
Armagh Meadowith 339. Reported SPs. 139

WAR DIARY or INTELLIGENCE SUMMARY.

Army Form C. 2118.

(Erase heading not required.)

Instructions regarding War Diaries and Intelligence Summaries are contained in F. S. Regs., Part II. and the Staff Manual respectively. Title pages will be prepared in manuscript.

Place	Date	Hour	Summary of Events and Information	Remarks and references to Appendices
	17th		No person used weather unfavorable. Carried on improvement & fencing lines for C of b trenches officers with reference to 6 & 7 rod.	
	18th		Memorial dinner with 444 Reported SP's 116. Total 2 foxes buggers at battalion hqrs in HINCHY. Party under LtKing lay line between 2 Brigades. Shortage of magneto wire.	
	19th		Menage dead work 301. Reported SP's 238. 87th Bde attack at 9pm All divisional lines told out either by direct line or alternative route. Brigade lines held out except to right battalion. All R.A. lines work well including O.P. lines.	
	20th		Menage dead work 478. Reported SP's 218. German dinner removed & several pairs lifted without result. Section of buzzery different - follows All lines ground in vicinity of Railway Triangle &	"A"

WAR DIARY
or
INTELLIGENCE SUMMARY.
(Erase heading not required.)

Army Form C. 2118.

Place	Date	Hour	Summary of Events and Information	Remarks and references to Appendices
	20th		Jerchy cut frequently. Has arranged for cavalry held work. Has been over to H.15.B.14 pro to workshops for complete overhaul. Likely period of absence 10 days.	
	21st		Tonnage dealt with 456. Registered SPs 208. Allotment of cable & telephone sent to 53rd AFA Bde in accordance with wire from A.D. Sigs. This probably take all week allotment. Lines still continue to be cut by shellfire but with assistance of alternative routes no trouble experienced. Halford Lacy sent to workshops to have front axle straightened. Supplies hitherto important - arranged from No. 1 dump "B". Tonnage dealt with 375. Registered SPs 243.	
	22nd		Reconnoitre with 2nd in command for new route. Leave forward to include all RA lines. Decide to erect two routes one from NY cable head	

WAR DIARY
or
INTELLIGENCE SUMMARY.

Army Form C. 2118.

Place	Date	Hour	Summary of Events and Information	Remarks and references to Appendices
			Another from ONWARD cable head. Each route converging to a test dugout near south end of BATTERY VALLEY. Both routes avoid shelled area + roads. Cape signal under tape to rear test. Western route S.pair altho' only S.pair cap) by me. Bnos personnel construct southern route.	
			McKibben attacked bispole dugouts + Lofter layers awarded the military medal.	
	23ᵈ		Henryo dealt with 401. Reported SPs 213.	
			Ichend the route obtained from Corps 13 - 3R pola. 80 arms + insulators (bobbins) + 16 mls SA wire. Whelon lit arms + put an auditerian stop on each pole. Route again reconn'd with Cpl. Culver officers.	
			Henryo dealt with 405. Reported SPs 214.	

WAR DIARY
or
INTELLIGENCE SUMMARY.

(Erase heading not required.)

Army Form C. 2118.

Place	Date	Hour	Summary of Events and Information	Remarks and references to Appendices
	24th		Busy to very wet day. Building of route postponed. Got question attachment of 8 pioneers amt with labour.	
	25th		Xmas day dealt with 353. Reported SPs 194. Building of both routes commenced. Developed route. 30 poles erected & completed ends & wires. Line terminated & ready to pull on wheel insulators with Spindles are used. Cops boxes S.S. wages being made to carry stones these have enabled to move along the day near the back. The wind dropped while bathing. (2nd) Then again disclosure 16 408. Reported SPs. 315.	
	26th		Work continued on the two routes. All poles erected on southern route but wiring not complete. Northern route under Corps Subine officer. All wire to left bank near SCARPE. Shr. at 3.30 p.m. Shells land in killed 2 men & officers between wounded	

WAR DIARY
or
INTELLIGENCE SUMMARY.
(Erase heading not required.)

Army Form C. 2118.

Place	Date	Hour	Summary of Events and Information	Remarks and references to Appendices
	27th		All of 5th Section lines brought at 3.30 pm (awful attack). Message front with 422 Repr. level to SPs 194. Works continued on routes to R3 completed except for minor details. Party of Pioneers under an RE Corporal constructed lest point for 4 lines at N end of battery valley near railway. Message dealt with 418. Registered SPs 262.	"C"
	28		Poled cable route built to meet existing found lines running round the method as shown in sketch below used. [sketch: ground block slightly let in to pole. Beech wood used. Hop poles 10 ft long.] Message dealt with 468. Registered SPs 188.	

WAR DIARY
or
INTELLIGENCE SUMMARY.
(Erase heading not required.)

Army Form C. 2118.

Place	Date	Hour	Summary of Events and Information	Remarks and references to Appendices
	29th		Changing over to new route commences & new list points standard. Local lines to P of W cage, brakes & traffic post with 3 artillery groups not changes over but forward bde to see that all arrangements for the night attack are correct. An extra amplifier & pair buggs installed to the communications with front line. A message sent on power buggs & transmitted to bde by a day light lamp like 18 min. Messages dealt with 465. Reported SPs 2/3	
	30th		Night attack postponed 24 hrs. Remainder of change was completed. On the new system there are fewer test points & in consequence a saving of linesmen & in trenches there men are now available to carry out improvements to cable zone of the many miles of cable laying about the forward area.	

WAR DIARY or INTELLIGENCE SUMMARY

Army Form C. 2118.

Place	Date	Hour	Summary of Events and Information	Remarks and references to Appendices
	31st		Notification of relief received. 3rd Division send forward an advance party to reconnoitre lines in divisional area. Messages dealt with 520. Registered S.P's 234. All lines forward to Brigades + Battalion held during the night attack. The present line was up to the outpost trench. Our buggies working all night but only that messages were sent. Conduct officers round main lines to Brigades + Coy HQrs. Diagram of communications before change are attached. Messages dealt with 523. Registered S.P's 250. Note. Whole to 3rd Army S.P. outside Division only are repeated.	"D"

F.H. Major
to be field by R.E.
H.C. 20th field by R.E.

War Diary

SECRET.

86th Brigade.
87th Brigade.
88th Brigade.
C.R.A.
C.R.E.
Officer i/c Signals.
29th Division.

The following will be the arrangements for communications during the operations on 19th instant.

1. BETWEEN THE DIVISION AND BRIGADES.

   (a) Telephone and telegraph lines are duplicated to each forward Brigade.
   A forward lateral line between the Brigades and flank Division Brigades. There will also be a lateral between the two advance Division exchanges at RAILWAY TRIANGLE and ESTAMINET CORNER.

   (b) A Wireless Telegraph Station is working at each forward Brigade Headquarters.

2. BETWEEN RIGHT SECTOR BRIGADE AND BATTALIONS.

   (a) Lines in duplicate to each Battalion. Some lines armoured, some laddered.

   (b) A power buzzer with each attacking Battalion working to an Amplifier at Brigade Headquarters.

   (c) Visual from Crucifix at MONCHY to Bde. hqrs.

3. 14 pigeons will be available for issue to the Right Brigade for distribution as far as Battalion Headquarters only.

C.T. Miller Capt
Lieut-Colonel, G.S.
29th Division.

18th May, 1917.

FD.

War Diary

86th Brigade.
87th Brigade.
88th Brigade.
C.R.A.
C.R.E.
1/2nd Monmouth Regt.
Officer i/c Signals (for information)

The following is a telephone message picked up by the listening set in the 29th Division area.

"The men will advance at 7 o'clock
Two minutes warning before fire opens"

Now that our line has been practically stationary for some time, it is likely that the enemy have established listening sets in the vicinity of their front line system and units should therefore exercise great care when using the telephone.

It is needless to point out that such messages as the one quoted above, might be of the utmost value to the enemy.

Lieut-Colonel, G.S.
16th May, 1917. 29th Division.

FD

War Diary.

S E C R E T. 29th Division C.G.S.44.

86th Brigade.
87th Brigade.
88th Brigade.
C.R.A.
C.R.E.
Officer i/c Signals. ✓
56th Division.

Reference C.G.S.44 dated 18th instant re signalling communications.

To para 2 add

(c) A visual station will be established close to the Crucifix in MONCHY which will work back to Brigade Headquarters.

May 19th, 1917.

C.T. Miller Capt
for Lieut-Colonel, G.S.
29th Division.

FD.

From Lt. T. G. Jawett R.E.
B.S.O. 88th Bde.

To O/C Signals 29th Division.

Ref (a) Delay in repair of div. lines
(b) Death of Y Y Cable-Section men.

Sir:-

I have the honour to submit the following report:-

About 3.30 P.M. yesterday a salvo of shells fell into the gun pits at bde. hdqrs. There was no previous warning of shelling.

Delay in Repair of div. lines.

A dump of Stokes ammunition and Mills grenades in the southern gun-pit was blown up, and all brigade lines to forward battalions were broken.

Hostile shelling continued until 4 P.M. At 3.40 P.M. all divisional lines were dis.

We were unable to leave the dugouts as salvos of shells were bursting in and about the hdqrs.

At 4 P.M. I sent a party to repair battalion lines. At the same time divisional linesmen went out.

My forward lines were through at 4.30 P.M. Divisional lines as follows:-

PY 35	---	5.05 P.M.
YL 21	---	5.07 -
CP	---	5.35 -
YL 30	---	5.45 -

New pieces of D twin Cable were let into divisional lines for a distance of 200 yds behind bde. hdqrs. My men assisted in this.

The lines were also broken further back along the railway in a number of places.

Two men of YY Cable Section were killed by the explosion of the dump.

Death of two men of YY Cable Section.

They were lying in a dugout a few yards from the dump. Several attempts were made to bring these men out during the shelling, but it was discovered they were dead.

We removed them yesterday and buried them on the other side of the railway this morning.

The bodies were in such a state that we could identify them only by pay books.

The shaft in which my men live is very damp, and these two men preferred to live above.

One Sergeant and four men of the right brigade, 51st Div. Signals were also killed by the explosion.

Driver E. Day was wounded in the left arm by a piece of shell and was admitted Hampour Dressing Station.

I have the honour to be, Sir,
Your Obedient Servant,

26/5/17

H. Fawcett Lt RE.

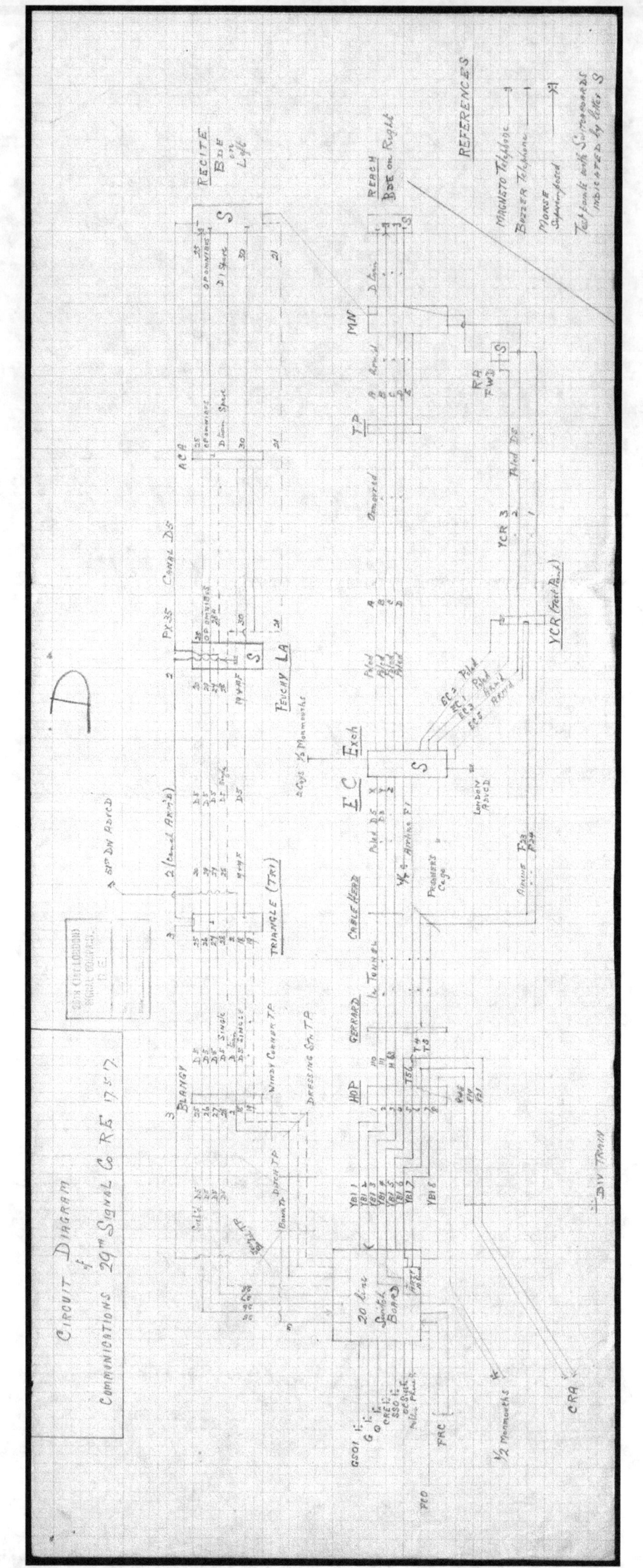

CONFIDENTIAL.

War Diary

of

29th (1st London) Divisional Signal Co., R.E.

From 1st June, 1917.   To 30th June, 1917.

VOLUME XII.

29th Signals R.E. Army Form C. 2118.

June 1917

WAR DIARY
or
INTELLIGENCE SUMMARY.
(Erase heading not required.)

Place	Date	Hour	Summary of Events and Information	Remarks and references to Appendices
ARRAS	1st		System via BV exchange finally completed. Linemen of 3rd Div Sigs go out to out stations to learn lines. Usual difficulties in region in front of FEUCHY. OC Signals 3rd Div. comes over to make final arrangements of relief. Messages dealt with 525. Registered S.P.'s 216	
	2nd		Relief of out stations by 3rd Div. completed, and 229 YB¹ linemen withdrawn except for small reliefs at each post. YC moving into separate HQ so connect at our system at HQT. Advance party despatched in the lorry to BERNAVILLE. Messages dealt with 414. Registered S.P's 211	
	3rd		Shelling during night 2nd/3rd cut Southern route to BV. Relief at 10am disorganized by shelling of new 3rd Div. HQ. 3rd Div. decide to move into our HQ, which therefore ordered the move WARLUS. This was carried out with aid of E.L. lorry only. Half the lorry bke's stores and personnel to BERNAVILLE. Coy. marches to LUCHEUX, where Staff of lorry rejoins. One cable detachment under 2/Lt Huddersmith left behind for R.A. communications. Messages dealt with 184. Registered S.P.'s 86	

A6945 Wt. W14142/M1160 350,000 12/16 D.D.&L. Forms/C/2118/14.

WAR DIARY
or
INTELLIGENCE SUMMARY.
(Erase heading not required.)

Army Form C. 2118.

Place	Date	Hour	Summary of Events and Information	Remarks and references to Appendices
BERNAVILLE	4th		Ditto move from WARLUS to BERNAVILLE E.L. tony convoys store and signal office personnel Coy. marched from LUCHEUX to BERNAVILLE. Halford tony convoy QM stores rations, with COMS and cooks. Billets etc. BERNAVILLE all fixed up by advance parties of 2nd, 3rd inst. Messages dealt with 156. Registered S.P.'s 72	
	5th		Bde HQrs in FIEFFES, FIENVILLERS and PERNOIS with superimposed move to each from BERNAVILLE. Coy. employed on cleaning up and overhauling equipment. Messages dealt with 238 Registered S.P.'s 128	
	Period from 6th to 22nd		This period utilised for training. Special attention was paid to improvement of turn-out, condition of horses, driving drill, overhauling and painting of cable wagons, instruction of new hands in cable wagon drill, and recreation for the men. Reorganization of brigade sections to new establishment was completed.	

WAR DIARY or INTELLIGENCE SUMMARY

Army Form C. 2118.

Place	Date	Hour	Summary of Events and Information	Remarks and references to Appendices
	6th to 22nd		"A fullerphone class was held three signallers from each battalion attending. The course lasted five days. Most of the men attending knew something about the instrument, but particular attention was paid to manipulation and a system of working the more awkward types involved, with a view to its employment within the division. Two courses were held: and those attending were instructed to teach what they had learnt to the remainder of the signallers of their battalion. There was insufficient time to hold a third course.	

Date	Mss. dealt with	Registered S.P's	Date	Mss. dealt with	Registered S.P's
6th	163	118	13th	152	54
7th	287	167	14th	154	80
8th	221	165	15th	173	70
9th	189	98	16th	188	80
10th	212	84	17th	131	86
11th	147	94	18th	166	78
12th	167	82	19th	169	76
			20th	150	96
			21st	147	86
			22nd	179	105

Army Form C. 2118.

WAR DIARY
or
INTELLIGENCE SUMMARY.
(Erase heading not required.)

Instructions regarding War Diaries and Intelligence Summaries are contained in F. S. Regs., Part II. and the Staff Manual respectively. Title pages will be prepared in manuscript.

Place	Date	Hour	Summary of Events and Information	Remarks and references to Appendices
BERNAVILLE	23rd		Advance party of 1 NCO & 2 men move to POPERINGHE area for Billeting purposes. Normal daily routine with training. Competition wrestling on horseback won by 2nd Lt. P. Griffin. Mess dealt with 176 Registered S.P.'s 67	
	24th		Normal daily routine. Sunday. Mess dealt with 215 Registered S.P.'s 81	
	25th		Est. bly. proceeds to PROVEN with advance party 87th Bde., and stores. Returned in evening. Lines to PERNOIS, BERNEUIL, LANCHES, and GORGES relaid. Other detachments employed. Mess dealt with 166 Registered S.P.'s 70	
	26th		Company entrained for PROVEN. Two officers move to PROVEN area and visit 38th Divn. Sig. Co. preparatory to taking over trunk system. Halt for tea breakdown between PREVENT and ST POL. Mess dealt with 381 Registered S.P.'s 70	

A6945 Wt. W14422/M1160 350,000 12/16 D.D. & L. Forms/C./2118/14.

Army Form C. 2118.

WAR DIARY
or
INTELLIGENCE SUMMARY.
(Erase heading not required.)

Place	Date	Hour	Summary of Events and Information	Remarks and references to Appendices
PROVEN	27th		86th, 87th & 88th Bdes all moved to PROVEN area. Communication very difficult as there are no lines available, and area is congested.	
			Advance party of company move to H.Q. 38th Div: from whence sent out for marking best dug-outs W.K, Z, A.	
			Mss draft mk 153. Registered S.P.'s 66	
	28th		87th Bde relieves Brigade of 38th Divn in line.	
			More men sent up to 38th Div. H.Q. including mounted orderlies.	
			29th Sig Co. "Wireless Section" comes from 5th Army.	
			Mss. draft mk 174. Registered S.P's. 78	
POPERINGHE	29th		29th Division takes over from 38th Division at 7am. Some lines between "C.B.D." and "N" in 15th Corps area B.S. Endeavours to obtain necessary lines in 15th Corps area, but not yet available owing to congestion.	
			Company arrives 1:30 pm and moves in to camp vacated by 38th Sig. Co.	
			Msi draft mk 441. Registered S.P's. 72	

Army Form C. 2118.

WAR DIARY
or
INTELLIGENCE SUMMARY.
(Erase heading not required.)

Place	Date	Hour	Summary of Events and Information	Remarks and references to Appendices
	3/4		Working party of 150 men complete 210 yds of buried to the RedHouse. Fault faulty on one line to forward brigade (F.D.) between 'Z' & 'W' Brigades. Cleared by 4pm. Both lines was used for telephone more troop superimposed on one pair. Army area officer attacked and back to Army for short rest, having been employed for sometime on work in front line. Messages dealt with 433. Registered S.P.'s 105	

L Stoll Major
O.C. 29th Sig. Coy R.E.

29/II (1st LONDON)
SIGNAL COMPANY.
R.E.
177

WAR DIARY
or
INTELLIGENCE SUMMARY.

Confidential

War Diary

of

29th Divisional Signal Co. R.E.

From 1st July 1917 to 31st July 1917.

(Volume IV)

Army Form C. 2118.

WAR DIARY
or
INTELLIGENCE SUMMARY.
(Erase heading not required.)

Instructions regarding War Diaries and Intelligence Summaries are contained in F.S. Regs., Part II and the Staff Manual respectively. Title pages will be prepared in manuscript.

Place	Date	Hour	Summary of Events and Information	Remarks and references to Appendices
VOORMEZEELE	July 1st		Another 210 yds of bury completed. Work of putting in tap leads and wiring continued. Nothing else of importance. Messages dealt with 409. Registered S.P's 89	
	July 2nd		220 yds of bury completed. Other work as usual. Some earth faults on bury between Wand K. rectified during afternoon. Messages dealt with 488. Registered S.P's 76	
	3rd		220 yds of bury completed. N.C.O. on wiring dug-outs reports crossing between B4 and Staenyzelle Road cut. Otherwise wiring continued. Course of instruction begun in Pigeon work for dismounted of 85th Bde commenced. Messages dealt with 443. Registered S.P's 113	
	4th		210 yds of bury completed, bringing trench within 50 yds of Red House on Y-Red House route. Normal work otherwise. Rope of 14 grads, 100 yds long made with wires to crossing canal by causeway near G.W. bridge. Messages dealt with 488. Registered S.P's 90	

WAR DIARY
or
INTELLIGENCE SUMMARY.
(Erase heading not required.)

Army Form C. 2118.

Place	Date	Hour	Summary of Events and Information	Remarks and references to Appendices.
	5th		220 yds of track completed — two finishing Y- Red House route, and beginning Red House — Elverdinghe Chateau route. Rope of 28 parts good covered. Placed across canal at causeway (side walk with) this was hoisted about 3ft up in zone half-completed portion of causeway and rests on bottom of canal in outer portion not yet started. This should bring cables at least 6ft underground when causeway is finished. Messages dealt with 463. Registered S.P's 88	
	6th		200 yds of track completed. Rodents near 86th & 87th Bde HQs behind St Sixte commenced. Shore traverse at 9.0am and apex etc letterbox poles at commencement of route 1200 yds finished by 7pm. Wiring of dugouts etc continued. Messages dealt with 393. Registered S.P's 90	
	7th		220 yds of track completed, bringing within 30 yds of Elverdinghe close. 2,500 yds of open wire route to 86th & 87th completed, bringing 87th Bde into communication at 6.0 am working via JN Bn coke route. Messages dealt with 400. Registered S.P's 76	

WAR DIARY
or
INTELLIGENCE SUMMARY.
(Erase heading not required.)

Army Form C. 2118.

Place	Date	Hour	Summary of Events and Information	Remarks and references to Appendices
	8th		Owing to heavy rain + cattle burying in early morning postponed. Line to 56th Bde completed about 3 pm, with about 1000 yds of D3 cable, with bury crossings under main roads. Neo Ye moving forward dug-outs withdrawn for two days rest. Messages well with 409. Registered S.P's 98.	
	9th		Busy to Elverdinghe Chateau completed + 200+ strands left front completed digging in the heavy moving to recent rains. Lines at Y dug out led in + stay there. Same done at Red House + Chateau lines linked out + labelled. All found OK except one pair between Y + Red House. Party sent out to stay + generally straighten up 2 pm route to 67th + 66th Bdes. Lines buried in 18th Corps area from up on being allotted [?] by 14th Corps. Henages duct with 529. Registered S.P's 113.	

Army Form C. 2118.

WAR DIARY
or
INTELLIGENCE SUMMARY.
(Erase heading not required.)

Instructions regarding War Diaries and Intelligence Summaries are contained in F. S. Regs., Part II. and the Staff Manual respectively. Title pages will be prepared in manuscript.

Place	Date	Hour	Summary of Events and Information	Remarks and references to Appendices
	10th		Completed section to Z dugout via left front line. Continued tresthem [trestleway?]. Half supply working party 160 OR's commence work at 5am. Party shelled while at work. 9 men wounded. NCO & two sappers continue work on dugouts. Wires tested out, labelled & terminal boards erected. Submit to AD Sigs a complete resume of wires in Corps dugouts. Photograph of this corps unable to supply — Cable airline stores & small part to Cinement repairs chiefly required. Going to constant change from Corps to Corps & Army to Army very important in extending some as far back as April — message dealt with 466 Repro [Repeated] and SP's, 105	
	11th		Working party did not work, rain owing to inclement weather.	

A6945 Wt. W14422/M1160 350,000 12/16 D. D. & L. Forms/C/2118/14.

WAR DIARY
or
INTELLIGENCE SUMMARY.
(Erase heading not required.)

Army Form C. 2118.

Instructions regarding War Diaries and Intelligence Summaries are contained in F. S. Regs. Part II. and the Staff Manual respectively. Title pages will be prepared in manuscript.

Place	Date	Hour	Summary of Events and Information	Remarks and references to Appendices
			Wiring party continue to work on testing & erecting terminal boards.	
			Party left for forward Brigade with armoured cable to a party of 6 men. The latter with the assistance of wire party carry cable to WELSH HARP ready for burying. Reconnoitre found from cable head to WELSH HARP to find most suitable route for trench.	
	12th		mirages dead north 627. Repr. but Prs. 128 200 yds of bury completed from cable head towards W.H. Owing to the tank 40 men were sent back without doing their job. Buried lines forward changed from 18 d Corps Area to 14 d Corps Area two lines do not work satisfactorily Total with allotment of buried lines received from Corps. Artillery require work allotted of the Sgnls D A	

WAR DIARY
or
INTELLIGENCE SUMMARY

Place	Date	Hour	Summary of Events and Information	Remarks and references to Appendices
	13th		Every bty hole allotted & some spares held in hand. All artillery pump hose filled up complete with lines at boards. Also all loose pumps & cable head (in trays) fitted up complete. Took completed by Menages Sect 2 in Sept. 4.22. Received SPs 119 Party to digging rounds now in dumps ready to continue work on trench but so alarm to march sounded & the O.C. lay orders men to march home. Consequently no work done. Stores drawn for the building of a two pair route from the line at X 27 a 7-4 to Marcus many the Belgian route (poles only) for the last 2 kilometres. Took over line for 38th DA continued. Only left with DA Spuls insufficient to carry on work required. Menages dealt with 60. Reported SPs 100.	

WAR DIARY or INTELLIGENCE SUMMARY

Army Form C. 2118.

(Erase heading not required.)

Place	Date	Hour	Summary of Events and Information	Remarks and references to Appendices
	14		Party of 120 men turn out to continue bury [?] near Webb Harp. Owing to discharge of gas by us party be to cease work at 1.30 p.m. Trench with cables had not filled in. Party of 2 M Co's & 1 man proceed to Proven to commence route from Brigadan to Infantry Progress made. Party of 5 N Co's proceed to 8th C.fr. Woolen School for a 7 days course. Any refugees with 5 after completing a course of similar duration, through deal with 613. Reinforced 80's 96 during night 14—15. 107 men sent to a trench to connect the two main forward roads which serves as a lateral. H.Q. Sigs considering there here in future then are trying to dig to forward area. This party completes latter 160 yds.	
	15			

WAR DIARY
or
INTELLIGENCE SUMMARY.
(Erase heading not required.)

Army Form C. 2118.

Place	Date	Hour	Summary of Events and Information	Remarks and references to Appendices
			Good progress made on route to Army, building from Orion to Combe be & allotting to 2 pairs over construction parties on meeting the Army route. 3 duct kits on cables trench (forward spurs) 8 inch penetrable & cut all cables. Heavy Kaffic on both Corps lines all day. Henage Walker to be repaired 81½ Mts.	
	16.		Good progress made on Y-A-O lahead 10x. Wire dug & route plate 210 yards. Cable laid & trench filled in. Working party disturbed by current from shelling. Lt T.R. King proceeds to Campagne for a twelve course. Own detachment. ten officer & 4 men withdrawn from Canal bank to Corps hqrs.	

WAR DIARY
or
INTELLIGENCE SUMMARY.

(Erase heading not required.)

Army Form C. 2118.

Place	Date	Hour	Summary of Events and Information	Remarks and references to Appendices
	17.		Open route forward to commencement of heavy cut by still fine. One hour carried with brigade on alternative route. Menage dealt with 596. Rejoined SP's 126. 240yds of bury completed, tunnelling under a railway line. Cables laid & finish filled in. Crying on canal at W.H. all cut. Previously 7pm but 12 tons thorough. Two hrs brigade complete. Army units formed thorough. Army commences leading to & at Rovers end. Open route from again cut during the night. Menage dealt with 600.	
	18.		Bury 6 PAROY FM complete & 150 yards Reg'n to'yd SR 134. Dug a cut leading to O dugout. At 11 pm sinking party had to cease work on	

WAR DIARY or INTELLIGENCE SUMMARY

Army Form C. 2118.

(Erase heading not required.)

Place	Date	Hour	Summary of Events and Information	Remarks and references to Appendices
			for relief. Infantry remained until 1:30 am as there was no abatement went back to bivouac only for hy had to remain out till daylight as they were unable to see their way in the dark. Took then to bury as felt then work to then bury in abeyance to coming relief. Cpl Rynds died to take over confusion of party to O Shell hopped nr signal office and & Sherba penetrated building but no one was hit. Surope dealt with 665. Registered SPs 172. to walk alone on bury East of Canal (WH - ST B) owing to relief. Rgp 30th Dn send up some huns + stores. Officer at Bosan complete & 38th Dn move in Lines	
	19.			

WAR DIARY or INTELLIGENCE SUMMARY

Army Form C. 2118.

Place	Date	Hour	Summary of Events and Information	Remarks and references to Appendices
	20		Brigade of Lille were on 38th Bde. move to different side. Engineers detail with 688 Regs. and Sps. Res. Party of two proving detailed for work on W.H - ST.P route surveyed to complete the Survey of 600 yds. Party surveyed to peripheral line. Shelling including gas shells. After party recced work there was found to be only partially dug in many places. Superintending Signal Officer remained until daylight & spec covered cables cut in several places. Work here was cut from German line to Sept. then work was completed. Line was handed over to Sps. 88th in fair condition. All signal personnel employed in being withdrawn from Canal bank. Also 67 prisoners	

WAR DIARY
or
INTELLIGENCE SUMMARY.
(Erase heading not required.)

Army Form C. 2118.

Place	Date	Hour	Summary of Events and Information	Remarks and references to Appendices
			with instructions to	
			All work done while on line reconnoitred	
			with 2nd in command with a view to compiling	
			a report for handing over.	
			Report on work done attached as well as	
			a copy of the work required by the 33rd Divn.	
	21	10 am	Handed over arms equip. etc. (Kit & SPs, Pers being	"A"
			complete.	
Rouen			Spent office hours. In eve went to table. The	
			2 so little from front line.	
			Arrangements to ship the boy that were accomodation	
			was 1/2 mile from Wag office	
	5 pm		Through to be from Rouen	
			Ent party of 1 NCO & 20 men to CALAIS by	
			train to draw 40 reinvs to 27 of them have	
			returned from subsections o RA HQ. On train for	

WAR DIARY
or
INTELLIGENCE SUMMARY.
(Erase heading not required.)

Army Form C. 2118.

Place	Date	Hour	Summary of Events and Information	Remarks and references to Appendices
	22		No signals RA only handed over 8 draught horses. Menage dealt with 423. Reserve lied SP's 68	
			Day spent cleaning up + overhauling equipment. Menage dealt with 315. Reserve lied SP's 60	
	23		Reserve issue + an dis tributed - Harness fitted. Menage dealt with 236. Reserve lied SP's 48	
	24		Instrument repairs makes small 3 pair test & listening in app analie for Sirimus as below:-	

[diagram of rectangular box 14" × 6" with circles labeled, arrow marked "A", and note "Wiring from socket to terminals underneath board."]

While made with electric light socket + plugs + terminals. Instrument leads to on to "A".
2 of above used to each tube for trial purposes.
Menage dealt with 242. Reserve lied SP's 40.

Army Form C. 2118.

WAR DIARY
or
INTELLIGENCE SUMMARY.
(Erase heading not required.)

Instructions regarding War Diaries and Intelligence Summaries are contained in F. S. Regs., Part II. and the Staff Manual respectively. Title pages will be prepared in manuscript.

Place	Date	Hour	Summary of Events and Information	Remarks and references to Appendices
	25		Nothing of special interest to report. Our chaps	
			stand to cable wagon drill. Lt. Gold A.W. awarded	
	30		bar to M.M. for conspicuous gallantry during a raid on	
			enemy trenches in ZWANOFF SECTOR. Registered S.P.s 92	
	25th		message dealt with 358 245 do 63	
	26th		do 304 do 38	
	27th		do 361 do 61	
	28th		do 259 do 51	
	29th		do 238 do 61	
	30th		do	
	31		Attack on enemy trenches commenced at daylight	
			29th. No wounded reports no orders to move but at	
			3 hours notice.	
			Wrote letter to G suggesting that signal service	
			Officers should in future R.A. seconded officers. The	

WAR DIARY
or
INTELLIGENCE SUMMARY

Army Form C. 2118.

Place	Date	Hour	Summary of Events and Information	Remarks and references to Appendices
			Matters as far as this DA is concerned have not been forthcoming. Copy to A & Sig units of forthcoming message sent to 3 Bde. Reprinted SOs 23	
			Diagram of R.A. communication - a list of OPs	"B"
			connection attached	"C"
			Signal Plan for operation attached	

F. Stukk Major
OC 29th Signal Coy RE.
31-7-17

[Stamp: 29TH (1ST LONDON) SIGNAL COMPANY R.E.]

"A"

WORK TO BE DONE IN ORDER OF URGENCY.

BURIES.

1. Bury from WELSH HARP (WH) C.13.a.30.43 to Cable head at C.7.c.60.00 (Tunnelled dug-out 100 yards to the left of head of HARKNESS AVENUE)   (20 pairs).

2. Bury from STB (C.13.c.30.20) to WELSH HARP (WH) via Butt 22 (approx.)   (12 pairs).

    Note: Cables for this route were laid from STB to a point C.13.c.35.50 in bottom of trench, but trench has since been knocked in and I dont think anything but a new bury the whole way will be satisfactory.

3. Bury from ELVERDINGHE CHATEAU to RIGHT GROUP H.QRS. at RED HOUSE (B.15.c.20.70) 12 pairs.

4. Bury from RED HOUSE to "Y" dug-out (B.21.a.30.70) 12 pairs.

5. Bury from ELVERDINGHE CHATEAU to Left Group H.Qrs. 20 prs.

6. "   ". Left Group H.Qrs. to "Z" dug-out (B.14.c.70.55) 20 pairs.

    Note: Exact position of Left Group H.Qrs. has not yet been definitely decided, though it is certain to be in the neighbourhood of "Z" Dug-out. Both buries therefore, mentioned in 5 and 6 above,, can be combined into one 20 pair route from "Z" to ELVERDINGHE CHATEAU via Left Group H.Qrs.

7. Bury from LUNAVILLE via PARROY to nearest box on new Y-A route (12 pairs).

    Note: XIV Corps are digging a 50 pair route from Y - A with a test point every ¼ mile - the bury mentioned in 7 above will form a lateral between MN route and this new Y -A route.

8. Supervise 24 pair emergency canal crossing being made by Army Area Detachment at Bridge 6-W. This is being put in a causeway under construction.

DUGOUTS.

1. Complete cable head dug-out - 2 small elephants in front line at XXX C.13.2.

2. Strengthen test point C.13.c.30.20. with concrete blocks and pit props.

3. Construct small elephant test point at C.13.d.15.35. (Butt 15)

    Note: As this is in view, it will have to be carefully camouflaged - elephant well dug down and all spoil removed in sandbags before daylight.

REINFORCING.

1. Reinforce all canal crossings with logs, tree trunks and any old pieces of timber that can be found on the Canal Bank.

2. Protect cables where they cross trenches, especially in the neighbourhood of WELSH HARP, where I suggest the use of angle iron pickets and concrete block. - the angle iron picket being stayed at the top and the whole covered with a sandbag revetment.

WIRING OFFICES.

1. Wire up Brigade H.Qrs. at HUDDERSFIELD (HR).
2. "   "   "   "   " WEESH HARP (WH).
3. "   " Test point at C.13.c.30.20 (STB).
4. "   "   "   "   " Butt 15.
5. "   " Cable head " C.13.2.
6. "   "   "   "   " C.7.c.60.00.

Wiring up of these offices and test points consist of erecting terminal boards, leading in cables and labelling according to diagram.

WIRELESS.

1. Erect aerials for use at (WELSH HARP Brigade H.Qrs.
                             (HUDDERSFIELD Road "   "

See how they stand. I suggest that 3 aerials be erected at HUDDERSFIELD and one at WELSH HARP.

R.A.

A certain amount of assistance may be required by R.A. Signals in the preparation of Batteries, O.P. Exchanges and other positions.

[signature]

                            Major. R.E.
27/6/17.   O.C., 38th Div. Signals.

Copies to 29th Divl. Signals. ✓
      R.A. Signals.
      A.D. Signals.
      File.

The following work has been done while on block service in this sector.

(1) Burying live north slope C.13 d.30.43 to the emplaced deposit in Yorkshire trench. This work has proved very difficult as slides near the lower entrance. They will have to be corduroy'd on the bank. The covering at lower entrance might be improved....

(2) Burying gas & fluid trench from Hillside C.21.A.30.70 to R.E. house. Until 150 yards from the deposit the trench owing to moisture is not more than 4 feet deep, and well figures harding at this point. Also the crossing of a small dyke might be still further strengthened. It has received about 4 feet of sandbag supported by trench boards on trestles.

(3) Burying from R.E. House to Ebb dugout entrance completed. The crossing of the stream by the bridge is a weak point in this route.

38 groins have been laid under
the Busseah causeway in 3 different
reaches.

The leading in on the Eastern
bank of the canal is not completed
140 groins only have been laid — to
5 t 5.

On the Western side of the
canal a vie punt bank to E.D. is
as still required to complete the
leading in.

Some 28 groins have been
filled out and launched across
the causeway.

Dugouts — The site line the dugout
on the support line at C.B.2.
have been completed and the floor
slant. The elephant has to be
erected as projected.

The hut punt at
C.B.1 & 2 have been filled and
launched.

The elephant & the punt
at C.B.1, 2, 3, 4 & 5 at Butt 8, have
been completed.

4.

The small Carriages in the neighbourhood of Hall Sharp and E.T.H. have not been destroyed as laborers have been constantly at work repairing & keeping the covered ways.

Morning Offices — A certain fair terminal boards have been erected at Huddersfield. This is complete. The certain [air] tunnel [posts] have been erected at Hull, beside one here at E.T.B. We are now compelled to accept for the hearing of the E.T.B. — P.H. route which we hope is not [obstruction].

Four 6 pair [strain] at Leeds have been erected at Hull &c. which is now complete.

The [Northern] cable head has not been [wired], we have terminal boards, [keeps] but it is not due to [skilled] being still in progress by the [minister].

The [Southern] cable head has not been [wired]. The [board] is not yet ready.

[... have been stated]

on the following route.

K C to M
M Northern Cable Head
HK Ball 15
Ball 15 - Northern Cable Head

also E field through C T B to H K

In many cases the existing head routes were not laid out correctly. The faulty routes were to be filled by wires coming up to terminal boards.

<u>Wireless</u> Aerials were erected at Belah Camp and Huddersfield but those at Belah Camp did not remain erected for more than 36 hours. Other aerials were not erected. At Huddersfield head aerial was put up and they remained erected for 3 days, but later during one day in "blown down" twice. No fresh aerials were again erected and still remain

Much assistance has been given by the artillery of the 55th and 50th divisions. The assistance given by laying cable and putting through wires on the buried route as well as in helping to fill up

6.

the different group and sub-group Stations. The F.O.O. did not have the assistance of the cable detachment which they are entitled to. This involved extra work on my personnel in dealing with the artillery requirements.

The scheme for the trench mortars was not carried out according to instructions owing to those instructions being received only 12 hours before the commencement of the shoot. All assistance possible was given to the T.M.O. to enable him to complete his arrangements.

[signature]
OC 19th Div Sig Coy RE

Copies to CO Signals 14th Corps
           OC Signals 2nd Div

29th Sigs

"B"

Connections of O.P's to 'O' Exchange.

O.P.	Connected From	To Test Box	Line & Test Box No.
K 9	X Line B.11.d.	C.F.	25
K 10	JOYEUSE FARM	A.B.	14
K 11	TWIN COT	C.F.	26
K 12	CHEAPSIDE	C.F.	27
K 8	STRAND PALACE	W.T.	38
K 23	HUNTER STREET	D.H.	O.Q. 12
K 24	DOCTORS HOUSE	D.H.	O.Q. 10
K 25	RAILWAY STREET	W.T.	42
K 39	POST 36	W.T.	28
K 42	PERISCOPE TREE	W.T.	29
K 45	ROAD BRIDGE	D.H.	O.Q. 11
K 46	RAILWAY BRIDGE	S.C.H.	13
K 47	POST 4	S.C.H.	14
K 48	M.G. 11	W.T.	39
K 150	X Line B.12.c.	C.F.	43

Locations of Test Boxes.

    C.F. - HUNTER STREET TRENCH on South side, 50 yards beyond CHASSEUR FARM.

    W.T. - WAALKRANTZ TRENCH East side at about B.12.d.10.55.

    D.H. - In DOCTORS HOUSE below O.P.

    S.C.H. - In Front line trench, 50 yards South of point where Railway crosses the Canal.

    A.B. - About B.17.b.3.4.

E.E. Green
Captain R.E.,
Officer i/c Signals 20th Divl. Artillery.

19th July 1917.

Circuit Diagram – Rt. Grp –

BURIED SYSTEM FED FROM 'O' EXCH. — RIGHT GROUP

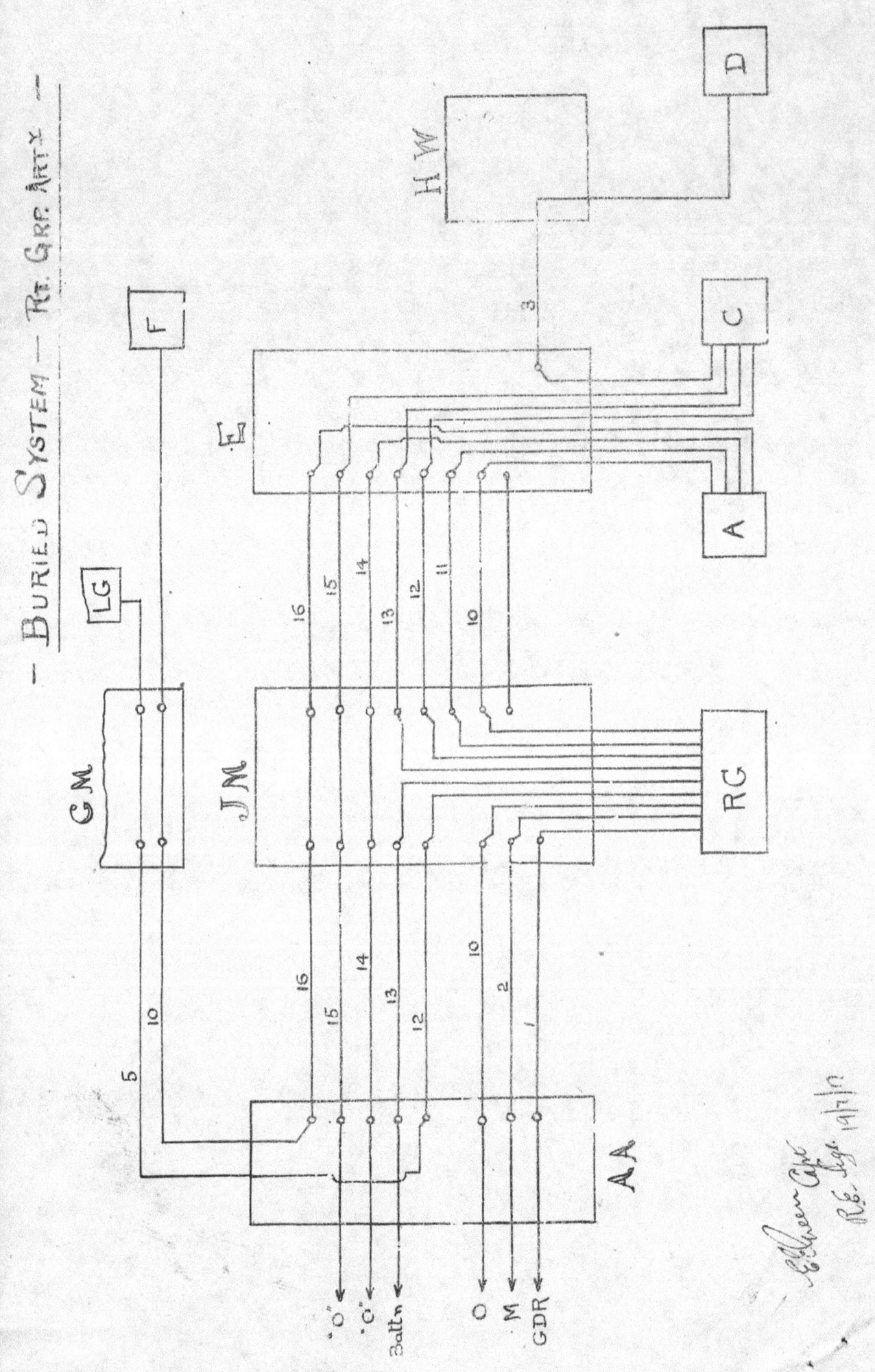

S E C R E T.   29th Division No.C.G.S.72/23.

29TH DIVISION OPERATIONS.

Instruction No. 4.

Communications.

GENERAL. 1. Owing to the Division being in reserve during the initial stage of the forthcoming operations, definite instructions for communication cannot be laid down.
Successful communications will depend upon :-

    (a) Commanders knowing and utilizing the various means for communicating that they have at their disposal.

    (b) Commanders assisting the Signal Service, by keeping them informed of the tactical situation and by moving their headquarters whenever possible along existing cable routes, instead of moving to a flank.

    (c) All Signal Officers being acquainted with S.S.148 and the amended instructions contained in para. 2 of XIV Corps Instructions No. 6, issued herewith.

TELEPHONE and TELEGRAPH Lines. 2. On taking over from any unit, their existing system will be adopted. Improvements will commence at once, but para. 2 of XIV Corps Instructions No. 6 will not be departed from.

WIRELESS. 3. One trench set complete with 2 operators will be issued on Z - 1 day to the 88th Brigade. A carrying party of 3 men will be detailed by the Brigade to accompany this set. Men so detailed should not be signallers but men temporarily unfit for the firing line.
A second trench set will remain with Divisional Headquarters and will be detailed as required.

AMPLIFIERS and POWER BUZZERS. 4. One amplifier with 2 operators will be issued on Z - 1 day to the 88th Brigade. A carrying party as in para. 3 will be required.
The Signal Officer of the leading Brigade will be issued with 2 Power Buzzers for distribution to battalions, to work to the amplifier.
A second amplifier with power buzzers will be kept in reserve.

VISUAL. 5. All visual stations will be taken over and manned. They will continue to work, until instructions are received from the O.C. Divisional Signals for their closing down.
Six men (including 1 N.C.O.) will be detailed by the O.C. 1/2nd Monmouths (Pioneers) to report to O.C. Divisional Signals on Z - 1 day for manning the divisional visual stations.

RUNNERS. 6. Each Brigade will have at their disposal the number of runners, as laid down in S.S.148, para. 5, page 18.
Motor cyclists or mounted D.Rs. will form the posts between Brigades and the Division.

PIGEONS. 7. Pigeons will be available and it is hoped that at least 2 pairs will be issued daily to battalions.

/ Brigade

- 2 -

Brigade pigeon men will refill daily at an intermediate point between the Division and Brigade Headquarters. The time for refilling and the place will be notified later.

Pigeon baskets to authorised scale as well as special assault baskets will shortly be issued.

CONTACT PATROL AEROPLANES. 8. The Instructions regarding Contact Patrol Aeroplanes are contained in Appendix "A" issued with 29th Division Instructions No. 2.

There will be a Divisional dropping station close to Advanced Divisional Headquarters. This spot will be marked with an ✕ made with strips.

GENERAL. 9. Position calls will not be used when once a unit moves forward after Zero. The new calls which have been recently issued will be utilized.

10. The following information regarding Signal Communications on the Left (Guards) Divisional front is circulated.

(a) <u>Buried Cable.</u>

Cable heads for Brigades are located :-

3rd (Left) Guards Brigade - B.6.c.3.3½. - N.C.H. (code letter)

2nd (Right) Guards Brigade)
) - B.12.b.3.3½. - S.C.H.
1st (Reserve) Guards Brigade) (code letter)

O.P. exchanges are to be at "O" dug-out (LUNAVILLE FARM) and "A" dug-out (B.24.b.10.6.).

(b) <u>Wireless.</u>

One trench wireless set is to be erected at Guards Brigade Battle H.Q. (B.11.d.6.3.) (Code letter C.F.), and to work to a Corps Directing Station at ELVERDINGHE CHATEAU. This set is to serve all three Guards Brigades.

(c) <u>Runners.</u>

Runner posts are being established at the following points between Advanced Divisional Headquarters (ZOMMERBLOOM) and Brigade Battle H.Q. at B.11.d.6.3.

B.9.c.3.½.
B.15.b.2½.9½.
B.16.a.2½.8.
B.10.d.5.1½.
B.17.a.8.10.

(d) <u>Forward Stations.</u>

It is intended to establish forward stations as follows :-

2nd (Right) Guards Brigade - C.1.c.6.4. and C.2.a.2.7.

/ 3rd

- 3 -

3rd (Left) Guards Brigade - C.1.a.½.6. - U.25.b.7.2.

1st (Reserve) Guards Brigade - C.1.a.4.1. - U.26.Central.

(e) Visual.

A Divisional Central visual signalling station is to be established at B.11.d.4.1. to work forward after Zero to the first series of Brigade forward stations, detailed in para.d. above.

When the forward stations move forward to their final positions, the Right Brigade intends to drop a Transmitting Visual Station in the vicinity of GABLE HOUSE (C.1.b.9.4½.).

(f) Cable Dumps.

Cable dumps are to be established as follows :-

Corps Dump - LUNAVILLE FARM.

Guards Divl. Dump - B.11.d.2.½. (near CHASSEUR FARM).

The position of the 29th Divisional Cable Dump will be notified later.

A C K N O W L E D G E.

C.F. Fuller.

Lieut-Colonel, G.S.,

18th July, 1917.   29th Division.

Copies to :-
    C.R.A. (38th Div.)   A.A. & Q.M.G.
    C.R.A. (29th Div.)   A.P.M.
    C.R.E.   D.M.G.O.
    86th Bde.   XIV Corps.
    87th Bde.   Guards Div.
    88th Bde.   20th Div.
    O.C. Sigs.   th Div.
    1/2nd Mon. Regt.   38
    A.D.M.S.   9th Squad. R.F.C.

M.

XIV CORPS INSTRUCTION NO. 6.

COMMUNICATIONS.

1.   Owing to the urgent necessity for quick and accurate information between Artillery F.O.O's and their respective Artillery Brigade Headquarters, as well as Battalion communication with their Infantry Brigade Headquarters, and at the same time also to arrange for liaison between Infantry and Artillery, the principle laid down in S.S.148 which only allows of 2 pairs of Cable from Cable Head to Brigade Forward Exchange, along which the whole of the information for Infantry and Artillery must pass, will to a slight extent be departed from.

2.   The method laid down in the accompanying diagram will be followed :-

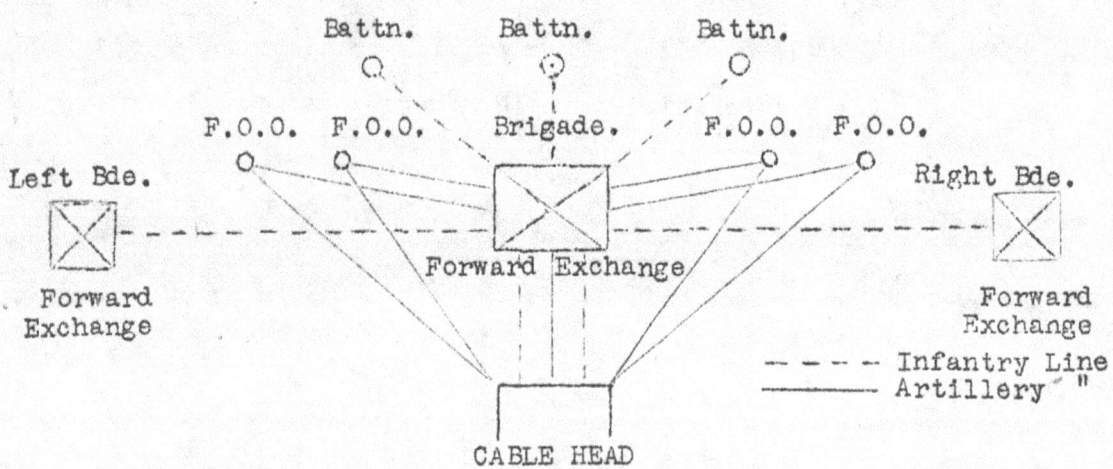

x x x x x x x x x x x x x x x x x x

On no account will any earth return circuit be employed. Metallic pairs (twisted cable) only are to be used.

                                          (Sgd) F. GATHORNE HARDY,
                                                Brigadier-General,
2nd July, 1917.   General Staff, XIV Corps.

CONFIDENTIAL.

War Diary

of

29th Divisional Signal Company R.E.

From 1st August, 1917 to 31st August, 1917.

VOLUME XIV.

-*-*-

WAR DIARY or INTELLIGENCE SUMMARY

Army Form C. 2118.

(Erase heading not required.)

Month: August

Place	Date	Hour	Summary of Events and Information	Remarks and references to Appendices
Hanwn	1st to 5th		Gunn in reserve. Training in cable wagon drill carried out. All men practice marching at night with respirators on.	
			1st message dealt with 216	
			2nd " " " 222	
			3rd " " " 221	
			4th " " " 230	
			5th " " " 245	
				Reported SP's 105
				" 96
				" 98
				" 103
				" 125
	6th		Orders received to relieve 1st Div. forward area. Reconnoitred & advance party sent up to learn routes etc.	
	7th		Messages dealt with 454. Stores sent with advance party sent forward. Captain Simpson proceeds to Loos blown to reconnoitre. Take over & stays there. Messages dealt with 526	Reported SP's 118 Reported SP 110

Army Form C. 2118.

WAR DIARY
or
INTELLIGENCE SUMMARY.
(Erase heading not required.)

Instructions regarding War Diaries and Intelligence Summaries are contained in F. S. Regs., Part II. and the Staff Manual respectively. Title pages will be prepared in manuscript.

Place	Date	Hour	Summary of Events and Information	Remarks and references to Appendices
J. Camp.	8	10 am	Intake over from had Division. Found on appears satisfactory except for the following points. a) H/T - 8ths withdrawn instead of being left up as requested. b) Certain auxiliary lines in towards were due to in bad condition. c) Schedule notified by Corps withdrawn in error. The whole system requires sharp heavy set heavy every available sapper employed in manning out points. Office telegraphists employed at J Camp. Loomes bloom & Chevron fine 2 b/rs employed as ex Operators at latter place to a month of above only some two day was available for work.	
	8		Message sent with 463 Regu End SP. 174	
	9		New lines laid out from Canal Pork to WOOD HOUSE.	

WAR DIARY
or
INTELLIGENCE SUMMARY

Army Form C. 2118.

Place	Date	Hour	Summary of Events and Information	Remarks and references to Appendices
			Reconnoitring forward areas with a view to making arrangements & forming a plan for the following day's attack.	
			On receipt of the portions of here the attached marked "A" was submitted to G.S. for approval. Message dealt with 523. Reported SPs 149	"A"
	10		Build 2 - 4pr pdr cable route from Chemin des Canal Bank. These routes refers a 7pr cable land by outgoing division. Cable slung on temporary anchor poles. Two lines run the Kinders little wounded while repairing lines between Canal and Wood House. Brigade hqrs ran back from WOOD H? to BOESINGHE. Signal depot advises no BSP available as reinforcements. Six duration message dealt with 538. Reported SPs 100	

WAR DIARY
or
INTELLIGENCE SUMMARY.
(Erase heading not required.)

Army Form C. 2118.

Place	Date	Hour	Summary of Events and Information	Remarks and references to Appendices
	11		Route between Chasseur Trees & Canal Bank completed. Two of the six men sent by Corps to assist with above wounded near BOESINGHE. Going to return afternoon in the day time. Further instructions are issued as attached marked "B" from operation at dawn STEEN BECK Crossed. PASSERELLE Captured. Pigeon message received from post to tablet at the letter plain.	"B"
	12		Message dealt with 582. Reported SPs 129. Application made to G.S. for 6 men from Pioneers Bn to assist carry cable to forward dump & lay armoured cable. Request granted. New type of light armoured cable not satisfactory & very little used. 16.213 about 4 cable hours difficult. Message dealt with 592. Reported SPs 129.	

Place	Date	Hour	Summary of Events and Information	Remarks and references to Appendices
	13.		Lt Hedderwick moves to CHASSEUR F.M. early of 4 men & 12 monaghs pioneers lay new line from Canal Bank to SAULES F.M. (battle hqs of 87th Bde) Another application made to Corps for telephones & buzzer units but same not available. Diagram of artillery commenced with instructions for FOO's marked "C" attacked Nothing definite can be met till then week for cable will not be met till then week further preparation on forward area. Reported SP3/20 card from Saules Fm to C.B. Area 2 pairs left side.	"C"
	14		Pioneers in draw returned. They escorted to carry up Stick D turns to head Vtrine Repo laid Vts 137	

Repo laid with 489

WAR DIARY
or
INTELLIGENCE SUMMARY.
(Erase heading not required.)

Army Form C. 2118.

Place	Date	Hour	Summary of Events and Information	Remarks and references to Appendices
	15.		Preparation completed. AAA Kuehn proved sent up to front area in accordance with plans. Amplifier & powr buzzer distributed to each the Coys. attched for 16 miles. Detonated. there is sufficient to the with to bt p.t. bo.	
Zermezeele Cabaret.		6 p.m.	Office of advance Coys open all lines through at appointed time. Working party proceed to CP to be employed in building field cable route et conditions allow. Message dealt with 656. Regd. SP's 111.	
	16	Zero 4.45 a.m.	at this hour all lines working to forward Coys. had left brigade at this forward station. Front established as pre mens. Cabaux alternative lines cut but at least one line worked to each the throughout the	

WAR DIARY
or
INTELLIGENCE SUMMARY
(Erase heading not required.)

Army Form C. 2118.

Instructions regarding War Diaries and Intelligence Summaries are contained in F.S. Regs., Part II. and the Staff Manual respectively. Title pages will be prepared in manuscript.

Place	Date	Hour	Summary of Events and Information	Remarks and references to Appendices
			Both YF stations worked all day & exchanged signals with CDS. DJ station only had one that at 8.31 a.m. & 6 hrs. The station did not have to signal was owing to the tops remaining at Saulo Twi. 82nd Bde wanted to relieve 82nd & 88th in the line will signal in as 110s. Ll. Aldersmith's party proceeded to the to continue lines from (3 pairs) of signal was Cable dumped found used from the pursue but storm made up a division but trying to keep this free this has pubes frequently for the of the 20 pairs of Pigeons issued to brigade only 11 pairs returned with messages. 13 birds returned without messages & 5 missing.	

WAR DIARY
or
INTELLIGENCE SUMMARY
(Erase heading not required.)

Army Form C. 2118.

Place	Date	Hour	Summary of Events and Information	Remarks and references to Appendices
	17		Poss began with not a previous Bath personnel requires more training. Messages dealt with 859 Replied SPs 116. Tried to signal two parties by earl during night but del sucked a during night early hour of morning that call was by S.S. at 5.10 am. Report was working of forward artillery communication attached marked "D".	"D"
	18		Messages dealt with 912. Replied SPs 105. Enemy fire much heavier. Messages to Bde kept more or less clear lines through Bde hqrs to Signal FM to Bde in wood. Hd. to 3 lines to Scarpa FM maintained to the Brigade. Diagram of communication forward of adv Hd's attached marked "E" with 863. Replied SPs 136.	"E"

WAR DIARY
or
INTELLIGENCE SUMMARY.
(Erase heading not required.)

Army Form C. 2118.

Place	Date	Hour	Summary of Events and Information	Remarks and references to Appendices
	19		to change hinage dealt with 429. Registered SPs. P10	
	20	1.20 pm	Orders received that advanced hqrs would close at 6 pm & reopen at J Camp. Delay at 6 pm in getting lines through due to Corps linesman not labelling lines taken off to the forward move.	
	21		hinage dealt with 462. Reported SPs 105. Lt Harvey & 15th Bde Subsection killed. Sgt Nightingale two N. 3 section taken his place.	
	22		hinage dealt with 403. Reported SPs 92. Following wounded during the night. The Cpl. Spr Cullers Sercesley & Bulworth. Gnr Abreer re- informed from base arrived. Cpl 12 men shot down brought to notice of D.D. Sigs. hinage dealt with 534. Registered SPs 95	

WAR DIARY
or
INTELLIGENCE SUMMARY.
(Erase heading not required.)

Army Form C. 2118.

Place	Date	Hour	Summary of Events and Information	Remarks and references to Appendices
	23.		No change.	
			Message dealt with SP 119. Registered SP. 25	
	24		Enemy in front area relieved otherwise no change.	
			Message dealt with SP. Registered SP. 133	
	25		Brigade relief. 87th Bde free to Stokes FM to relief of	
			WOOD HOUSE. This necessitates a Brigade	
			new hqrs & also two sub B Battalions	
			All arrangements made for move of right & left	
			Artillery front ps.	
			B213 asked 4 RSP & cable touch different to	
			reinforcements received for 5 hrs to enable	
			motor cyclist & 1 driver, latter refused to 48 Lys.	
			Orders for the relief of the division by French	
			division issued. Commander with frends on it	
			reference to advanced parties. Registered SP. 119	
			Message dealt with SP4	

WAR DIARY
or
INTELLIGENCE SUMMARY.
(Erase heading not required.)

Army Form C. 2118.

Place	Date	Hour	Summary of Events and Information	Remarks and references to Appendices
	26		Advance party of 9 mounts & 1 NCO arrived 9mmn Bloom with mounts left for out-standing stations. Artillery units receive 23 of smaller as reinforcements but this number still inadequate. Arrange with GOC to start a school to retrain officers newly Division received acting operations. Suggestion received & he attached marked "F"	"F"
			Messages dealt with 612 Registered S.P.'s 116	
	27		Advance party Guards division signals proceed to out-stations. Only three linesmen withdrawn by us however changed over, and certain office relief at CP taken over by Guards advance party. Lorry taken down of stores to PROVEN.	
			Messages dealt with 940 Registered S.P.'s 104	
	28		No change in station. All except 1 officer and 1 NCO at CP and one NCO at Canal Bank withdrawn from out-stations. Second lorry load to PROVEN conveys Office-relief, advance party and stores. Messages dealt with 650 Registered S.P.'s 91	

Army Form C. 2118.

WAR DIARY
or
INTELLIGENCE SUMMARY.
(Erase heading not required.)

Place	Date	Hour	Summary of Events and Information	Remarks and references to Appendices
	29		Guards div. takes over at 10 a.m. All our personnel withdrawn from outstations by 9 a.m. preceding by lorry direct to PROVEN. Remainder of company marched to PROVEN at 9 a.m. All flags withdrawn from brigade section to use at School commencing 31st. O.C. Sigs. 29 Div. Atty with R.A.M.C. Detachment and "S.B." Detachment all withdrawn to PROVEN with rest of Company. Lorry return to BOMMER BROOM to pick up have others on duty at Right Group. Messages dealt with 393. Registered S.P.s ////	
	30th		Instructor personnel to D.S. Signal School proceeds to BOLLEZEELE with recrecant stores. Personnel to H.Q.s reconnoitring with a h...... Company employed in cleaning up. Our Stretcher S.A. Cart ... Major F.H. OWEN M.C. gained a cattle w.p. on 2/I. Messages dealt with 277. Registered S.P.'s 67	

A6945 Wt. W11422/M1160 350,000 12/16 D. D. & L. Forms/C./2118/14-

WAR DIARY or INTELLIGENCE SUMMARY.

Army Form C. 2118.

Place	Date	Hour	Summary of Events and Information	Remarks and references to Appendices
	31st		Aerial attack commenced work. Rather hard to keep in touch with them as they are about twenty five miles from Div HQ. Second detachment "A" section under Sgt Bowman and Cpl Hanley being one hour (D.C.) to 86th Bde HQ. Distance about 1½ miles. Messages dealt with 226. Registered S.P.S. 41	

29TH (1ST LONDON)
SIGNAL COMPANY,
R.E.
No. 31.8.15
Date

O.C. in chair lap) R.E.
for O.C. 29 Div. Sig. C. R.E

Copy No. 4

"A"

Communication Instructions No 4 are cancelled and the following substituted :- (a) Communication before Zero
(b) " after Zero
(c) General,

(A) Communication before Zero

Telephone
& Telegraph
lines.

1. The main divisional route runs forward via CHASSEUR FARM to a test point on the canal about B.12.B.6.1 This route is poled cable. From Canal ground cable route runs to WOOD HOUSE (C.2.A.2.8.) via CANON FARM (C.1.C.6.3.) From WOOD HOUSE the route continues to CAPTAINS FARM (U.26.B.2.7). In addition 2 pairs will be laid from WOOD HOUSE to VULCANS FARM (U.27.C.1.7).

The above cable route will serve the 3 Infantry Brigades on their arrival in the forward area.

WIRELESS.

2. One trench set is erected at WOOD HOUSE (C.2.A.2.8) and works to Corps Directing station at ELVERDINGHE CHATEAU. Messages thence by telephone.

PIGEONS.

3. 7 pairs of birds will be available for each brigade and will be supplied to brigades under Divisional arrangements during afternoon of Y day. Each brigade will keep a reserve of 2 pairs at Brigade Headquarters. Arrangements for refilling will be communicated to Brigades on Z day.

VISUAL.

4. A transmitting station will be located at WOOD HOUSE (call W H) and will work back to CHASSEUR FARM (call C F). Messages thence by telephone. The 87th Brigade will establish a sending station about U.26.B.0.6 and the 88th Brigade one about U.27.C.1.8. All stations N E of WOOD HOUSE will send D D messages.

RUNNERS. 5. Runner posts will be established at BOESINGHE CHATEAU and WOOD HOUSE by 86th Brigade, CAPTAINS FARM by 87th Brigade and VULCAN FARM by 88th Brigade.
Each will consist of eight men.

AEROPLANES. 6. Communication with aeroplanes will be carried out as laid down in 29th Div Instructions No 8.

(B) COMMUNICATIONS AFTER ZERO.

Telegraph &
Telephone Lines. 1. Two pairs will be extended from Captains Farm to Signal Farm (U 21 C 20). As soon as **practicable the 87th Brigade will establish a Brigade Forward Station about U 21 A 2 4**

When the green line has been captured the 86th Brigade will lay lines to a brigade forward station about U 22 C 3 5. Each of these forward stations must be clearly marked.

Brigades will **lay lateral lines from** N to S. In addition the 87th Brigade will be responsible for the Liaison with the French.

A poled cable route will be built by division from Canal post B 12 B 6 1. to WOOD HOUSE.

WIRELESS 2. A trench set at WOOD HOUSE will be erected and working at Zero plus 1 hour at CAPTAINS FARM and will remain there until the green line is captured. This set will then move to SIGNAL FARM and three men will be detailed **by 87th Brigade** to accompany this set.

The set now at Wood House will not move.

Attention is called to 29th Div C.G.S **55/24** para 3

VISUAL. 3. WOOD HOUSE will become the Divisional Central Visual Station for receiving and transmitting all messages

3.

from the forward area. Forward stations will be
established about U 22 D 8 0 (call S A) and
U 21 A 4 5 (call W N).

The 1/2 Monmouths will place 10 signallers at
the disposal of O.C. Signals to assist with above.
They will report at Advanced Divl Headquarters on Y day.

RUNNERS. 5. Runners will be returned to Brigades as their
places are taken by mounted orderlies.

(C) GENERAL.

CABLE DUMP. Main dump will be at ZOMMERHOOM but a supply
of light cables and poles will be stored at B 12 B 4 1.

MOVES OF HQRS. It is important that as much notice as possible
is given of any intended move of Headquarters.

ARTILLERY. Separate instructions will shortly be issued for
artillery communications and artillery liaison lines.

AMPLIFIERS &
POWER BUZZERS. It is doubtful if personnel will be available for
working these instruments but further instructions will
be issued later.

Major.
O.C. 29th Divisional Signal Co. R.E.

Copy No 1 to General Staff
2 to A.D.Signals 14th Corps
3 to O.C.Signals 20th Div.
4 File.

"B"

Copy No. 8.

SECRET.

COMMUNICATIONS.

This office No 1096 dated 10/6/17 is cancelled and the following substituted:-

Telephone & Telegraph Lines.
1. The main divisional route forward runs via CHASSEUR FARM to a test point on the Canal Bank about B 12 B 6 1. From this point ground lines run direct and by alternative routes to WOOD HOUSE C 2 A 2 8 and SAULES FARM U 25 B 2 2.

88th Brigade will establish a forward station at VULCANS FARM U 27 C 1 7. After the capture of the Green line this forward station will move to RUISSEAU FARM U 21 C 7 2. Similarly the 87th Brigade will establish forward stations at Captains Farm U 26 B 2 7 and later SIGNAL FARM U 21 C 2 0.

Brigades will lay lateral lines from North to South. In addition the 87th Brigade will be responsible for the Liaison with the French.

When the RED LINE has been captured a poled cable route will be built from CANAL to WOOD HOUSE.

WIRELESS.
2. One trench set now working from WOOD HOUSE will not move.

A second set will be erected at SAULES FARM at Zero plus 1 hour. When the RED LINE has been captured this set will move to SIGNAL FARM. The 87th Brigade will detail 3 men to accompany this set. Both sets will work back to the Corps directing station at ELVERDINGHE. Messages thence by telephone.

PIGEONS.
3. 10 pairs of birds will be available for each attacking brigade and will be supplied to brigades together with special assault baskets during the afternoon of Y day. Each brigade will keep a reserve of 2 pairs,

at Brigade Headquarters.

In additiob to the above the 87th Brigade will be supplied with 5 pairs of French birds for liaison.

VISUAL. 4. A divisional central visual station will be established at WOOD HOUSE (call W H) and will work back to CHASSEUR FARM (call C F). The 88th and 87th Brigades will open up sending stations about U 26 D 7 7 (call M D) and U 26 A 9 6 (call C T) respectively. These stations will send D D messages and will be working by Zero - 6 hours. The 1/2 Monmouths will place 10 signallers at the disposal of O.C. Signals to assist with above. They will report at ZOMMERBLOOM by noon Y day.

RUNNERS. 5. A runner post consisting of 1 N.C.O and u 7 men will be established at BOESINGHE CHATEAU by the 86th Brigade. This post will work forward to WOOD HOUSE and SAULES FARM. 88th and 87th Brigade will detail runners as required to work back to the above post. All runners will carry their messages in the top right breast pocket.

AMPLIFIERS &
POWER BUZZERS. 6. Each brigade will be supplied with an amplifier and 2 power buzzers which will work between the brigade forward station and battalion headquarters. 2 operators will accompany each amplifier. Battalions will supply operators for the power buzzers.

AEROPLANES. 7. Communication with aeroplanes will be carried out as laid down in 29th Div Instructions No 8.

G E N E R A L.

CABLE DUMP. Main cable dump will be at ZOMMERBLOOM but a supply of cable and light poles will be stored at BOESINGHE CHATEAU.

29th DIVISIONAL ARTILLERY INSTRUCTIONS No 9

13th August 1917.

Communications with F.O.O's

1. **RIGHT GROUP.**

   (a). The pair of F.O.O's from each of the Brigades forming the Right Group will have their starting point at the Artillery Brigade Forward Station at U.26.c.9.5. (C.B.).

   This Station will be manned for telephonic and visual communication to the Brigades of the Group. Information received from the F.O.O's will be transmitted by the quickest means available.

   (b). From the Station C.B. each pair of F.O.O's with their party will lay out a telephone line to the forward O.P. which they establish. One telephonist of the party, with an instrument, will be left at C.B. for each F.O.O. line.

   (c). Each pair of F.O.O's will establish visual communication with the Artillery Forward Station C.B.

   Messages sent by visual must be preceeded and terminated by "R.A" repeated three times.

   Signallers will be detailed for duty at C.B. to read messages sent from F.O.O's by visual.

   (d). Upon arriving at their forward O.P., while one F.O.O. observes, the second will run out a line to the Infantry Brigade Station at RUISSEAU FARM (U.21.c.7.2.) which Station will be established after the capture of the Green Line.

   This will provide for an alternative means of communication with the Artillery, through the Infantry Brigade.

2. **LEFT GROUP.**

   (a). The pair of F.O.O's from each of the Brigades forming the Left Group will have their starting point at

2.

The Station will transmit information received from the F.O.O's to the Brigades or Group, by telephone or visual.

(b). From the Station at   each pair of F.O.O's with their party will lay out a telephone line to the forward O.P. which they establish. One telephonist with an instrument, will be left at the starting point, for each F.O.O. line.

(c). Visual communication between F.O.O's and the Artillery forward Station at   will be worked in the same manner as laid down in para 1 (c).

(d). Upon arriving at their forward O.P. while one F.O.O. observes the second will run out a line to the Infantry Brigade Forward Station at Signal Farm (U.21.c.2.0.) This Station will be established after the capture of the Green Line.

3. <u>Personnel and Signalling Equipment.</u>

Each pair of F.O.O's must be accompanied by:-

    3 - Signallers (one to be left at the Artillery Brigade Forward Station).
    2 - Linemen.
    2 - Runners.

Each party should be supplied with:-

    2 - D.S. telephones.
    1 - Lucas lamp.
    1 - Folding Signalling Shutter.
    2 - miles twisted telephone wire.

An Officer should be detailed from each Group to supervise the transmission of information at the Brigade Forward Stations.

                                           Captain R.A.
                     Brigade Major 29th Divisional Artillery.

3.

MOVES of HEADQUARTERS. It is important that as much notice as possible is given of any intended move of Headquarters.

ARTILLERY. Separate instructions will shortly be issued for artillery communications.

                            [signed] Major.
                            O.C. 29th Divisional Signal Co. R.E.

12th August 1917.

```
Copy No 1 to General Staff
        2    A.D.Signals 14th Corps
        3    O.C.Signals 20th Div.
        4    O i/c Signals R.A.
        5       "      "    86th Brigade.
        6       "      "    87th     "
        7.      "      "    88th     "
        8.   File
```

Communications — Left Arty

"D"

Forward Artillery Communications on night of 16th

1. Right Group.

F.O.O's 15th Bde. party were shelled and F.O.O. wounded. Party broke up and some returned. Remainder joined 84th F.O.O. party.

Major Ball has observed from CB during today, but Brigade have no communications forward of this station

17th Brigade. F.O.O. and party established and maintained a good line beyond the Wijdendrift.

Visual by lamp was established from several points en route and communication with CB was maintained throughout the day.

A line was laid back to Ruisseau Farm as ordered but no Infantry Forward Station had been established there up to late in the morning

84th Brigade F.O.O. and party established and maintained a good line to the Wijdendrift. As far as can be learned no definite O.P. was determined upon.

2. C.B. Communication was maintained by Brigades during the day except during short periods, when visual by Lucas lamp was worked to 15th Brigade

S.O.S. During the night the post C.B. will be used as an S.O.S. station

Communication with Brigades will be by (1) Telephone direct to Brigades (2) Telephone through Infantry Brigade at Wood House and thence direct to Right Group. (3) By Lamp to 15th Brigade

In addition Very Lights and rockets for repeating S.O.S. are being supplied for use at C.B.

2. Left Group.

F.O.O's One Brigade has a line through to the Wijdendrift from Fourche Farm station.
A second Brigade has a line to Craonne Farm
Visual has not been used for sending back messages but is possible from the Wijdendrift. Possibility from Craonne Farm is uncertain

To Fourche Farm The lines from Brigades have been maintained almost constantly.

Visual is in operation between Fourche Farm and a Battery of the 5th Brigade.

3.

S.O.S. Fourche Farm will be used during the night as an S.O.S. station

Communication with Bdes will be by (1) Telephone direct to Brigades (2) Telephone through the Infantry Brigade at Saules Farm thence direct to Left Group. (3) By lamp to a battery of 5th Bde, transmitted to Brigades

In addition Very lights and rockets for repeating S.O.S. are being supplied for use at Fourche Farm.

<u>Wireless</u> Wireless signals from Trench Set working at Saules Farm were received by the receiving set installed by Left Group at 74th Brigade Headqrs. No messages were sent to Right Group or Left Group by this means.

16.8.17.

CONFIDENTIAL.

War Diary

of

29th (1st London) Divl. Signal Co., R.E.

From 1st September, 1917, to 30th September, 1917.

VOLUME XV.

-*-*-

WAR DIARY or INTELLIGENCE SUMMARY

Army Form C. 2118.

Place	Date	Hour	Summary of Events and Information	Remarks and references to Appendices
PROVEN	1st		Training in Cable Wagon Drill. New line laid to 86th Bde HQ about Vlamber of Dalmes. Maintenance of existing circuits. Messages dealt with 195. Registered SP's 44	
	2nd to 7th		Nothing of Interest. Training of new hands in Cable wagon drill and line work generally. Maintenance as usual. Arty Brigades moved to POLINCOVE on 3rd with sub-sections. 2 O Cable Signallers sent to Corps school for Improvement. Messages dealt with 200-199, 30-187, 42-213, 55-207, 67-187. Registered S.D's 27-25, 20-43, 25-32, 55-27, 35-40	
	8th		87th Bde move to HERZEELE for training purposes. Switched over on to a new line from PROVEN TEST POINT. Obtain 85th worked telephone only for communication with Rear Office. Messages dealt with 192. Registered SP's 42.	

WAR DIARY
or
INTELLIGENCE SUMMARY.

(Erase heading not required.)

Army Form C. 2118.

Instructions regarding War Diaries and Intelligence Summaries are contained in F. S. Regs., Part II and the Staff Manual respectively. Title pages will be prepared in manuscript.

Place	Date	Hour	Summary of Events and Information	Remarks and references to Appendices
PROVEN	9th		One officer sent to W. Riding Dd. C. R. to train tree signallers. Otherwise nothing of interest. Recreation training – football & cricket. Messages dealt with 194. Registered S.P.'s 45.	
	10th		Cable wagon drill with old detachments to keep them up to the work, as the others are working to hear men. Normal maintenance. Messages dealt with 233. Registered S.P.'s 33	
	11th		20 Machine Gunners from School to learn "Telephony". T.E. to be trained as Telephonists only, as they are only to transmit at the School 10 days, this will be difficult. Normal routine on cable drill. Gunners looking well and dry weather helps. Hope time to get clean again. Messages dealt with 203. Registered S.P.'s 46	
	12th		Nothing of interest. 2/Lt KING rejoins M.R. from School Boulogne. Messages dealt with 210. Registered S.P.'s 49	

WAR DIARY
or
INTELLIGENCE SUMMARY.
(Erase heading not required.)

Army Form C. 2118.

Place	Date	Hour	Summary of Events and Information	Remarks and references to Appendices
	13th		Nothing to report. Signal School closes 18th & men return to unit.	
	to			
	21st		13th Messages dealt with 338 Reported SPs 54	
			14th " 227 " 72	
			15th " 263 " 81	
			16th " 186 " 53	
			17th " 280 " 83	
			18th " 284 " 94	
			19th " 266 " 45	
			20th " 396 " 71	
			21st " 446 " 44	
I Corps	22nd	10am	Take over from French Signals. Everything working OK. Horwich exchange moved from Zoom to Luvron 6 Elverdinghe Chateau	
			Messages dealt with 808 Reported SPs 83	
	23rd		Lines to forward areas cut of canal suffer badly cut	

A6945 Wt. W14123/M1160 350,000 12/16 D. D. & L. Forms/C.2118/14.

WAR DIARY
or
INTELLIGENCE SUMMARY

Army Form C. 2118.

(Erase heading not required.)

Place	Date	Hour	Summary of Events and Information	Remarks and references to Appendices
			to shell fire. Subunit to G. scheme for buying 21 prisoners from Canal to Saulis farm. This scheme will deal with the requirements of both infantry & artillery. Throughout died with 699. Reported 8.68	
	24		Heavy shelling East of Canal cut all lines to Ble hope also but avail down also Line to Hqs to Bdes cut. Ruenus unable to work satisfactorily in dark with Gas masks on Long duty on message.	
	25		Further F of C dealt with R 440. Reptim SPs 106 Further F of Canal in Groups tho from 17.40 am to 0 am (Uny light) Wistation observers report Repd Bed SPs 94 Reptd Bed SPs 97	

WAR DIARY
or
INTELLIGENCE SUMMARY
(Erase heading not required.)

Army Form C. 2118.

Place	Date	Hour	Summary of Events and Information	Remarks and references to Appendices
	26 to 30		Nothing of note to record. Enemy confined himself to shelling the village by night & wireway by day. We continued to shell his trenches & back areas. Our shells did not appear to have his usual effect in generating enemy strafes. Relieved on 30th inst. by 19th Divisional Signal Coy.	
			Messages dealt with:	
	26		964 Inward 894	
	27		833 "	
	28		732 " 843	
	29			
	30			
			Controlled 890 74 " 94 " 73 " 91 " 135	

L.H.H. Hayter
HQ 29th April Coy R.E.

29TH (1ST LONDON)
SIGNAL COMPANY
R.E.
1/5/17

Army Form C. 2118.

WAR DIARY
or
INTELLIGENCE SUMMARY.
(Erase heading not required.)

Vol 16

Confidential

War Diary
of
29th Divisional Signal Co. R.E.

From 1st Oct: 1917 to 31st Oct 1917.

(Volume 16)

WAR DIARY
or
INTELLIGENCE SUMMARY.

Army Form C. 2118.

20th Div Signal Coy R.E. OCTOBER 1917

Place	Date	Hour	Summary of Events and Information	Remarks and references to Appendices
Camp	1st		Another 200 yds of bury from Cavell track to Woodhouse completed and tested. Was considerably damaged as a result of storms last night. Messages dealt with 824. Registered S.P.S. 114	
	2nd		Bury continued. 300 yds done with assistance of 46 men from the Battery. All lines OK throughout night. Messages dealt with 1064. Registered S.P.S. 133	
Elverdinghe	3rd		Bury continued. 300 yds done in Yeakesbury Amiltza section (440 yards) tested and utilised. All lines again opened up safely. Div. H.Q. moved from Ticket to Elverdinghe Chateau at 6pm. More cavalry network laid except for two pairs to Corps found down. Messages dealt with 1124. Registered S.P.S. 144	

WAR DIARY
or
INTELLIGENCE SUMMARY.
(Erase heading not required.)

Army Form C. 2118.

Place	Date	Hour	Summary of Events and Information	Remarks and references to Appendices
F.C.	4th		No trouble on account of Aeroplanes. Battalion (R Det Battery) on night Dir Post checked and found effective. Battalion HQ telephone communication from 84+3de Sauces Farm checked. Bde HQ Signal Farm by telephone lies visited & have traces of 2 cupper Degrees ducks of signatures fitted. Who established at Signal Farm working to Capt Drake? Skeleton Bof engine. Message dealt with 1121. Registered SP6 149.	
	5th		Busy continued, 230 yds dug leaving one more days work to reach Wood House. Otherwise normal maintenance and work. Inspection's operation Power buzzer and Amplifier direct from Signal Farm. Glare of Park not very successful. Working via Martins Mill proved OK. All found communication working. Message dealt with 1158. Registered SP6 157.	

WAR DIARY
or
INTELLIGENCE SUMMARY.
(Erase heading not required.)

Army Form C. 2118.

Place	Date	Hour	Summary of Events and Information	Remarks and references to Appendices
F.O.	6th		Bury to WOOD HOUSE completed. Obs. 3 pairs of lines D⁹ busted cable laid from WOOD HOUSE (WH) to VULCAN CROSSING (VC). Lineman post established. WH consisting of 2 linemen. Messages dealt with 647. Registered S.P's 132.	
	7th		87th Bde HQ move to VC from SAULE'S FARM at 9am. a Guards Brigade move into SAULE'S FARM at that hour. Communication maintained to both throng night 7th/8th. Six additional pairs WH to VC laid in morning. W/T set moved to SIGNAL FARM to VC, and one at SAULE'S FARM returned to Div H.R. Messages dealt with 696. Registered S.P's 153.	

WAR DIARY
or
INTELLIGENCE SUMMARY.
(Erase heading not required.)

Army Form C. 2118.

Place	Date	Hour	Summary of Events and Information	Remarks and references to Appendices
F.C.	8th		Preparations for offensive (completed) as follows: (see accompanying A)	
			(a) S.P.s (bulgarian) laid between VLAMERTINGHE and AU BON GATE, and extend between 4 two near front line	
			Each brigade laid two pairs to its forward station	
			(b) Amplifiers installed in Brigade forward station	
			Power buzzers with attaching batteries to go forward after capture 2nd objective and 1 F.[Stn](?) Battn HQ	
			(c) 1 pair of pigeons issued to each brigade	
			(d) Visual station established at MARTIN'S MILL	
			LANGEMARCK CHURCH, or AU BON GATE, & VULCAN CROSSING	
			No signalling forward except to answer receipt of a visible message	
			(e) W/T stations established at AU BON GATE and VULCAN CROSSING	
			Bde HQs move - 88th to MARTIN's MILL, 86th to AU BON GATE, 87 to CARIBOU CAMP / R Oskirrs(?)	

Mss dealt with 507   87 #6

R Oskirrs S/3 161

WAR DIARY or INTELLIGENCE SUMMARY

Army Form C. 2118.

Place	Date	Hour	Summary of Events and Information	Remarks and references to Appendices
F.C.	9th		Shooting successful. Communication maintained to brigade. Though difficulties experienced WH to VC have been and to obs't [observation] posts. Wireless rangefinders not successful. Left Bde. registered by marky [marking] ground. Right Bde. by loss of accumulators through shellfire. Visual quite successful. Diagram of lines attached Appendix "A". Messages dealt with 960. Registered SP's 98	"A"
	10th		17th Div. signals stated to relieve us. Artillerie arrived 8am and all except wheelers [?] translation of ours returned. Relief of Brigadier completed by both being relieved by one Brigade. Difficulty in arrival [?] as result of sudden Left Brigade left the very late, but total relief finally combined by about 11 hrs. Major BIRTH leaves Coy as the commanding 2Ways of Messages dealt with 498. Rangers SP's 42	

Major BIRTH

WAR DIARY
or
INTELLIGENCE SUMMARY.
(Erase heading not required.)

Army Form C. 2118.

Place	Date	Hour	Summary of Events and Information	Remarks and references to Appendices
PROVEN	11th		Div. HQ moved to PROVEN. Leaving area to 17th Div at 8am. Bivouacs at PL-D5 and S.6 area to PROVEN neighbourhood.	
			30ks switchboard loaned to 17th Sig Coy & they rely on ours if 20 tie circuits of Coy march from DRAGON CAMP to PARDOT CAMP near PROVEN. Messages dealt with 301. Registered SPs 48	
	12th			
	13th		Nothing of importance. Coy. employed cleaning up as far as breath wire permits. Messages dealt with 12th 293 54 13th 242 Registered SPs 55	
	14th		Name as 12th & 13th 15. Heavy load sent to BASSEUX with office returns and stores. Messages dealt with 299. Registered SPs 89	

WAR DIARY or INTELLIGENCE SUMMARY

Army Form C. 2118.

Place	Date	Hour	Summary of Events and Information	Remarks and references to Appendices
	15th		Coy marches to entraining station HOPOUTRE leaving PROVEN	
		7.30am	7.30am waited for Goods. Ambulance arrives from BASSEUX about 8pm after engine trouble. 87th Bde closes down and entrains for BAILLEULMONT. Messages dealt with 163. Registered S.P's 98	
	16th		E.L. lorry leaves PROVEN 10 am with loss of officers kits, office furniture, instruments, w/t officers tools and six men. Albion lorry engine but right by 12 noon & leaves for BASSEUX with W/T gear, instruments and CRME stores. E.L.lorry arrives 7.30am. Coy arrives BASSEUX about 3pm. 87th Bde in touch at BAILLEULMONT. Messages dealt with 83. Registered S.P's 105	

WAR DIARY
or
INTELLIGENCE SUMMARY.

(Erase heading not required.)

Army Form C. 2118.

Place	Date	Hour	Summary of Events and Information	Remarks and references to Appendices
	17th		Albroisbury arrived 2am	
			88th 88th Bde in touch by Bow, horses at BLAIRVILLE hutted at POMMIER	POMMIER
			Company employed cleaning up Horse lines at BASSEUX.	
			are a considerable improvement on those at PROVEN.	
			Messages dealt with 234. Registered S.P's 130	
	18th		Division in rest. Work done mainly consisting of:-	
	19th		(1) Training of Infantry Brigadiers in Power Buzzer, Amplifier,	
	20th		and Visual (Lucas Lamp).	
	21st		(2) Training of Cable Detachments	
	22nd		(3) Buzzer Matters and for Improving accommodation	
	23rd		(4) Training of Brigade Sections in Wireless.	
	to		(5) Signal School for Artillery.	
	31st		(6) Reorganization of Divisional Artillery Section.	
			(7) Maintenance of existing Back Area Communications.	
			Messages dealt with 18th 214 Registered S.P's 130	

WAR DIARY
or
INTELLIGENCE SUMMARY.

Army Form C. 2118.

Place	Date	Hour	Summary of Events and Information	Remarks and references to Appendices
			Message dealt with 19th 219 Registered Etc 150	
			20th 230 124	
			21st 222 121	
			22nd 286 106	
			23rd 195 110	
			24th 218 121	
			25th 198 102	
			26th 247 141	
			27th 249 130	
			28th 232 130	
			29th 251 146	
			30th 288 150	
			31st 301 139	

A Simpson Major RE
O.C. 56th Div Signal Coy RE

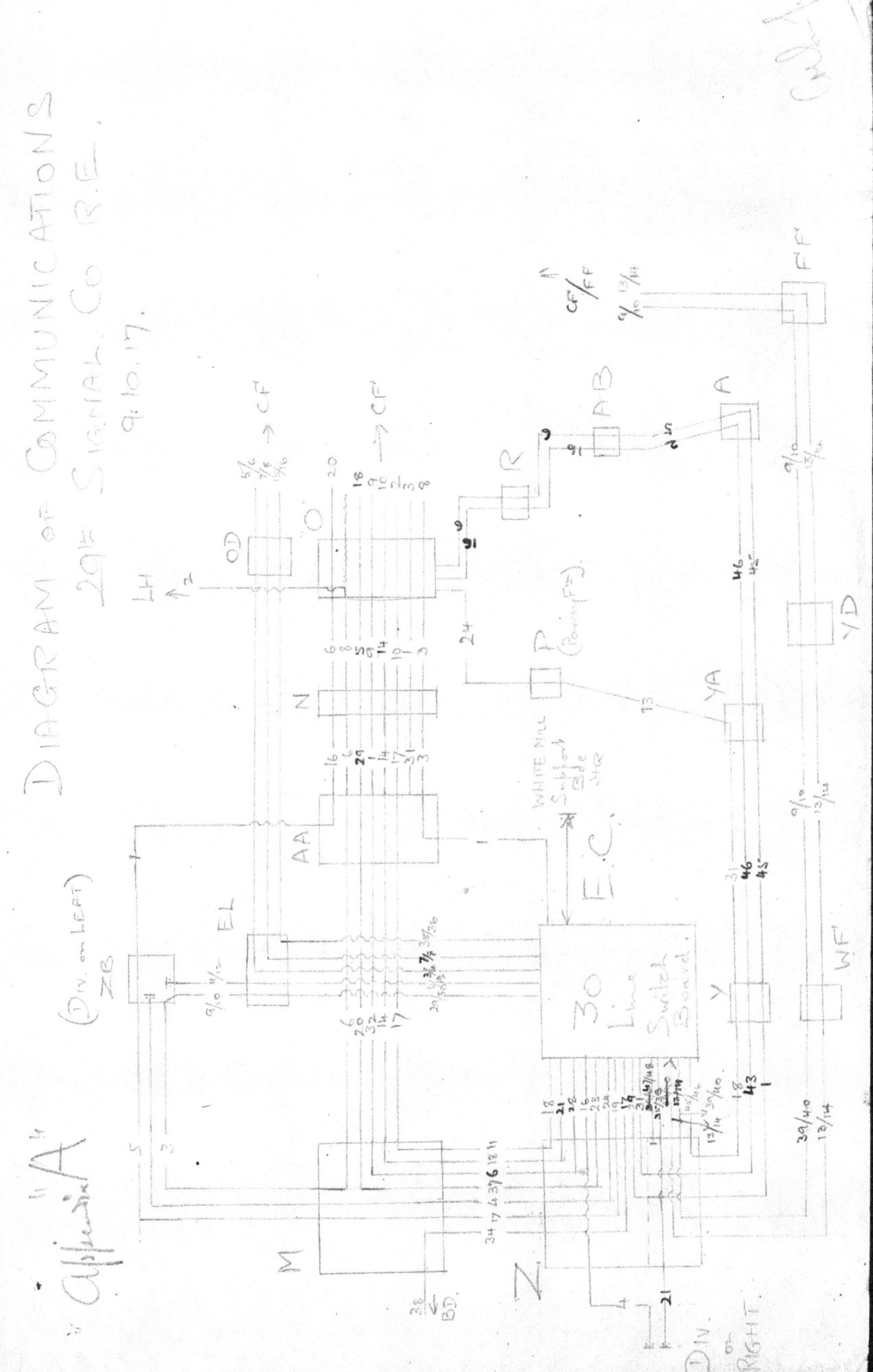

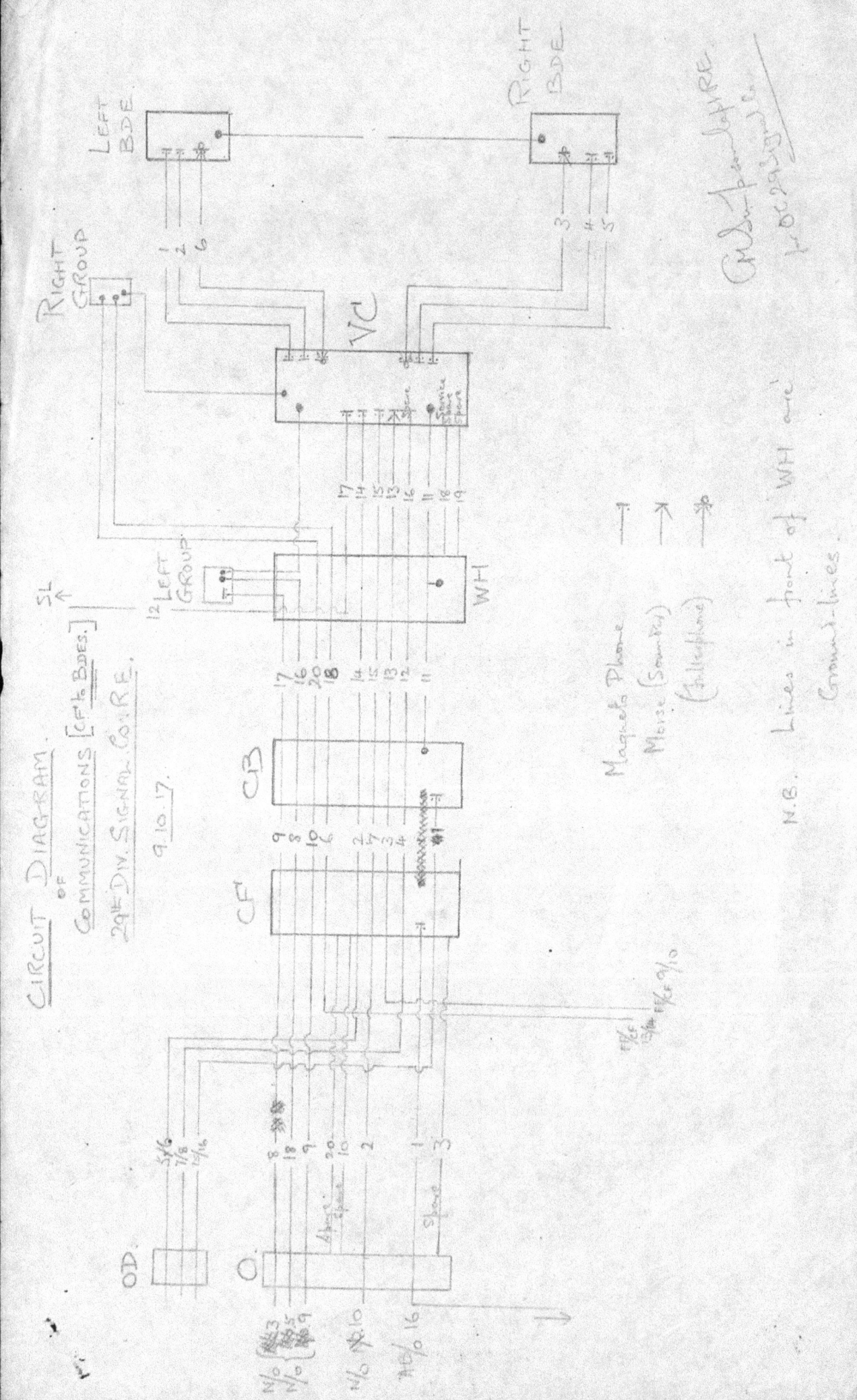

CONFIDENTIAL.

WAR DIARY.

OF

29TH DIVISIONAL SIGNAL COY., R.E.,

VOLUME 17.

(November 1917)

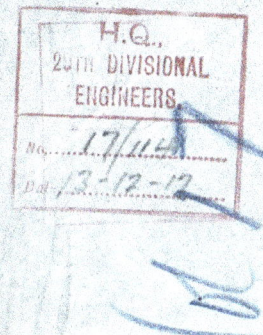

WAR DIARY
or
INTELLIGENCE SUMMARY.

Army Form C. 2118.

(Erase heading not required.)

Place	Date	Hour	Summary of Events and Information	Remarks and references to Appendices
Busseux	Aug 1-17		Division in reserve area. Training of personnel and maintenance of existing stores were carried out. Most of the work that was carried out, in addition, stated were erected and huts were built in camp. On the 12th, No. 1 coy were sent to 9th Corps to assist in construction of cable trenches and cable routes for forthcoming offensive. This number was increased to 22 by the addition of 6 men of 2nd Artillery Sig. Detachment. Schemes were carried out with Lucas Lamp and wireless working in with Brigade section and Brigade section training consisted of a line net. in visual practice with Lucas lamp. 1 Day trip carried from BAPAUME to BASSEUX to MOISLAINS, thirty three 16th Personnel by rail travelled night 14/15 — arrived MOISLAINS 16th. Camp night 15/16.	
MOISLAINS	15		Brigade at HAUT-ALLAINES and MOISLAINS. 87 O.R. 88 O.R.	

WAR DIARY
or
INTELLIGENCE SUMMARY.
(Erase heading not required.)

Army Form C. 2118.

Place	Date	Hour	Summary of Events and Information	Remarks and references to Appendices
QUENTIN MILL	19th		H.Q. only connected by telephone only. Brigades moved to ETRICOURT, FINS, SOREL, night 18/19th. Div. Hq. moved to SOREL (rear Hq) and QUENTIN MILL 800 yards east of GOUZEAUCOURT (Advanced Hq). Night 19th at 1.30 Brigades to assemble area northwest of GOUZEAUCOURT. Communication to one Brigade Hq by telephone. The other two allowed wires to proximity to remainder. Hq to B.G.C. 1st Brigade. 8 8 & 88th wires Hq ready for 87th Brigade. At Hq 10.30 am Brigades ordered to carry out programme issued some time before the 20th and 12 Mr. Winsome first intimation received. Division to be ready to Brigades in that infant land here (communication by telephone) to Brigades with 3 minutes of order. German front line through to half mile East	
QUENTIN MILL	20th		of front line of trenches to their hexagon. VILLIERS PLOUICH, thence by Mme. F. 1600 yards East to the 29th Divn. at Hq. 10.30 am Cuptein. to advance. Reach Brigade.	

WAR DIARY or INTELLIGENCE SUMMARY

Army Form C. 2118.

Place: QUENTIN MILL 16 March

With the assistance of Pte Lowman retailed lines have been extending working telephone lines in addition an advanced construction party collected two poles from cable heads to L34D5½ to establish ground advanced telegraph office & Laid a Laid complete to advanced station interrupted by wire 500 yards forward of office where it should have been. The wires which for both by pigeons will restored by ab 2.30 pm. Lines communication being of surviving links and messages to Brigade were interrupted. At 4 pm Sergt LOWMAN with two mounted men was sent forward to get to the 83rd Bde Hq sent back message 4.30 to their Hq at 5 pm. Visual communication with 86 & 87 Brigade Hq established from the advanced horsemen station. No messages for to station were sent. During night 20/21st of June were sent from the advanced station to Brigade Hq but

A6645 Wt. W14422/M1160 350,000 12/16 D.D. & L. Forms/C/2118/14.

WAR DIARY
or
INTELLIGENCE SUMMARY.

(Erase heading not required.)

Army Form C. 2118.

Place	Date	Hour	Summary of Events and Information	Remarks and references to Appendices
QUENTIN MILL	20th (cont)		Owing to darkness and the nature of the ground very little of Tanks progress could be seen or noted through during the fight.	
			WIRELESS. The 86th & 88th Brigades were accompanied by wireless Tanks, these however did not function until the 21st and were therefore useless during the outflanking of the afternoon of the 20th.	
			RUNNERS. Owing to the difficulty of locating positions of Brigade HQ and the error in the position of advanced station, and also the great distance covered, runners were unable to find Bn destinations readily and messages sent by this means took up to four hours to arrive.	
			PIGEONS. Owing to mist and there no pigeon messages were received.	
QUENTIN MILL	21st		Went forward to locate the advanced Station and found that it was in the wrong place. I checked	

Army Form C. 2118.

WAR DIARY
or
INTELLIGENCE SUMMARY.
(Erase heading not required.)

Place	Date	Hour	Summary of Events and Information	Remarks and references to Appendices
QUENTIN MILL	24th (cont)		Issued ML job form of armoured cable link to MARCOING and MASNIÈRES and maintenance of existing cables continued. Wireless working satisfactorily from both stations. Motor cyclist DRLS managed between Hy. and 3 Brigades during daylight.	
DITTO	25-29th		WORK. A new power armoured route constructed between Hy and A dugout (1000 yards north-west of VILLERS PLOUICH). Lines between F cabins and ML hutto also the existing route between ML and Brigades were failed when the stations attacked. Trouble from hostile shell fire particularly increased and four cables were found unsatisfactory for the forward area. Owing to short state of roads motor cyclists unable to proceed MARCOING and MASNIÈRES at night.	

PTO

Army Form C. 2118.

WAR DIARY
or
INTELLIGENCE SUMMARY.

(Erase heading not required.)

Place	Date	Hour	Summary of Events and Information	Remarks and references to Appendices
QUENTIN MILL	22nd	contd	Then to move its position to the correct place viz L 34 D 27. This was carried out having the Wagon line to Brigade line completed by this by 4 P.M. Two Fuller phone advanced station sets & advanced Div Hy were opened at the same time and communication by telephone from advanced Div to Brigade became more or less possible.	
QUENTIN MILL	23rd		87th Wireless Set with advanced station has moved to 88th Brigade Hy near MASNIÈRES and Wilson's set was sent IA to MARCOING — two power B5 were laid from Cable head to advanced station. Direct Fullerphone working from Divisional Div Hy to Brigade was established and horse supervised station Div Hy and the advanced station (ML).	
do	24th		The 2 pdr Area Detachment loaned to assist in construction first are line armoured cable from Cable head to ML.	

PTO

WAR DIARY
or
INTELLIGENCE SUMMARY.

Army Form C. 2118.

Place	Date	Hour	Summary of Events and Information	Remarks and references to Appendices
	23-29th(cont)		D.A.L.S at night was therefore carried out by mounted orderlies.	
QUENTIN MILL	30th		Attack by enemy on whole front. At 8.45 am enemy within 100 yds of Bde HQ, was Bde Hq surrounded. Impossible to depart personel [sic] or establishment about 19. In consequence a defensible Bde Hq established until 5 hours in advance Bde HQ was forced 600 yds back of BEAUCAMP. Remainder very slowly by wireless to Corps and by mounted orderly to Brigades via RIBECOURT. Rear HQ remained at SOREL. Transport captured ore distinguished communicates to two officers two men including RE. Entire light horse also left behind owing to a railway from [?] blocking it. Across the road and thirty [?] on south-easterly Bde Brigade [Counter] attacked	

P.T.O

Army Form C. 2118.

WAR DIARY
or
INTELLIGENCE SUMMARY.
(Erase heading not required.)

Place	Date	Hour	Summary of Events and Information	Remarks and references to Appendices
	30th March		direction from MARCOING. Both 87th & 88th Brigades turned sectors and MARCOING wireless station turned out and counter-attacks both the infantry returning to their normal duties when enemy was repulsed. to Divisional Commissioners are working all three were employed at the capture of QUENTIN Mill. 12/4/17	

Cont. signs. Major R.E. [illegible]
for O.C. Div. Signal Co. R.E.

CONFIDENTIAL

WAR DIARY

OF

29th DIVISIONAL SIGNAL Co. RE

1/12/17 TO 31/12/17

Army Form C. 2118.

29th Div. Signal Coy

WAR DIARY
or
INTELLIGENCE SUMMARY.
(Erase heading not required.)

DECEMBER 1917

Place	Date	Hour	Summary of Events and Information	Remarks and references to Appendices
	1st		HR. from BEAUCAMP to TRESCAULT. Communication by telephone working in RIBECOURT to 87th Bde. Great deal of trouble beyond Ribecourt from shell fire. Nounds DR's motorcyclist DR's work given to 87th Bde. three by runner to 86th + 88th. During night 86th Bde withdrawn from MASNIÈRES, with Trench Set – which had been working continuously since dawn of Nov 30th with conspicuous success.	
	2nd		Line held by 87th + 88th (left to right) New telephone pair laid at dawn to 87th Bde and they had line to 88th. New telephone line from shell fire 4 linemen killed. At 3pm exchange at Ribcourt received direct hit amongst about 100 yards. Only 3 casualties from this. Telephones etc saved from old HR. Q'nary at QUENTIN MILL. Enemy had done no material damage to instruments (unable to salve F.L. etc) as enemy had broken the magneto.	

WAR DIARY
or
INTELLIGENCE SUMMARY.

Army Form C. 2118.

Place	Date	Hour	Summary of Events and Information	Remarks and references to Appendices
	3rd		Lines as before. Hawincourt extremely difficult. 86th Bde in front around to HAVRINCOURT wood. 87th relieved by Bngds of 6th Div. moved to close support. HQ near RIBECOURT. In touch by telephone. 86th Bde under tactical command of 6th Divn. Communications handed over. Artillery command also passed to 6th Div Arty — who took over RIBECOURT exchange	
	4th		No change in situation. Prepare to move to BAPAUME in evening. 36th Divn relieved by 87th & 88th Brigades. HQ move to SOREL at 9pm, closing TRESCAULT at that hour. Brigades to FINS, EQUANCOURT and ETRICOURT.	
	5th		Div HQ LE CAUROY. Transport marches via BAPAUME. Remainder to LE CAUROY area by tactical trains	

WAR DIARY
or
INTELLIGENCE SUMMARY.
(Erase heading not required.)

Army Form C. 2118.

Place	Date	Hour	Summary of Events and Information	Remarks and references to Appendices
	6th to 16th		Lines to all brigades at LIENCOURT, SUS-ST-LEGER, and HUMBERNES all quite satisfactory but required a working party at first. Time spent in obtaining reinforcements, reequipment, training, and maintenance of lines. Reinforcements very slow. Only 8 out of 30 horses arrived, and about 20 out of 50 men. 2/Lt Shirrell R.E. — vice 2/Lt MACLACHLAN wounded on 30th November — arrived on 12th, both also No 1 Sec. vice 2/Lt ROSS to No 3 Sec.	
	16th		Company commenced three days march to new area leaving after relays to work Sig. Office until move of Div HQ first days march to PETIT-FILLIEVRE.	
	17th		Second days march to FRESSIN.	

Army Form C. 2118.

WAR DIARY
or
INTELLIGENCE SUMMARY.
(Erase heading not required.)

Instructions regarding War Diaries and Intelligence Summaries are contained in F. S. Regs., Part II. and the Staff Manual respectively. Title pages will be prepared in manuscript.

Place	Date	Hour	Summary of Events and Information	Remarks and references to Appendices
W	18th		Arrival at HUCRULIERS. Office closed at LAUROY, and reopened HUCRULIERS at same hour - communication to Brigades by telephone telegraph. Coy arrived at Hucqueliers about 4 pm (horses) trace another 3 kilom. to PREURES and there was no accommodation in former. March extremely difficult owing heavy snow drifts. The only unit except MMP to arrive for programme.	
	19th to 31st		Training & re-equipment. Few reinforcements not arrived - no remounts. Two cable wagons and one Arty telephone wagon supplied. All training greatly hampered by snow which impeded all vehicles. Work mostly confined to indoor lectures and squad drill.	

CWJohnson
Lt Col
OC 2nd Div Sig Co
March '15

A6945 Wt. W11422/M1160 350,000 12/16 D. D. & L. Forms/C./2118/14.

CONFIDENTIAL.

WAR DIARY.

of

29th DIVISIONAL SIGNAL COMPANY R.E.

From 1.1.1918. to 31.1.1918.

WAR DIARY
INTELLIGENCE SUMMARY

JANUARY Army Form C. 2118.
29th Divn Sig Coy RE

Place	Date	Hour	Summary of Events and Information	Remarks and references to Appendices
HUCQUELIERS	1st to 2nd		Rest. Training as far as snow permitted. Maintenance of lines very difficult owing to weather. Stations length.	
	3rd	9.0 am	3rd Inst. Coy moved off by route march to FAUQUEMBERGUES. Roads very difficult & slippery. Arrived about 2 pm into temp. billets. Advance party to WIZERNES with stores by lorry. 2nd Inst. Message dealt with 502. Registered S.P's 266.	
	"			
WIZERNES	4th		Div HQ. closed HUCQUELIERS 10 am, reopened WIZERNES at that hour. Signal Coy. arrived at 2.0 pm. Billets good – all horses under cover. Lines to 87th, 88th Bdes (87th moved to WIZERNES men 19th, 88th Bde Line about 10 miles long (about) early in month.) See diagram A. attached. A lot of trouble. Message dealt with 120. Registered S.P's 98.	

29 Div. SRE.

Army Form C. 2118.

WAR DIARY
or
INTELLIGENCE SUMMARY.
(Erase heading not required.)

January

Place	Date	Hour	Summary of Events and Information	Remarks and references to Appendices
WIZERNES	5th to 13th		Training as follows: Courses for each brigade in Pigeons, Power Buzzers and Amplifiers. Brigade Pools of 16 men for P.B. & Amplifiers now formed. Courses within company for training of linesmen. Normal maintenance of lines.	
	14th		Remounts to complete arrived 14th. Wagon drawn also completed to establishment. Reinforcements of men insufficient. Messages dealt with 1955. Registered SP6 1119	
	15th		Advance Party of linesmen with all instruments sent up to 8th Div. HQ, CANAL BANK, DEAD END, YPRES. Messages dealt with 183. Registered SP6 123	
	16th		Lorry returned from 8th Div. HR. Nothing of importance. Messages dealt with 201. Registered S.P.6 1115	

29 DIV SIGS

Army Form C. 2118.

WAR DIARY
or
INTELLIGENCE SUMMARY.
(Erase heading not required.)

January

Place	Date	Hour	Summary of Events and Information	Remarks and references to Appendices
WIZERNES	17th		Second Advance Party with Wireless Section under 2/Lt Crow, proceeded to 8th Div HQ. All personnel and stores required to take over from 8th Div. now in this area (lorry returned)	
EWIZERNES			Coy. Transport marched to ZERMEZEELE	
			Nee. March with 174. Registered S.P.S 118.	
	18th		Lorry with COMS stores to MERSEY CAMP (8th Div Signal Transport), under L/Cpl DAY. After unloading, lorry returned to ZERMEZEELE	
			E.L. Lorry to 8th Div. HQ. Messages dealt with 260. Registered S.P.S. 110.	
DEAD END YPRES	19th		29th Div took over from 8th Div. at 12 noon in sector N of PASSCHENDAELE. One brigade with 2 battns holding the line. Bn HQ at GALLIPOLI with burned lines back to Division. Messages dealt with 385. Registered S.P.S. 119.	

A6945 Wt. W14421/M1160 350,000 12/16 D. D. & L. Forms/C.2118/14.

29 Div: Sig:

WAR DIARY
INTELLIGENCE SUMMARY

Army Form C. 2118.

January

Place	Date	Hour	Summary of Events and Information	Remarks and references to Appendices
DEAD END YPRES	20th		Situation normal. Communication as follows:-	
			86th Bde (in Line). Forward - Ground Lines, Visual, Wireless, Buzzer Amplifier.	
			Rear - Buzzer Lines, Wireless	B. Dn 6 Bdes.
			88th Bde (in Support) Forward - Ground Lines, Wireless	C. Bde in line forward
			Rear - Airline, with alternative buzzing.	D. Wireless
			Diagrams B, C, D attached	
			87th Bde (in Reserve) Permanent routes.	
			Normal maintenance and reconnaissance of area to	
			front work required	
			Messages dealt with 400. Registered S.P's 1/13.	
	21st		29 Div. Arty take over from 8th Div. Arty. Arty Brigades	
			at WIELTJE and at close to WIELTJE - ST JULIEN Road	
			(15th RHA & 17th RFA respectively). Communication by airlines &	
			alternative buries.	
			Messages dealt with 422. Registered S.P's 1/32	

A6945 Wt. W14422/M1160 350,000 12/16 D. D. & L. Forms/C/2118/14.

29D.S.C.R.E

Army Form C. 2118.

WAR DIARY
or
INTELLIGENCE SUMMARY.

January

(Erase heading not required.)

Place	Date	Hour	Summary of Events and Information	Remarks and references to Appendices
DEAD END YPRES	22nd to 31st		Normal maintenance of all means of communication. Systematic clearing of the area by small parties, especially on Tracks 5 and 6, and the plank road. Chief difficulties experienced (a) Getting forward stores, accumulators, rations and working parties. (b) Earthing and other faults on buzzer system. (c) Inexperience of new drafts on twisted cable test point work. On 25th 15th Bde R.H.A. moved to tunnelled dugouts 750 yds W. of GALLIPOLI communication by ground lines on trestles to G.P. Very little trouble from shell fire experienced. Divisional Signal School for 60 signallers commenced at BRAKE CAMP on 28th under 2/Lt Turney, RFA (from 29th D.A.C.) Messages staff with 3641 Registrn. DSPS 1325 CMS in base MajorRE at 24thD.v.S.GRE	

29th DIVISION
HACK
1325

CIRCUIT DIAGRAM.
29TH DIVISIONAL SIGNAL COY.
9TH JAN. 18.

A.

St Omer — Tilques Ex. YB1 — Exchange
→ To Tilques Exchange

Wizernes — 29th Div. — St Omer Ex. K — NZHH, NZHG, NZHF
Connections to: CRE, RTO, Div Train, DADOS, G, Q, Sigs, DGO

Boisdinghem — YB1 K — 88th Bde

Hallines — YB1 K — 86th Bde

Lumbres — YB1 K — 87th Bde
→ To Fruges Exchange

NOTE: — 29TH DIV ARTY AND 29TH AM SUB PARK THROUGH LUMBRES AND FRUGES.
29TH. DIV. S.C. THROUGH ST. OMER AND TILQUES.

Legend:
⊢ MAG. TELEPHONE
K " WITH SUP. SOUNDER.
⊠ MAG. EXCHANGE

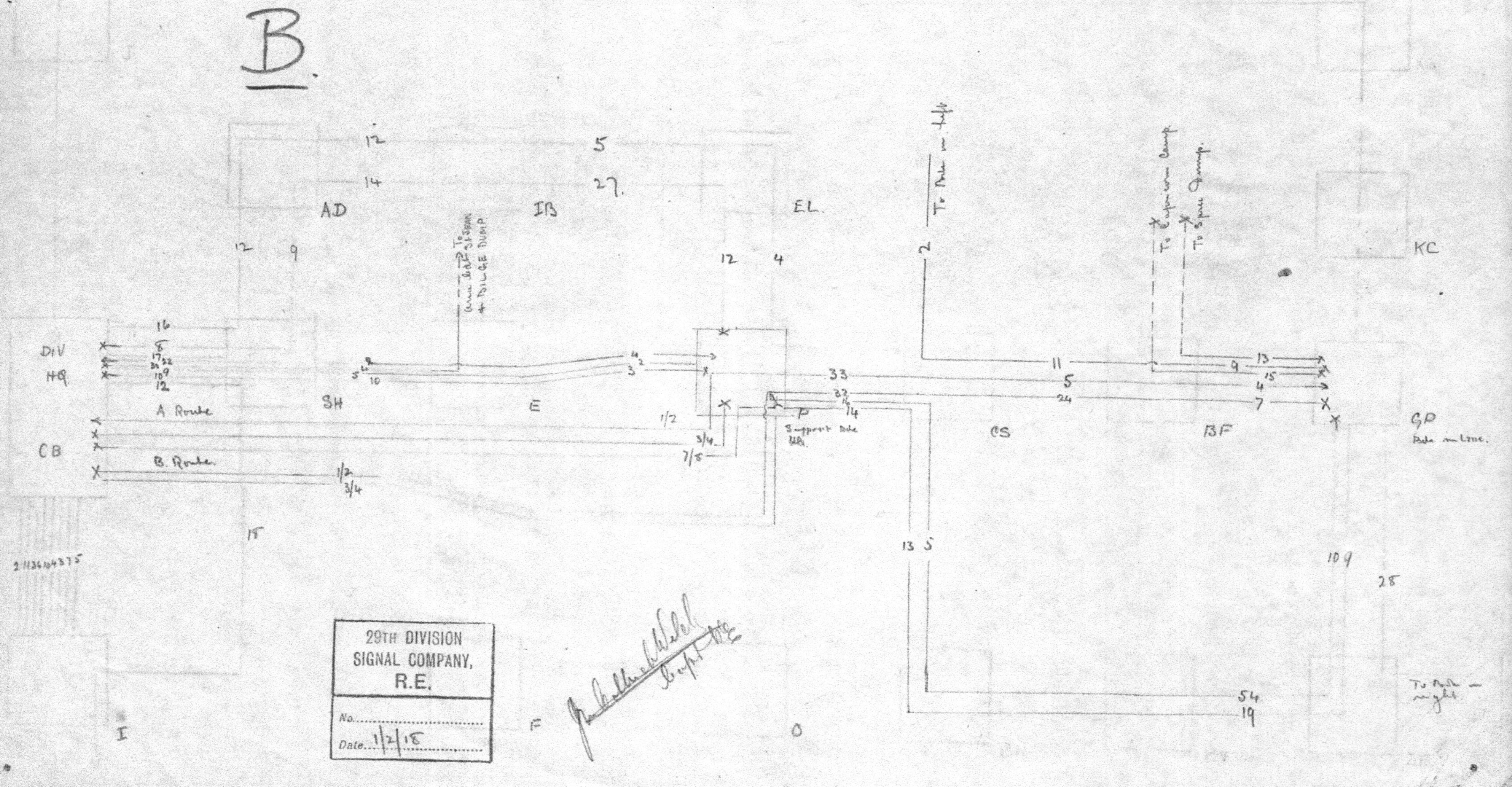

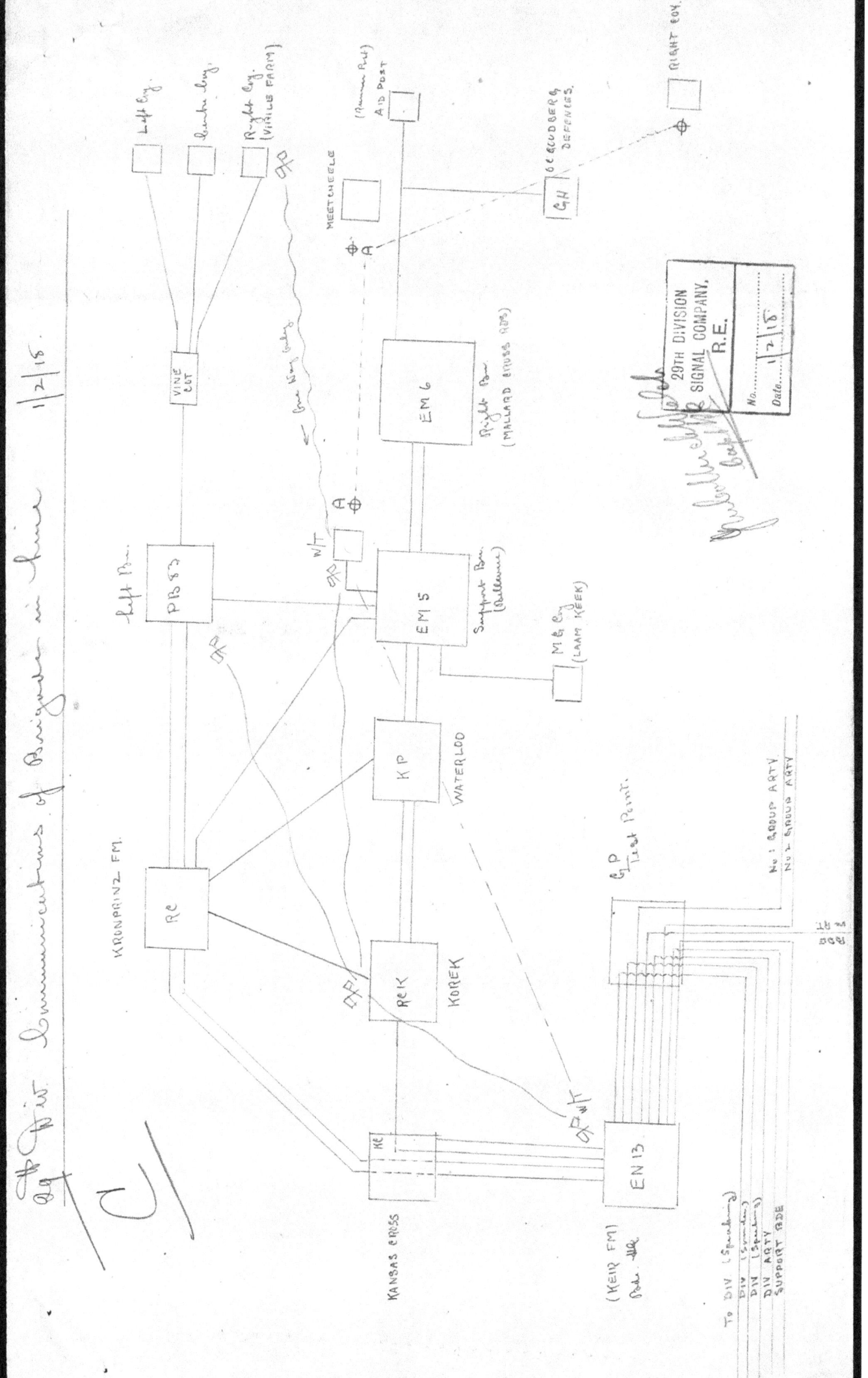

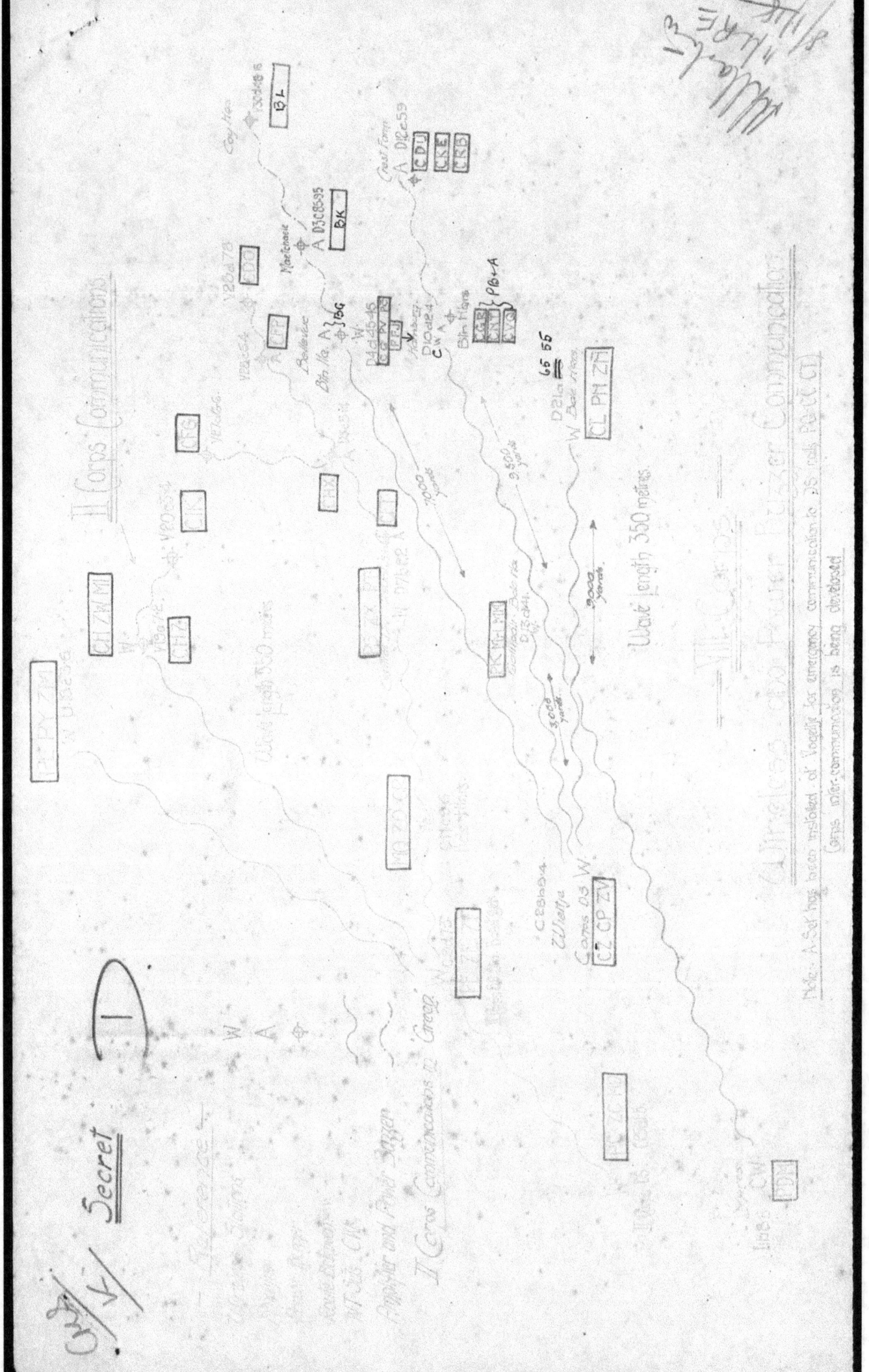

CONFIDENTIAL

WAR DIARY.

of

29th Divisional Signal Coy R.E.

From 1/2/18. To 28/2/18.

VOLUME No..........

WAR DIARY
INTELLIGENCE SUMMARY

Place: YPRES ST JEAN
Date: 1/2/15

Commencement moved in Divisional Reserve in the whole of the last month. Very little trouble was experienced. Relief from + Relief of been from Bn. Hd. Qs. to Bn. Hd. Qs. (2A/D13 at 10.10). The system was thoroughly excellent and some casualties occurred but at points difficult were no improvement. The men had been during his 4th tour in the trenches. Bn. Hd. WIELTJE was found by platoon during the field with route from Bn. Hd. to OS half plus 9 which was unpleasant. The events that occurred were caught up again in Appendix I. It represents movement from ABEEVILLE to supply Depot when we left had but it begins from hyment is again in the B.H. — 2E routes were done as there occurred well such expected in relieving at that could be expected in retiring from 9 to 6 p.m. Our casualty will essentially will assembled in The excavaten will subsists.

10

WAR DIARY
or
INTELLIGENCE SUMMARY
(Erase heading not required.)

Army Form C. 2118.

Place	Date	Hour	Summary of Events and Information	Remarks and references to Appendices
	1st		At Corps Signals for return. Reported Abraham never going. Was very overdue.	
			Instruction of Motor Cyclists & Infantry Personnel continued at Divisional Signal School at BRAKE CAMP.	
	6/2/15		Found by Pulse Shaft that Divisional Hd. was not full up and left by two Motors of No. 1 Right Res. Hd.	
	6/2/15		at WATERLOO (28/D.9.60.80) and left Res. Hd. at KRONPRINZ (28/D.3c.50.45). To provide telephone communication by air lines was impractical to establish & forward Divisional exchange on operating Res. Hd. at "GALLIPOLI". Sounds commence when by cannon shots on G.P. just pointed. The remaining Divisional A. and Corps telephone 2 exchanges ??????, the Divisional exchange/telephone 2. It was necessary to install new set at WATERLOO and me at KRONPRINZ	
			to remain ????? at GALLIPOLI. The whole BELLEVUE to ??????.	
			DRLS by Auto Cyclist DR to GALLIPOLI three by ????? to ????? Hds. All Motor Cyclists ready at GALLIPOLI for return of ????	

WAR DIARY
or
INTELLIGENCE SUMMARY.

Army Form C. 2118.

Place	Date	Hour	Summary of Events and Information	Remarks and references to Appendices
			Visual communication from Gr. to KOREK, BELLEVUE, KRONPRINZ and WATERLOO.	
	9/2/15		Readjustment of visual system effected 9/2/15 and all afternoon were furnished to commanders concerned with list of any kind.	
	10/2/15		Tel. line + telegraph line remained through	
	11/2/15		Whence tents of linesmen were transferred upstairs to huts now built & still ground accommodation in use by H/Q gunners.	
Canal Bank YPRES	11/2/15		New tent duly established being lorry to DROGLANDT.	
			Arrival of new commission to the H.Q. just being due at STEENVOORDE 10 am. Corps forwarded to billets in STEENVOORDE	
STEENVOORDE			Relined engagements at DROGLANDT by letter which at WINNEZEELE, WATOU and POPERINGHE. New communication direct to billets at WINNEZEELE & WATOU and through VIII Corps Signal Office to POPERINGHE, hence mainly on Army Command Routes.	
	12/2/15		G DA H.Q. closed down at Canal Bank & reopened POPERINGHE.	

WAR DIARY
or
INTELLIGENCE SUMMARY.
(Erase heading not required.)

Army Form C. 2118.

Place	Date	Hour	Summary of Events and Information	Remarks and references to Appendices
			Telephone communication in permanent routes through VIII Corps at POPERINGHE exchange. Telephone lines in permanent circuits at POPERINGHE exchange.	
			During the firsts months of operations construction of maintenance of stables, common rat by [?] [?] [?] say eng, included in field park, huts first, huts, [?], [?] in shelter dugouts.	
	19/7/15		98 1 Pole at WINNEZEELE moved to N6 in POPERINGHE quarters by St J Pole moved to EECKE [?] [?] to [?] at EECKE established by means of already existing [?] permanent [?].	
	21/7/15		Arranging with R. Police for supply of suitable room for Divnn Supervisor & Amplifier house at [?] Girls School	Appendices 3 + 4
	22/7/15		Div Supts. Servants & personnel consisted of 1 officer + 10 O.R.	
	24/7/15		Div Supvr & Amplifir house at Girls School dispersed at 9.00 [?] [?]	

WAR DIARY
or
INTELLIGENCE SUMMARY.

Army Form C. 2118.

Place	Date	Hour	Summary of Events and Information	Remarks and references to Appendices
	26/2/18		At 1 Probn at WATOU moved to HQ at POPERINGHE and to 2nd S Probn moved back to WINNEZEELE. Their ennumerators in future. Remarks to Corps + 1 Probn Ennumts supervised in Telephone Lines. Charts of Telegraph + DRLS Circuits held with by this HQ Signals Office during month shown on Appendices 5 + 6	

20TH DIVISION
SIGNAL COMPANY.
R.E.
No. 1.3.18

Appendix I.

LINES - LEFT DIVISIONAL ARTILLERY, VIII Corps.

31/1/6

From	To	Type	Circuit
D.A. H.Q.	15th Bde. RHA.	S	CS-37/C-P-19-CS-19-BF-21-GP
D.A. H.Q.	" "	TB	CS-4-SH-3-AD-13-13-22-ZE-5-P-3-CS-24-BH-50-ZE-7-GP
DA. H.Q.	17th " RFA	T	CS-B5/3-P
D.A. H.Q.	" "	T3	CS-5poled cable-CS-14-BF
D.A. H.Q.	86th "	T	CS-A5/6-P
D.A. H.Q.	" "	T	CS-25-SH-55-E-25-F-18-C
D.A. H.Q.	Inf.Bde.inLine	T	CS-4 poled cable-CS-17-BF-22-GP
15 Bde. R.H.A.	BT exchange	T	GP-15-ZE-40-WH-10-LC-44-BT
17 R.F.A.	Inf.Bde.inLine	T	BF-24-GP
D.A. Res.Bde.	"	T	O-35-BE-27-Z3-58-GP
86thBde.R.F.A.	Batteries	T	CS-25-BF
		T	CS-22-BF
86 Bde. R.F.A. Batteries.	OP	T	BF-5-GP
B F	"	T	BF-11-GP
JRB (17 Bde Battery Ex.) 29th Div.Art.	WH	T	GP-1-WH
	DTO	T	CS-3-SH-7-AD
	Counter Batt.	T	CS-39/10-P
	Support Bde.	S	CS-22-SH-X-X-4-P
Div. H.Q.	"	T	CS-A3/4-P
" "	"	T	CS-B3/4-P
" "	Bde. in Line	S	CE-A1/2-P-53-CS-5-3B-4-GP
" "	"	T	CE-A7/C-P-14-CS-13-BH-19-ZE-9-GP
" "	"	T	CS-21/2-P-52-CS-24-BF-7-GP
" "	Bde. in Line	T	P-16-CS-S-EH-54-ZE-10-GP
Support Bde.	Bde. on left	T	GP-9-MF-11-C3-10-P-ground line-OW-4-OL-10-HC
Bde. in Line	" right	T	GP-28-ZE-45-WH-2-EH-2
Div. H.Q.	Bilgo Dump & Area Gdt.St.Joan	T	CS-30-SH-4-E
" "	CHS.VLELTJE	T	CS-10-SH-10-E-3-P
" "	Spree Dump	T	GP-15-BF
Bde. in Line	Capricorn Camp	T	GP-15-BF
" "	Pioneers	T	CS-10-I
Div. H.Q.	Div. on right	T	CS-7-I-32-A →

LINES - LEFT DIVISIONAL ARTILLERY, VIII CORPS.(cont)

From	To	Type	Circuit
Div. H.Q.	Div. on left	T	CE—local—CL—18—VR—13—J—18—RH—local
" "	2do. in Res.	S Smp	CE—11—I—1/2—Z
" "	VIII Corps H.Q.	T	CE—2—I—3/6—Z
" "	" " "	T	CE—9/10—LV
" "	" " "	S Smp	CE—5—I—17/13—Z
" "	W.R.Fd.Co.RE. } Kent Fd.Co RE }	T	CE—11/12—LV
		T	CE—23—LG—24—SC

Appendix 2.

Programme of Work for Establishment of Communications for BDE HQs and WATERLOO and KRONPRINZ.

Twisted D8 lines will be laid under Divisional arrangements as below:—

(1.) One pair from EN13 through KC to KRONPRINZ for ringing exchange line.

(2.) Existing line will be used as buzzer exchange line.

(3.) One pair will be laid from GP through KC to KRONPRINZ and connected to BF4 for Sounder to Div. HQ (local no. 27. Existing local to EN13 will be disconnected.

(4.) Existing lines will be joined through at KOREK and used on ringing exchange.

(5.) One pair from GP through KC and KOREK to WATERLOO and connected to GP-25-BF for sounder to Div. HQ.

The above are numbered as in brackets. Speaking line on buzzer exchange will be provided via BT. Pair to be laid from EN13 to GP connected to ZE23 and line to be laid from BT (connected to 90) to WATERLOO.

Cable required 8 miles twisted D8.

Disposition of Linemen.

(a). EN13.   SGT. OWEN with PO44, Spr Goddard, Pnr Blakey
(b). KC.   L/Cpl. JONES, Sprs Gooldon and Harvey.
(c). WATERLOO. L/Cpl. Harvey, Spr. Constant.
(d). KRONPRINZ. Spr. Heath, and Pnr. Masters
(e). KOREK.   L/Cpl. Goldsmith and Spr. Whall.
(f). GP.   Spr. Maidment.

(a). SGT. OWEN i/c forward lines,
     Spr. Goddard and Pnr. Blakey will assist.

(b). to lay lines 1. and 3.

(c). will be responsible from WATERLOO.

(d). will be responsible for service line to KOREK and will assist (b).

(e). will be responsible for lines 4. and 5.

(f). Test point duty.

For maintenance Divisional parties will work towards each other.

Exchange at EN13.

1 x 10 lines cord~~less~~.

2 x 4 + 3 Buzzer boards ~~are with transfer to 10 line cordless~~.

Manned by Sappers Fry and Sheppard.

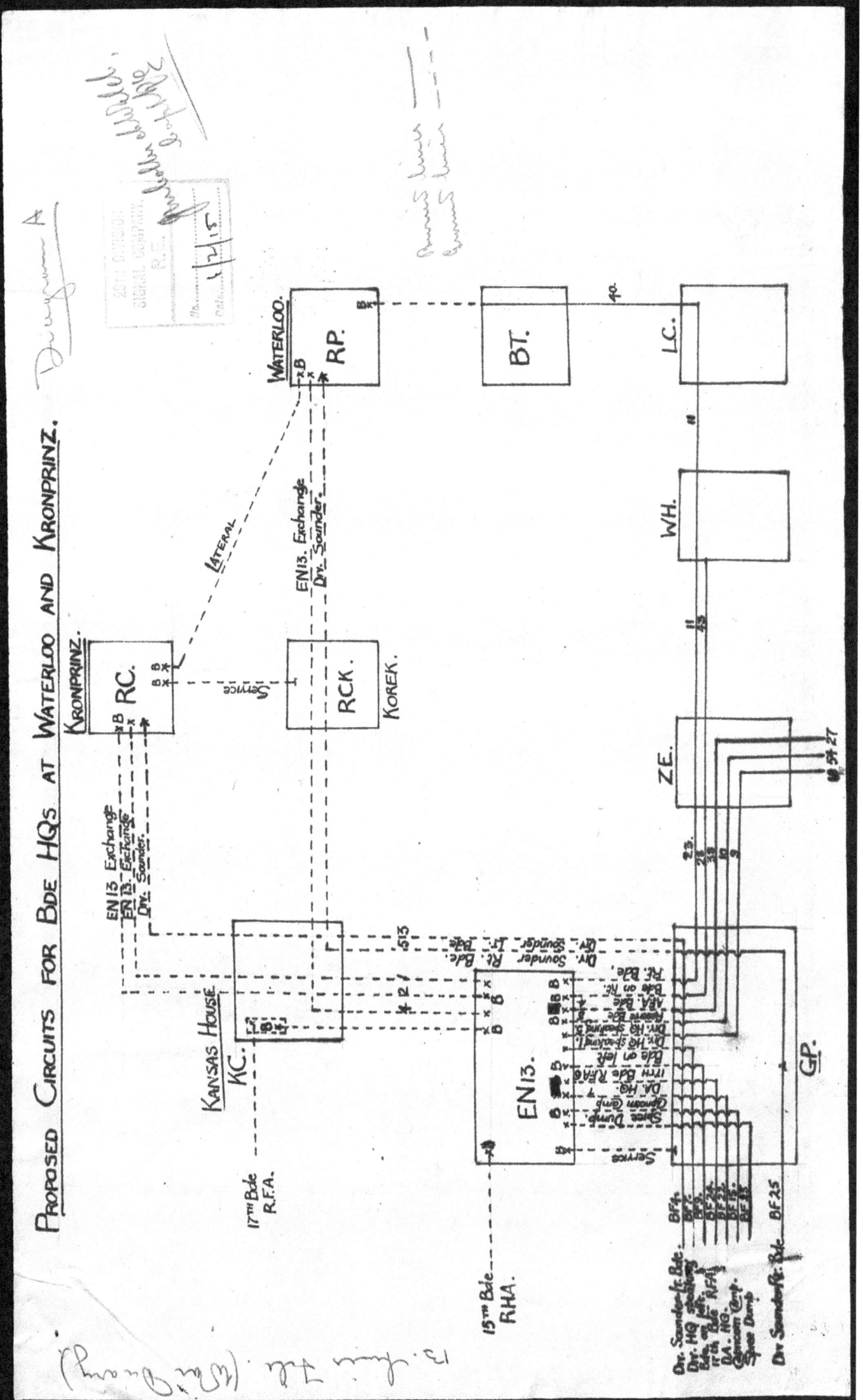

87th Inf Bde.   War Diary.   Appendix 3
88th Inf Bde.

Refce. G.S. 8/20.   d/- 19-2-8

Will the following arrangements for training an
extra 12 men in Power Buzzer and Amplifier suit please?

1. The present (one week) course for training in
Power Buzzer and Amplifier will disperse on Sunday
24th inst.

2. The 2nd course will assemble on Sunday 24th
inst and disperse on Sunday March 1st.

3. 12 Signallers per Bde (i.e. 4 signallers per Battery)
will be detailed for the 2nd Course.

4. They should be fully trained signallers able to
send on Buzzer at rate of 10 words per minute at least.

5. They should take blankets and one day's
rations.

6. A lorry will call at 87th Bde HQ at
3 pm and at 88th Bde HQ at 11 am on 24th inst.
O.C. Sigs. 87th and 88th Bdes will arrange guides
for these lorries to the B'ns. HQ's of their respectively, where they will pick up signallers detailed and
convey them to the School.

C M Simpson
Major R.E.
O.C. 29th Div. Sig. Co. R.E.

29TH DIVISION
SIGNAL COMPANY.
R.E.
Date 21/2/15

86th Inf Bde.   War Diary   Appendix 4

Refce. GS 8/20   d/- 19-2-18

Will the following arrangements suit you please?

1. A course will assemble at Divl Signal School DROGLANDT on Sunday 24th inst. for the training of 24 Signallers of 86th Inf. Bde. in Power Buzzer and Amplifier. The course will last one week dispersing on March 3rd.

2. 8 Signallers per battalion should be detached, and should include 4 Signallers per battalion already partially trained.

3. Signallers detailed should take one day's rations and blankets.

4. A lorry will call at each battalion HQ between 3 and 4 pm on 24th inst to collect signallers detailed and to convey them to the School. Lorry will call at 86th Bde HQ at 2.45 pm, and O.C. Sigs. 86th Bde. will arrange for a guide for it to the three Battn. HQs.

A. Simpson
Major R.E.
O.C. 29th Div. Sig. Co.

29TH DIVISION
SIGNAL COMPANY.
R.E.
No. ....
Date 21/2/18

SP21 Sealed Packets

Appendix 5   Febru 1915

Feby 1.	150		B/ford	2,480
2	139	Feby 18		104
3	170	19		77
4	177	20		64
5	137	21		105
6	174	22		108
7	194	23		66
8	172	24		84
9	157	25		57
10	230	26		73
11	130	27		66
12	94	28		95
13	112			
14	112		Total	3,419
15	103			
16	138			
17	91			

c/ford 2,480

29TH DIVISION
SIGNAL COMPANY,
R.E.
No.
Date 1.3.18

Appendix 6

Telegrams
February 1918

1	417	15	205
2	456	16	223
3	401	17	172
4	451	18	180
5	397	19	211
6	349	20	201
7	465	21	243
8	367	22	236
9	487	23	265
10	566	24	218
11	526	25	224
12	350	26	153
13	226	27	187
14	170	28	187
	5628		2905
			5628

Total. 8533

29TH DIVISION
SIGNAL COMPANY
R.E.

No.
Date 1.3.18

CONFIDENTIAL

WAR DIARY.

of

29th Divl Signal Co. RE

From 1/3/18. to 31/3/18.

VOLUME No..........

WAR DIARY
or
INTELLIGENCE SUMMARY.

Army Form C. 2118.

29th Divl Sig Co R.E.

March 1918

Place	Date	Hour	Summary of Events and Information	Remarks and references to Appendices
STEENVOORDE	1st		Division in Reserve. 86th Bde Sector EECKE 87th Bde POPERINGHE 88th Bde at WINNIZEELE. Communication on Army yorks via STEENVOORDE exchange	
	6		Usual forward training	
	5th		NCOs & Sappers loaned to 1st K.T.M. Corps for burying cable in forward area. Remainder of linesmen employed on linemen's course of instruction	
			2nd Staff Ride	
			Divl Signal School DROGLANDT passed out 16 men on Mar 3rd. Equivalent number of men untrained men sent to school by units	
			Division found in reserve 2/4 Battalion Lincolnshire for brigade work	
			[illegible] through Power Buzzer and Amplifier course. Messages dealt with × 1129 Registered SP's × 421	See appendix E
	8th		Advance parties of 87th & 14 Bde section proceeded to forward area preparatory to relief of left half Sector, 6th Division communications. Two army heads of skins from STEENVOORDE to MERSEY CAMP. Messages dealt with 199. Registered P.S 75	

Army Form C. 2118.

WAR DIARY
or
INTELLIGENCE SUMMARY.
(Erase heading not required.)

20th Div Sig. Co. R.E.
MARCH 1917

Title pages II

Place	Date	Hour	Summary of Events and Information	Remarks and references to Appendices
STEENVOORDE	7th		Advance parties to 8th Division and to 8th Divisional Sig. Coy. left Section VIII Corps. Forward sent as follows	
			(a) 25th Bde (N°4) Section to WIELTJE and WATERLOO relieving right of 25th Bde.	
			(b) Wireless Section to all wireless posts, including attached infantry for power buzzer and amplifier, to P.B. Amplifier posts.	
			(c) Linemen forward forward Lineman's posts, and visual personnel.	
			(d) One officer relief for Hdqrs, WIELTJE, GALLIPOLI enlarged	
			All found stations including visual relieved by 4 p.m. No stores except instruments for bz-relief were sent up	
			Messages dealt with 210 Registered S.R.S. 154	
CANAL BANK DEAD END YPRES	8th		Relief complete at 10 a.m. Trouble with Electric Light Scheme owing to difficulty of starting.	
			All former lines O.K. see steps taken to procure at once with investigation	
			of KRONPRINZ (BM) and BELLEVUE (UR10) lines on the	
			All Wireless Stations in good working order. also Visual.	
			Messages dealt with 414 Registered S.R.S. 145	

WAR DIARY or INTELLIGENCE SUMMARY

Army Form C. 2118.

2nd Div Sig Coy R.E.
MARCH 1917

Place	Date	Hour	Summary of Events and Information	Remarks and references to Appendices
DEAD END CANAL BANK YPRES	9th		Normal maintenance. All forms of communication including Wireless (supply of accumulators)	
			Buried wires tested and found as follows:-	
			(a) from CALGARY GRANGE to KRONPRINZ repairable.	
			(b) from " " 6 THY test box, 300 yds W. of BELLEVUE	
	19th		These were repaired and strengthening work was continued.	
			Ex Visual. Extra spare batteries and bulbs were supplied to each visual station. Indented wrtg/sigd frequently	
			Wireless. A Power buzzer Amplifier combined was received by us and tried. After slight alterations it was placed in O.P. at PASSCHENDAELE on evening of 19th inst, and worked satisfactorily by MEETCHEELE	
			1st Bgd RHA	
			Personnel. 2 men were transferred from Infantry to assist in the formation of No 3 section, for extra work entailed by addition of M.G. Battalion.	
			Messages dealt with *5094 Registered SP's *1761 Geographx E	

D. D. & L., London, E.C.
(A7883) Wt. W8o9/M1672 350,000 4/17 **Sch. 52a** Forms/C/2118/14

WAR DIARY
or INTELLIGENCE SUMMARY
(Erase heading not required.)

29th Div. Sig. Co. R.E.

MARCH 1917

IV

Army Form C. 2118.

Place	Date	Hour	Summary of Events and Information	Remarks and references to Appendices
YPRES (Dead End Canal Bank)	20th		Normal F.W. day apart from heavy shelling of track areas and consequent difficulties on all routes behind Div'l H.Qrs. Forward cable routes were also repeatedly cut but were soon repaired — and no more than one wire was 'down' at any one time. At 6pm, heavy shelling o/ KRONPRINZ FM., HQ LEFT. INF. BDE caused considerable interruption in communication, but one line from EN 58 (left Art'y Bde) was open to EN III (KRONPRINZ) held. Communication by wireless also attempted owing to destruction of Aznl. Shelling died down 6.30pm, and at 6.40pm two more lines with but through and communication by wireless resumed. Heavy shelling on whole area throughout night. Messages dealt with 489. Registered S.P.s 148.	
	21st		Heavy shelling particularly with gas, in early morning, slightly interrupted telephone communication with left Inf. Bde. Subsequent investigation proved Azl. KRONPRINZ – CALGARY GRANGE bury wire not destroyed by shelling yesterday evening. 20th inst. This was brought into use, therefore, at once — though not technically completed. *(Continued on page V.)*	

WAR DIARY
or
INTELLIGENCE SUMMARY.

Army Form C. 2118.

29th Div. 8y C.R.E.
MARCH 1918

Place	Date	Hour	Summary of Events and Information	Remarks and references to Appendices
YPRES	21st		In addition to shelling of KRONPRINZ on evening of 20th a barrage was placed	
Dras Ends			down behind or W. of BELLEWE. All lines were cut by power buzzer	
Canal Bank			Amplifier communication was maintained, in addition to visual.	
			To-day 21st an East was placed inside the main dug-out of	
			BELLEWE which provides a base of 40 yds. This base is completely	
			shell proof, and communication is still maintained when it is used, with	
			WATERLOO, Right Infy Bde, at a range of 750 yds; and should be completely	
			reliable under all conditions.	
			Message dealt with 602. Registers S.P's 195	
	22nd		Normal maintenance. During morning Calgary Grange – Kronprinz bury	
			was scout at crossing of stream.	
			Work commenced on strengthening Ft CALGARY-GRANGE Test-point.	
			Message dealt with 479. Registered S.P's 180	

Army Form C. 2118.

WAR DIARY
or
INTELLIGENCE SUMMARY.
(Erase heading not required.)

29th Div Sig¹ Co R.E.
MARCH 1918

Place	Date	Hour	Summary of Events and Information	Remarks and references to Appendices
YPRES Dead End	23rd to 25th		Normal maintenance work continued. Power Buzzer Amplifier from 2/E Passchendaele continued to work satisfactorily. Lt F.S. SHRUBB sent to GP exchange to be in charge of forward communications. An additional N.C.O also sent to assist in supervision of work. On Sunday 24th inst. Div. Signal School moved to TEN ELMS Camp — to join canal Bank teacher Corps Signal School. Messages dealt with 1462. Registered S.P.s 441	
"	26th to 31st		Normal maintenance. Lt T.G. FAWCETT relieve WILTSHIRE at GALLIPOLI Exchange. Work done — (1) Test point at CALGARY GRANGE rebuilt and line properly led in on terminal boards. (2) Bury from CG to KRONPRINZ looked up thoroughly. (3) Bury KANSAS HO. to KOREK looked up for 400 yds near KOREK. Power Buzzer Amplifier and Visual communication O.K. Messages dealt with 2663. Registers S.Ps 548	

A.J.Austin Major R.E.
O.C. S'pals 29 Div.

Army Form C. 2118.

WAR DIARY
or
INTELLIGENCE SUMMARY.
(Erase heading not required.)

VII

Place	Date	Hour	Summary of Events and Information	Remarks and references to Appendices
			Summary of Appendices	
			A. Signal Communications – Left Sector – VIII Corps.	
			B. Diagram of Circuits at Divl. Report Centre – GALIPOLI exchange 7/3/18	
			" (2)	12/3/18
			C. Diagram of Communications Left Brigade 17/3/18.	
			D. " " Right Brigade 29/3/18.	

W. Simpson Major R.E.
O.C. No 29th Divl Sig Co R.E.

[Stamp: 20TH DIVISION SIGNAL COMPANY. R.E. 2.4.18]

To ~~Hitchinson~~ file

War Diary

(A)

ref CGS 12/3
of 22.3.18

Signal Communication - 29th Division
Left Sector - VIII Corps.

1 <u>Telegraph and Telephone</u>

A <u>Infantry Brigades to Battalions and Companies</u>

All Companies, Battalions, and Brigades are connected from front to rear by ground telephone and fullerphone lines. Most companies are connected laterally, but those in the left battalion sector are not.

All Battalions within the Division and the two Brigade H.Q. are connected laterally; Brigade H.Q. are also connected to the Brigades of other divisions on their flanks.

Fullerphone only is used for telegraph working in front of Brigade H.Q.

B <u>Division H.Q. to Infy. Brigade H.Q.</u>

Telephone and Telegraph lines run along the following main routes, viz:

By Airline or Poled Cable to WIELTJE, thence by buried lines to GALLIPOLI, via BANK FARM with alternative route via BAVARIA HOUSES and ZEVENCOTE. From GALLIPOLI via KANSAS HOUSE, KOREK, CALGARY GRANGE - to KRONPRINZ for left Brigade, or test-box at D9.b.5.4 an thence by ground line for Right Brigade.

Also

Also from GALLIPOLI via ZEVENCOTE to BOATHOEK thence by groundline for Right Brigade.

There are exchanges at WIELTJE to serve Battalions in Reserve, and at GALLIPOLI for Artillery liason purposes and to form an Advanced Divisional Exchange.

C. Artillery to Infantry

Artillery Liason lines are provided from Artillery Brigades direct to Infantry Brigades; and also through GALLIPOLI Exchange.

Divisional Artillery HQ have in addition a direct line to GALLIPOLI Exchange.

2. Visual

(a) From front to rear only, has been arranged
 (1) From all Coy HQ's except VALOUR FARM, to Battalion HQ.
 (2) From KRONPRINZ to Central Visual Station at KOREK.
 (3) From WALLEMOLEN to WURST FARM.

(b) Both ways, has been arranged
 (1) From KRONPRINZ and WATERLOO to BELLEVUE
 (2) From BELLEVUE and WATERLOO to KOREK.
 (3) From KOREK to GALLIPOLI.
 (4) From batteries to Artillery Brigade HQ. whenever feasible. Artillery also have a Central Visual Station at WARWICK CASTLE about D 15 b.1.9.

3. <u>Power Buzzer, Amplifier, and Wireless</u>

Power Buzzers are installed at
1. Coy H.Q. V.28.c.7.5.55
2. Coy H.Q. V.30.d.30.15

Power Buzzer Amplifiers are installed at
1. Artillery O.P. D6.c.5.6
2. MEETCHEELE
3. BELLEVUE
4. WATERLOO

Wireless Trench sets, working to Corps Directing Station at C.29.c.2.7 are installed at
1. Left Brigade H.Q. KRONPRINZ
2. Right Brigade H.Q. WATERLOO

All the above are working satisfactorily.

4. <u>Pigeons</u>

4 pairs of Pigeons per day are sent up, one pair to each Battalion. In the event of operations being imminent or expected, up to 20 pairs per day obtained.

5. <u>D.R.L.S. and Runners</u>

Motor cyclists proceed as far as GALLIPOLI. From there to the front all sealed packets are carried by runner - runs being made to time-table as far as Battalion H.Q.

Runner Posts are situated at

(1).

Runner Posts are situated at
(1) GALLIPOLI
(2) Brigade HQ's
(3) Battalion HQ's
(4) VINE COTTS (Coy HQ)
(5) MOSSELMARKT (Coy HQ)
(6) Coy. HQ.

Major R.E.
OC. 29 Divisional Signal Co.
R.E.

War Diary

(B1)

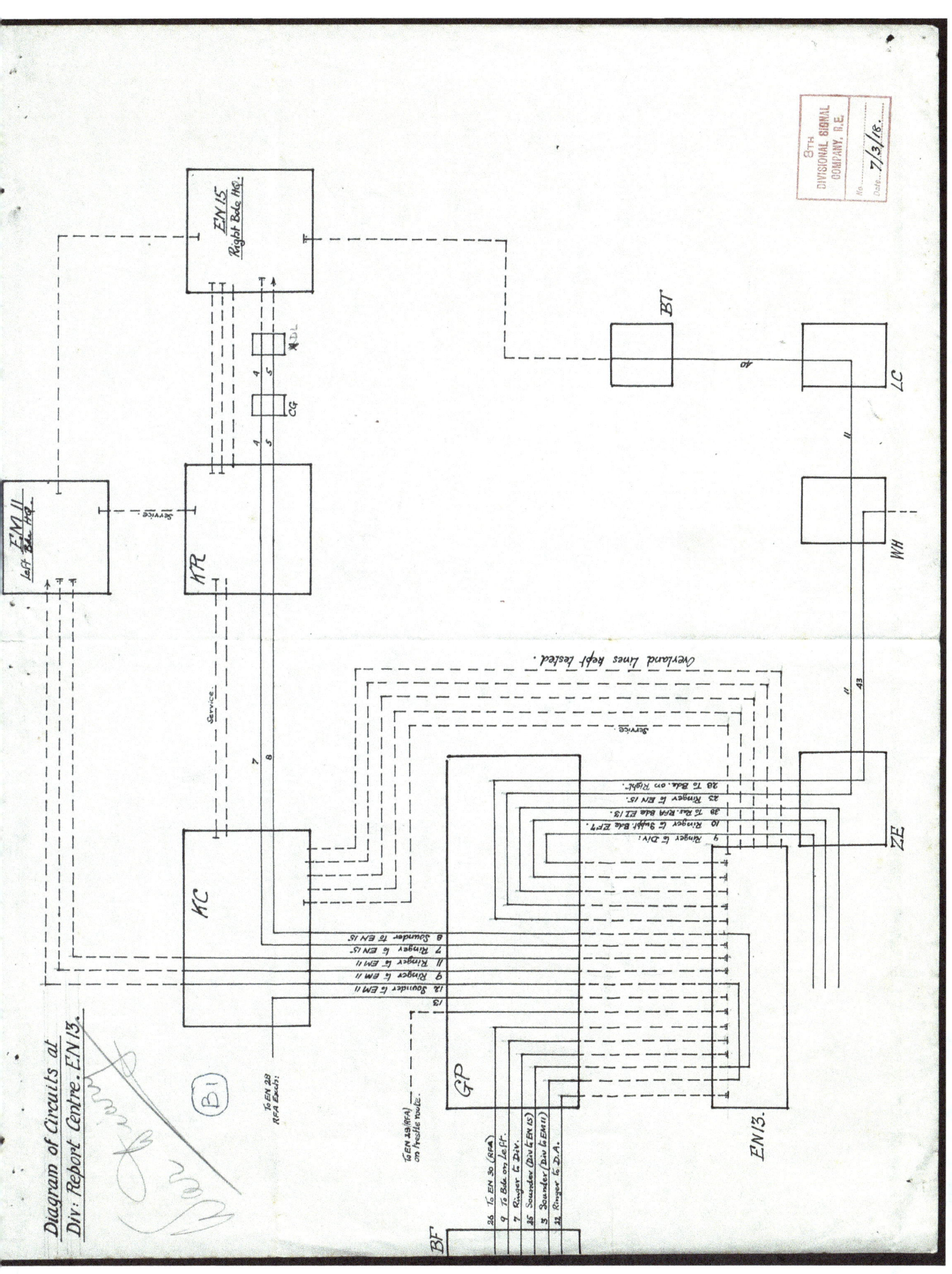

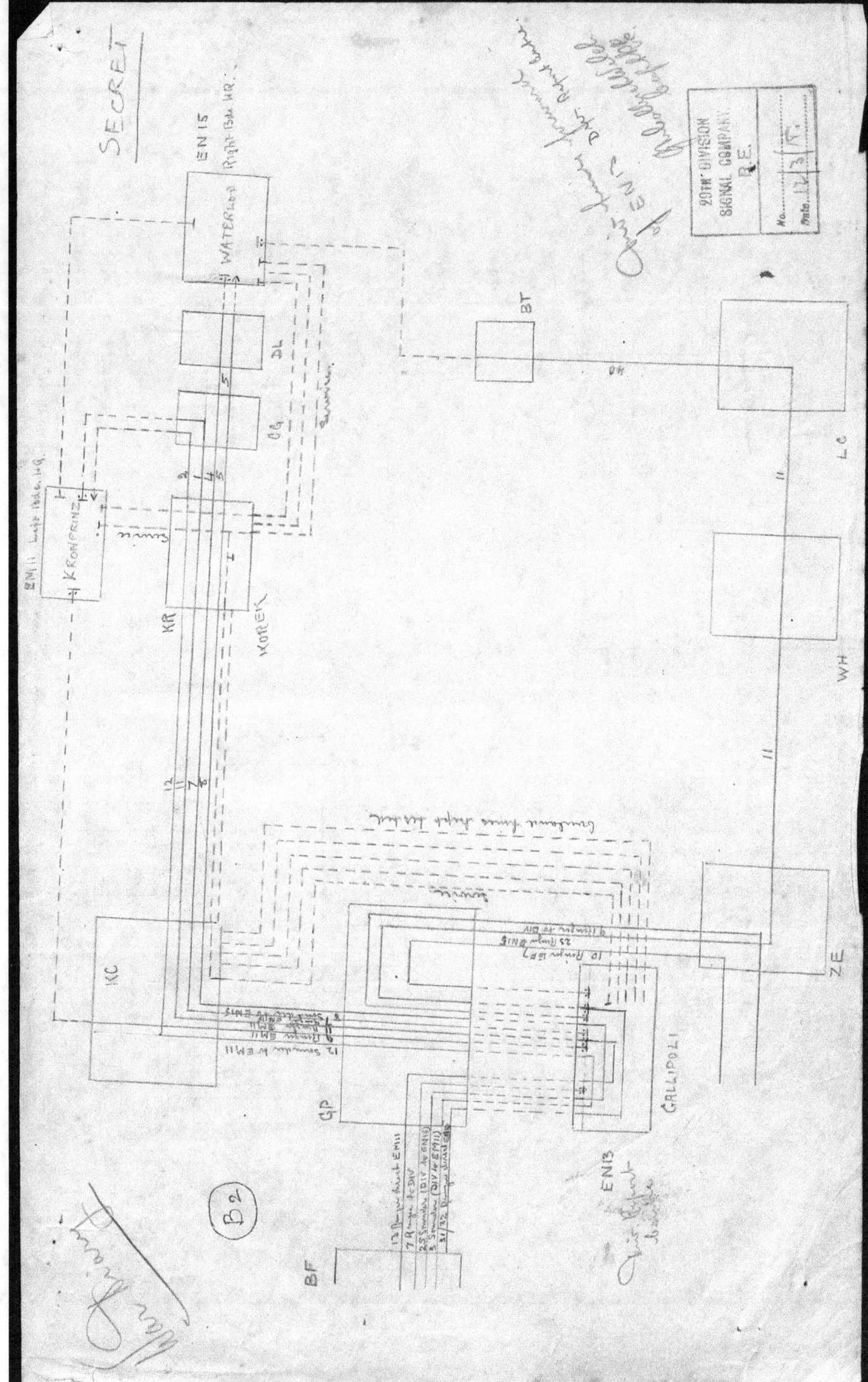

Left Brigade –

Brand Diagram

1 Forward Commander (arrow)

17/5/15

Right Bde.   29/3/18

DIAGRAM OF BATTN. COMMUNICATIONS.

War Diary
(D)

EZ 5 — L.Coy. L.Bn.
EV 33 — R.Coy. L.Bn. / L.Coy. R.Bn.
EV 35 — R.Coy. R.Bn.

EZ 4 — Supp. Coy. L.Bn.
EV 34 — Supp. Coy. R.Bn.
PB — ROSSELMARKT

To Support Coy of Bde on Right.

MEETCHEELE

UR 6
UR 16

FROM WATERLOO
EM 5
M.G. Coy
LAAM KEEK

20TH
SIGNAL COMPANY,
R.E.
No.   Date

Appendix E
Summary of messages dealt with – March 1918

		Bt Fwd	5859
1	203	17	368
2	225	18	394
3	176	19	413
4	253	20	489
5	272	21	602
6	197	22	477
7	200	23	525
8	414	24	484
9	468	25	453
10	473	26	476
11	545	27	407
12	455	28	427
13	565	29	504
14	473	30	400
15	492	31	449
16	448		

Total 12,727

Carrd Fwd 5859

Appendix E

Dr L.S. Summary
of Lp's for March 18

Mch			Bt ford	2,224
1	67	Mch		
2	104	18	135	
3	72	19	197	
4	95	20	148	
5	88	21	175	
6	78	22	180	
7	154	23	149	
8	145	24	133	
9	164	25	145	
10	171	26	120	
11	186	27	188	
12	133	28	131	
13	153	29	127	
14	129	30	137	
15	192	31	175	
16	167			
17	134	Total	4,364	

Cd ford 2,224

SIGNAL SERVICE

Army Form W 3023
(In pads of 100)

Despatch Rider Letter Service

To_____

No.	Identification No.	Addressed to	Signature of Recipient
1			
2			
3			
4			
5			
6			
7			
8			
9			
0			
1			
2			
3			
4			
5			
6			
7			
8			
9			
0			

Sig. Mr. Despatching Office. | Despatch Rider.

Despatched at_____ Received at_____
    Date Stamp.   Date Stamp.

Forwarding Office.   Receiving Office.

(12532) Wt. W 5513—M 2568. 25,000 pads. 7/17. D & S. E 1256A.

29th Divisional Engineers

29th DIVISIONAL SIGNAL COMPANY R.E.

APRIL 1918.

C O N F I D E N T I A L

WAR DIARY.

of

29TH DIVISIONAL SIGNAL CO. RE.

From 1st May 1918 to 31 May 1918.

VOLUME No..........

CONFIDENTIAL

WAR DIARY.

of

29 Divl Signal Co.

From 1/4/18 to 30/4/18

VOLUME No..........

WAR DIARY
or
INTELLIGENCE SUMMARY.

29th Div 25C RE.
APRIL 1918

Army Form C. 2118.

Place	Date	Hour	Summary of Events and Information	Remarks and references to Appendices
YPRES.	1st to 8th		Normal maintenance and work on lines. From 4th to 7th 86th Inf Bde take over left Bde front of 33rd Div on our right. Bde HQ near Zevencote. Three power buzzers and two Amplifiers taken over in this section. Communications quite satisfactory – between Wie.33.b HQ and open ground lines forward, in front of LEWI COTTAGES. Loop-set established between PASSCHENDAELE O.P. and LAMKEEK. Working not satisfactory owing to insufficiency of training; and one portion of set being sent up wrongly wired. On night 7th/8th 86th Bde were relieved by a brigade of 41st Divn. Bde moved to BRAKE CAMP. On night 8th/9th 87th Bde were relieved by a brigade of 41st Divn and moved to ST JAN TER BIZEN. Communications via 8th Corps. Messages dealt with :- Registered SP5. 1st 460, 2nd 440, 3rd 516, 4th 521, 5th 546, 6th 546, 7th 360 1st 121, 2nd 130, 3rd 149, 4th 130 8th 682 5th 203, 6th 175, 7th 161, 8th 152	

Army Form C. 2118.

WAR DIARY
or
INTELLIGENCE SUMMARY.
(Erase heading not required.)

29th Div Sig Co. R.E.

APRIL 1918

Place	Date	Hour	Summary of Events and Information	Remarks and references to Appendices
YPRES	9th		Relief for forward stations, wireless stations and linesmen's posts sent up by 11th Division Signals by lorry in morning. Office ships and linemen for Headquarters sent up during the afternoon. All spare men returned to MERSEY CAMP during afternoon. Orders issued for move onto to ST POL area and lorry, under Lt FAWCETT R.E. sent to ST POL area with Advance Party.	
		6pm	Orders re move to ST POL area cancelled, and warning orders for move to MERVILLE - NIEPPE front area issued. M/C Despatch Rider contd Lt FAWCETT instructing to return to report to AD Sigs XV Corps. Lt SHRIVELL proceeded by motor cycle to report to AD Sigs XV Corps. La MOTTE to keep touch with situation.	
		11pm	One cable section and lorry load of linemen and office telegraphists sent to LES LAURIERS (about 22 miles from MERSEY CAMP). Messages dealt with ££ 747. Registered SP's 138.	

Army Form C. 2118.

29th Div Sig Co. R.E.
APRIL 1918

WAR DIARY
or
INTELLIGENCE SUMMARY.
(Erase heading not required.)

III

Place	Date	Hour	Summary of Events and Information	Remarks and references to Appendices
LES LAURIER N.W. of MERVILLE	10th	7am	Div HQ opened at 7am. Brigades (less 88th Bde) having moved from POPERINGHE by motor-bus. Coy transport less no 1 Cable Section marched from MERSEY CAMP at 5am with orders to rendez-vous at STRAZEELE. Communication to Inf Brigades by permanent airline while cable is laid out by cattle wagons. Little shelling during morning, heavy afternoon.	
		4:30pm	Bde HQR moved to 1½ miles E of NEUF BERQUIN - lines extended by cattle wagon. Advd Div Report Centre established at NEUF BERQUIN. One trench Wireless set with each Bde HQR and WILSON. set with Div HQR — Communication O.K. but jamming by flank Divisions very noticeable. Messages dealt with 731 Registrars + SP's 39	

WAR DIARY
or
INTELLIGENCE SUMMARY.
(Erase heading not required.)

Army Form C. 2118.

29th Div. Sig. Coy R.E.

APRIL 1918

Place	Date	Hour	Summary of Events and Information	Remarks and references to Appendices
LES LAURIERS N.W. of MERVILLE (about 2½ mile)	11th	9am	Advcd Report Centre moved about 1000 yds WNW of NEUF BERQUIN owing to heavy shelling. Additional lines laid by cable wagons to Inf. Bdes. but some difficulty was experienced by wagons in returning to Headquarters owing to hospital advance on Right flank of the Division	
		3.30pm	Div.HQ moved to LAMOTTE. At the same time, HQrs 86 & 87 Inf Bdes moved back in a N.W. direction about 1500 yds, while enemy reached a point (about 5.30pm) within 200 yds of Advcd Report Centre, and crossed over sections of two lines between LES LAURIERS & Advance Report Centre. Instructed Advcd Report Centre (now no longer needed as such by G.S.) to move back past the 1500 yds along route of one line. Owing to Bdes moving off momentarily, no line (telephone) communication was established with the Advce Report Centre and Inf. Bdes. Communication by Wireless obtained at 4.45pm when Bdes arrived.	
			Completed this move.	
		6pm	At 6pm decided to re-establish telephone communication via VIEUX BERQUIN	
		10pm		

WAR DIARY
or
INTELLIGENCE SUMMARY.

(Erase heading not required.)

Army Form C. 2118.

29th Divl. Signal Co. RE
APRIL 1918

V

Place	Date	Hour	Summary of Events and Information	Remarks and references to Appendices
LAMOTTE	11th	1 pm	LT FAWCETT RE closed Advanced Report Centre and moves to 31st Divl A.D.O.S. at VIEUX BERQUIN, where a party was sent by lorry to lay a line to the Brigades and another line outskirts return from B.de to VIEUX BERQUIN Lines were blown between LAMOTTE & VIEUX BERQUIN on a permanent airline route	
		11.30pm	Cable wagon sent out from LAMOTTE to lay to brigades at for out of six of Battery sent to VIEUX BERQUIN who mistook their way and became involved in some fighting, became casualties. Difficulties of laying cable on a crowded road at night very great, and progress slow Messages dealt with 259 Registered SPs 18	

Army Form C. 2118.

WAR DIARY
or
INTELLIGENCE SUMMARY.
(Erase heading not required.)

29th D??? Brigade RE
APRIL 1918

Place	Date	Hour	Summary of Events and Information	Remarks and references to Appendices
CAESTRE	12th		At 9.15am Div HR closed LA MOTTE and moved to CAESTRE. Communication to higher command obtained to 2nd Army via Army Test Hut. Lt SHRIVELL sent out to discover Lt FAWCETT who was laying lines between LA MOTTE and Bde HR's (which moved at 4 am to BLEU) 1000 yards E. of VIEUX BERQUIN) and re-direct him to CAESTRE. At 12 noon Two Infantry Brigades were moving to MERRIS and ROUGE CROIX reorganized cable wagons to get a line through to STRAZEELE to MERRIS. In the meantime Brigades were hiding, preparing to move to LE PARADIS 1500 yds N.N.W of VIEUX BERQUIN. At 3.15pm O.C. Details 92nd Inf Bde came on to line laid to MERRIS and informed General Staff that enemy was outside Eastern outskirts of the village. Lt SNRIVELL who had a telephone on this line at STRAZEELE was advised to remain there and await further instructions while a G. Staff officer went out to tell Brigades to move to STRAZEELE. They however moved to LE PARADIS. A party was then sent out to SHRIVELL by	

WAR DIARY
or
INTELLIGENCE SUMMARY.
(Erase heading not required.)

29th Div.[S]ig. Coy R.E.
VIII (7)
APRIL 1918

Army Form C. 2118.

Place	Date	Hour	Summary of Events and Information	Remarks and references to Appendices
CAESTRE	12th		motor lorry to extend line to LE PARADIS. This was through at	
		5.30pm		
			Wireless Communication was maintained throughout but	
			difficulties were (a) Jamming (only slightly here)	
			(b) Runners owing to enciphering deciphering	
			Messages dealt with 401. Registered S.P.'s 61	
	13th		Two additional lines were laid out one about ½ mile W. of STRAZEELE	
			between BORRE & PRADELLES, the other SEC BOIS to Bde	
			H.Rs. in LE PARADIS. Bde HRS were at 12 noon to AME NOLEGHEM	
			about 10 yds. Not LE PARADIS. tel exch R3 on line and telephone	
			to Stou. Telephone communication was not interrupted.	
			During the night the division was withdrawn from the 1st Australian	
			Division. Transport & Signal Co was sent from CAESTRE to ST SYLVESTRE	
			CAPPEL	
			Messages dealt with 380. Registered S.P.s 36.	

Army Form C. 2118.

WAR DIARY
or
INTELLIGENCE SUMMARY.
29th ~~30th~~ "A" Div. Sig. Co. R.E.
APRIL 1918
(Erase heading not required.)

Place	Date	Hour	Summary of Events and Information	Remarks and references to Appendices
ST SYLVESTRE CAPPEL	14th		Div. HR about CAESTRE (to-day) ST SYLVESTRE CAPPEL. 86th Bde HR about ½ mile E. of ST SYLVESTRE CAPPEL. In the SE of the village. Both in touch by telephone by 12 noon 14th.	
	15 to 18th		On night 15th/16th 29th Composite Bde under GOC 87th Bde were to take over Sect CAESTRE with Bde HR at LE PEUPLIER about 1½ m. SW of CAESTRE, to assist if necessary operations being carried out by 133rd French Divn near MEREREN and to be taken over, between 133rd Australian Division and the 133rd French Divn. On night 17/18th this Bde returned to original headquarters before this move. No special arrangements for communication with refused – but wireless was set up to this brigade though never used. Telephone lines were laid out and reeled up. Training in cable wagon drill, netting and boundaries. Amplifiers were carried out.	
			Messages dealt with 1374 Registered S.P.E. 357 See Appendix A	

Army Form C. 2118.

WAR DIARY
or
INTELLIGENCE SUMMARY.
(Erase heading not required.)

24th Div¹ Signal Co.
APRIL 1918

Place	Date	Hour	Summary of Events and Information	Remarks and references to Appendices
HONDEGHEM	18th		Div HQ closed at ST SYLVESTRE CAPPEL and opened at HONDEGHEM at	
	19th	10am	Divn. 86 & 87 Bde HR's — 86 — HONDEGHEM — 87 about 1½ miles	
			S.E. of 1st village. Communication by telephone & runner.	
	20th		En 21st, 88th Bde arrived to reinf Divn. after fighting with 29th & 34th Divs. — BAILLEUL — NEUVE EGLISE area. Casualties to Bde Signal section had losses in stores small throughout the brigade. Training carried out in cable-wagon drill — wireless found buzzer, visual, as usual. 20/21st Messages dealt with 1693. Registered SP's 643	
	27th		Advance party to man office (message forts) visual + wireless power buzzer amplifier stations at 31st Divn. and SWALTON CAPPEL and out stations in 31st Divn. area, preparatory to relief of 31st Div by 29 Div. Messages dealt with 339. Registered SP's 120.	See Appendix A

WAR DIARY
or
INTELLIGENCE SUMMARY

29th Divl. Sigs. R.E.

APRIL 1918

Place	Date	Hour	Summary of Events and Information	Remarks and references to Appendices
WALLON CAPPEL	29th		D.H.Q. closed HONDEGHEM and opened WALLON CAPPEL at 10 a.m. when command of Right Sector XV Corps passed to G.O.C. 29th Division.	
			Bde H.Q.s R&W 86th at farm 200x N. of IR-TIR ANGLAIS	
	30th		Left " 87th about 1000 yds N.E. of 86th Bde.	
			Communications scheme	
			(a) Telephone & telegraph lines via exchange WGD passed to Brigades and thence Brigade to Battalion and company by field cable laid along hedges and in ditches	
			(b) Wireless between Bde HRs & Div HQ (9 spark system) Power Buzzer Amplifier between Right Bde and its Battalions and between Left Bde & its Right Battalion	
			(c) Visual between Bde HQ & Div HQ via two transmitting stations	
			On 30th 6 messenger dogs were sent to each Bde HQ to work between Brigade and Battalion on a first trial.	
			Message traffic 28th 450 Registered SPs 28th 140.	
			29th 635 29th 153.	
			30th 595 30th 125.	

28th DIVISION
SIGNAL COMPANY,
R.E.

O.C. 29th Divl. Signal Co. R.E.

APPENDIX A

April	Telegrams	Registered Packets
1	460	121
2	440	130
3	516	149
4	521	130
5	546	203
6	576	175
7	360	161
8	682	152
9	747	138
10	731	39
11	259	18
12	401	61
13	380	36
14	275	42
15	240	46
16	220	79
17	235	53
18	216	64
19	188	73
20	129	42
21	160	86
22	202	68
23	240	105
24	310	104
25	245	95
26	377	143
27	339	120
28	450	140
29	635	153
30	595	125
Totals	11675	3051

WAR DIARY
or
INTELLIGENCE SUMMARY.

29th Divisional Sig. Co. RE Army Form C. 2118.

May 1918.

Place	Date	Hour	Summary of Events and Information	Remarks and references to Appendices
WALLON-CAPPEL	1st to 7th		Normal maintenance of lines. Poling of cable completed, where required, and considerable alterations made in the routes of lines in front of G.d HASARD to avoid the shelled areas as much as possible. Considerable use made of ditches which are fairly deep in this country. 87th Inf. Bde. prepared to move to house in G.d SEC BOIS and lines were accordingly extended from their existing Headquarters. Wireless and visual communication as usual.	
	8th to 10th		88th Inf. Bde. relieved 87th Inf. Bde. in the left sector of the line on the night 8/9th. On the 10th they moved their Headquarters to E.11.b.0.9. (Sheet 36A - 1/40,000) about 1000 yards behind the house chosen by the 87th Inf. Bde. The original extension of lines was used for the new Headquarters. An Exchange was established at the old Headquarters known as AS. Apart from the above, normal maintenance of lines and other lines of communication. Power Buzzer	

WAR DIARY 29th Divisional Sig. Co. R.E.

or

INTELLIGENCE SUMMARY.

(Erase heading not required.)

Army Form C. 2118.

II May 1918

Place	Date	Hour	Summary of Events and Information	Remarks and references to Appendices
WALLON - CAPPEL	8th to 10th		(Continued) Power Buzzer Amplifier arrangements were not affected by the above	
	11th to 14th		Work commenced to reorganise Visual communications to Brigades. Two rear terminal stations in touch with each other were established, each of which worked to one of the Brigades in the line, thus making four terminal stations all in communication with each other, should lateral communication be required. Screens were erected at the rear stations with small apertures in them to permit working from rear to front by heliograph or lamp. The system worked satisfactorily. On the night of the 13/14th the 87th Inf. Bde. relieved the 88th Inf. Bde. Power Buzzer Amplifier stations were moved about to meet the moves of the Battalions the principle being to have one P.B.Ar. set in each Brigade sector, and at each Brigade Headquarters. Wireless	

WAR DIARY
or
INTELLIGENCE SUMMARY.

(Erase heading not required.)

Army Form C. 2118.

29th Divisional Sig. Co. R.E.

May 1918

Place	Date	Hour	Summary of Events and Information	Remarks and references to Appendices
WALLON -CAPPEL	11th to 14th		(Continued) Wireless trench sets moved with Brigade Headquarters and worked satisfactorily.	
	15th to 20th		In this period the 29th Divisional Artillery came in and Headquarters relieved the 38th Divisional Artillery. The 17th Brigade R.F.A. came into the line as Right Group. On the night 19/20th the 88th Inf Bde relieved the 36th Inf Bde in the Right Sector.	
	21st to 28th		The normal maintenance of lines was carried out and Visual communication from the main Visual Station to Artillery Brigades was obtained and tested. Normal maintenance of lines and further improvements in routes effected, as particularly shelled areas became more obvious, and extensive use made of field ditches. A Wireless loop set was installed between Left Brigade Headquarters	

WAR DIARY 29th Divisional Sig Co R.E.

or

INTELLIGENCE SUMMARY.

(Erase heading not required.)

Army Form C. 2118.

May 1918.

IV

Instructions regarding War Diaries and Intelligence Summaries are contained in F. S. Regs., Part II. and the Staff Manual respectively. Title pages will be prepared in manuscript.

Place	Date	Hour	Summary of Events and Information	Remarks and references to Appendices
WALLON -CAPPEL	21st to 28		(Continued) Headquarters and PETIT SEC BOIS (HQ of OC PETIT SEC BOIS defences) This worked satisfactorily. Power Buzzer Amplifier communications were again reorganised as follows. - One PBAr was installed at each Brigade Headquarters and one at SWARTENBROUCH to serve the Battalions in line of each Brigade, (two Battalions in all). Forward Power Buzzers were installed at one Bn HQ in the line of each of these Battalions for SOS purposes. Visual and Wireless as usual. On the night 27/28 the 86th Inf Bde relieved the 87th Inf Bde in the left sector.	
	29th to 31st		Normal maintenance of lines. Successful test with contact aeroplane of the new Popham T. Signalling Panel was carried out on the morning of the 30th. Otherwise nothing of particular interest occurred.	

Army Form C. 2118.

WAR DIARY 29 Divl Sig Co~RE
or
INTELLIGENCE SUMMARY. May 1918
(Erase heading not required.)

Place	Date	Hour	Summary of Events and Information	Remarks and references to Appendices
WALLON -CAPPEL			Casualties:- Lieut V.R KING died of wounds on the 13th of the month. The average of casualties was 7 per week chiefly due to ordinary and gas shelling.	
			Summary of Appendices	
			A.B and C. Three circuit diagrams marked A.B.C are attached	
			D) Shows the number of Messages and Sealed Packets handled in the Signal Office for each day	

C.W Simpson Major RE

OC. 29th Divl Sig. Co. RE.

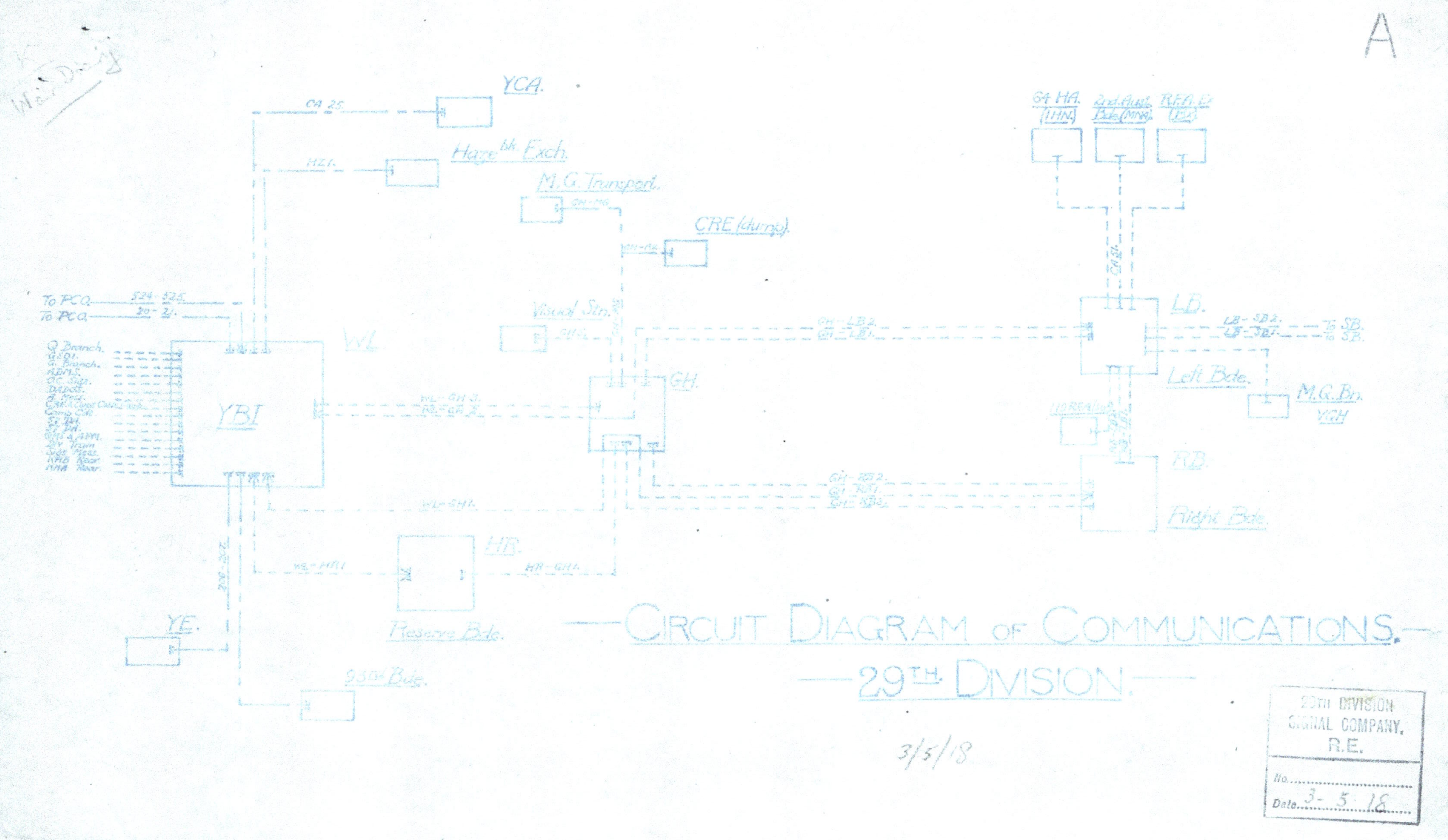
A
YCA.
CA 25.
Haze bk. Exch.
HZ1.
M.G. Transport.
CRE (dump).
Visual Stn.
To PCO.
524-525.
To PCO.
20-21.
WL.
YBI
GH.
HB.
Reserve Bde.
YE.
93rd Bde.
64 HA. (IHN)
2nd Aust. Bde. (MNR)
R.F.A. D. (EE)
LD.
Left Bde.
M.G. Bn. YGH
RB.
Right Bde.
To SB.
To SB.
Circuit Diagram of Communications.
29th Division.
3/5/18
29th DIVISION SIGNAL COMPANY, R.E.
No.
Date 3-5-18

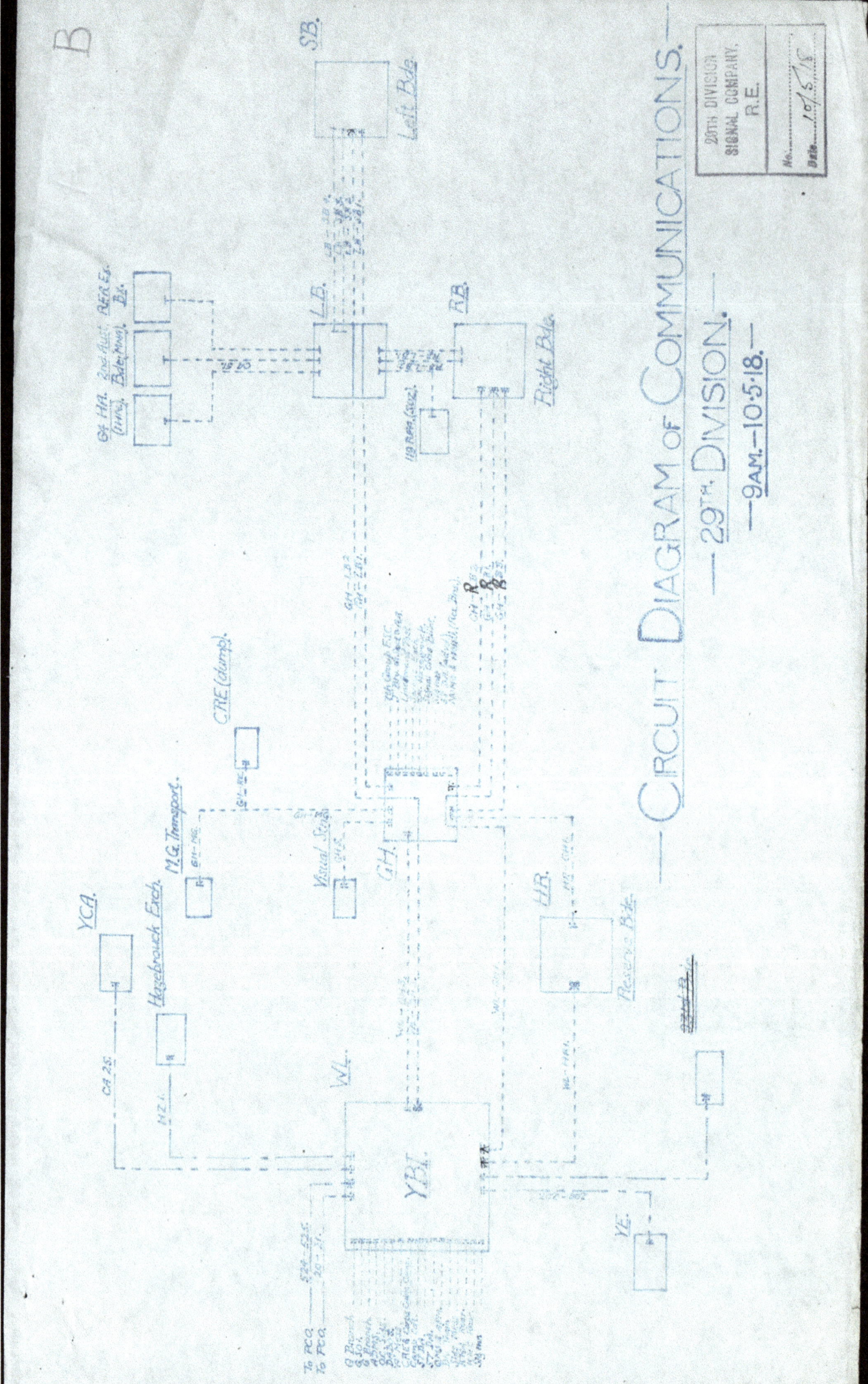

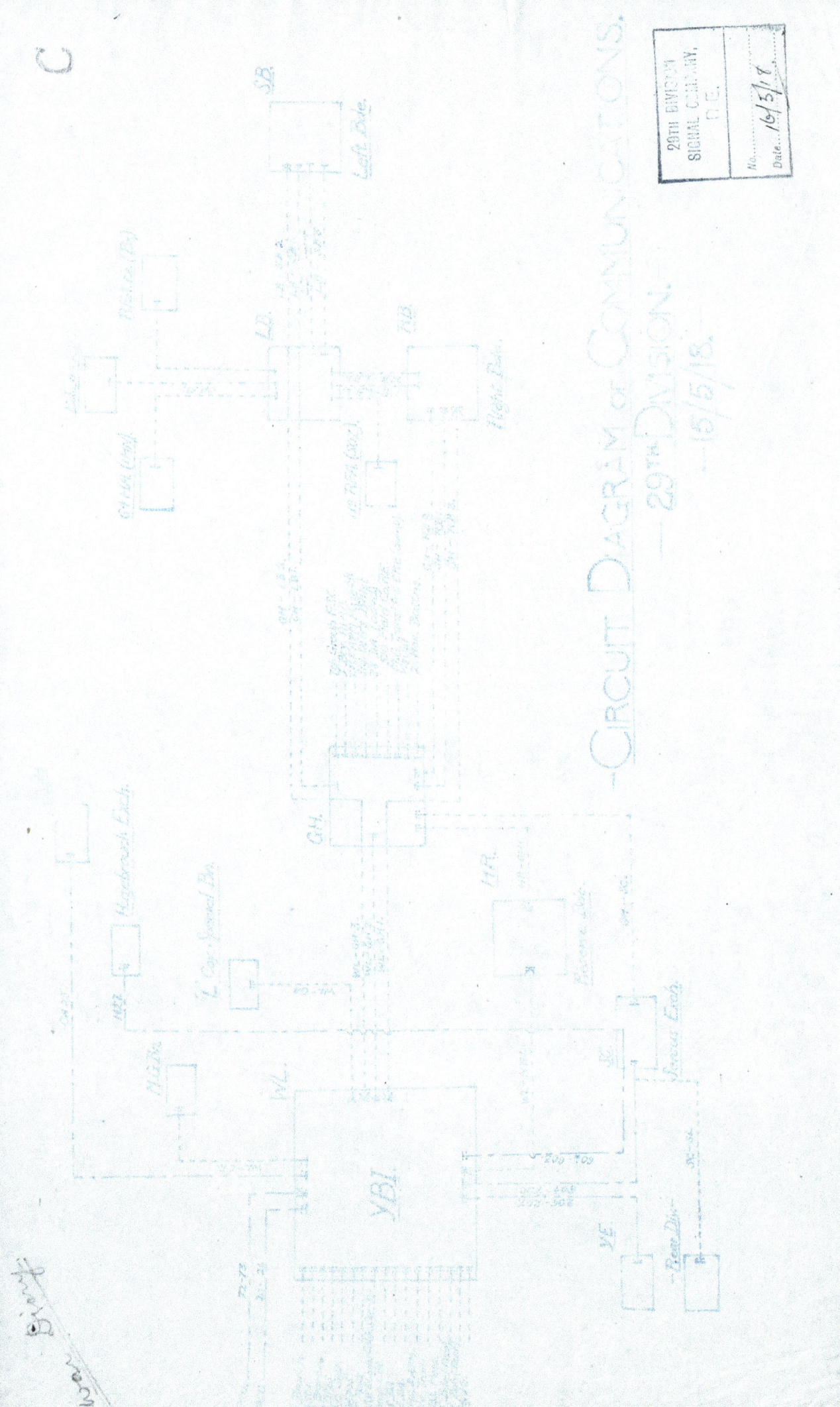

WAR DIARY
or
INTELLIGENCE SUMMARY.

Army Form C. 2118.

29th Divisional Sig Co RE

May 1918

D2

(Erase heading not required.)

Summary of Events and Information

Place	Date	Hour	Number of messages and Registered dealt Rickets with									Remarks and references to Appendices
			Date	No. of Messages	No. of Regd S.P.	Date	No. of Messages	No. of Regd S.P.	Date	No. of Messages	No. of Regd S.P.	
WALLON -CAPPEL			1918 1 May	652	133	Bf Fwd	6802	1969	Bf Fwd	13395	4765	
			2 "	601	138	12 May	628	299	22 May	653	238	
			3 "	512	152	13 "	731	277	23 "	638	251	
			4 "	591	187	14 "	816	316	24 "	603	192	
			5 "	565	124	15 "	716	321	25 "	546	210	
			6 "	635	121	16 "	636	364	26 "	703	209	
			7 "	614	149	17 "	666	306	27 "	567	229	
			8 "	724	213	18 "	639	236	28 "	580	224	
			9 "	678	144	19 "	548	218	29 "	614	248	
			10 "	489	222	20 "	604	222	30 "	495	201	
			11 "	741	386	21 "	609	215	31 "	640	171	
			Cd Fwd	6802	1969	Cd Fwd	13395	4763	TOTAL	19494	6936	

Vol 24

CONFIDENTIAL

WAR DIARY.

of

29th Division Signal Coy, RE

From 1st to 30th June 1918 inclusive

VOLUME No.

Army Form C. 2118.

WAR DIARY
or
INTELLIGENCE SUMMARY.
(Erase heading not required.)

June 1918

Place	Date	Hour	Summary of Events and Information	Remarks and references to Appendices
WALDON	1st		The hours are shown in the right below 18th Royal Ir	
CAPPEL	16		Div. Inspected below in part of the area of	
	21st		NIEPPE FOREST	
			LINE COMMUNICATION	
			Telephone and telephone have been very well	
			Although a certain amount of trouble was experienced from	
			gas shelling at night (which put the wires of some	
			batteries V.A. out of action) yet, our construction in	
			airline cable at the rate of a mile to a stream	
			some miles about 3 or 4 with back the wire	
			system. G.H.Q. advanced telephone exchange to the	
			rear of Div. Hg. and to A.S. Co. Sig. are both well	
			laid. Divisional artillery the wires have well	
			on the whole, but again through more occasion from	
			depots who were closing the wires of such as	
			Innes Brown Brigade the wires felt very well, but	
			(and a [illegible])	

Army Form C. 2118.

WAR DIARY
INTELLIGENCE SUMMARY.
(Erase heading not required.)

29 Division Signal Co. R.E.

JUNE 1918

Place	Date	Hour	Summary of Events and Information	Remarks and references to Appendices
WALLON CAPPEL	1st	21:30	(Continued) no sound wires being used. Owing to enemy gas shelling it was difficult to maintain communication.	
			WIRELESS. From WALLON CAPPEL to the Brigades wireless communication was much more efficient. All power buzzers and amplifiers were found to be considerably more satisfactory than the power buzzers given to the Field Coy. It was thought that this could be carried out between Divisional H.Q. and Division to between Divisional Headqrs and Brigade Headqrs worked satisfactorily. Also sent Wilson Hughes Trailing Set constructed in the forward area for the 10th Bn. stations. Continued on Page III	

Army Form C. 2118.

WAR DIARY
INTELLIGENCE SUMMARY.
(Erase heading not required.)

29th Division Signal Coy
June 1918

Instructions regarding War Diaries and Intelligence Summaries are contained in F. S. Regs., Part II, and the Staff Manual respectively. Title pages will be prepared in manuscript.

Place	Date	Hour	Summary of Events and Information	Remarks and references to Appendices
WALLON CAPPEL	22 to 30		(Contd) VISUAL. Visual arrangements were carried out during the summer period. Owing to no aerial activity it was not possible to test for visual other than from our own stations. PIGEONS and DOGS. Pigeons were employed from the front line with considerable success and with few casualties. On 29th June two relieves by the 31st Infantry Brigade were carried out in WALLON CAPPEL & WAERDRECQUES with units in billets at LUMBRES, RACQUINGHEM and PONT ASQUIN. This ____ into which ____ in reserve and training lines. (Contd on MMIV)	

Army Form C. 2118.

WAR DIARY
or
INTELLIGENCE SUMMARY.
(Erase heading not required.)

29 Divisional HQrs   IV   June 1918

Place	Date	Hour	Summary of Events and Information	Remarks and references to Appendices
WARDRECQUES	22		Carried out ordinary	
	to		training as soldiers —	
	29		Not carrying out Chaplain duties and instructions	
			were given and examined. A few	
			No. 3 visitors which were sent in to	
			HQ carried out visual duties at Chaplains	
			Services as well as delegated communications	
			duties.	
	30		On June 29th the 86th Brigade moved forward	
			into the 31st Divisional area as a support	
			Brigade. Our Hqrs were established at LE TIR ANGLAIS	
			On the 30th the Brigade relieved the Divisional	
			front line occupied by the 31st Division Communications	
			were established with the 87th to the 31st Divisions while	
			they were engaged *(continues on page V)*	

Army Form C. 2118.

29 Division Signal Co [?]
June 1916

WAR DIARY
INTELLIGENCE SUMMARY.
(Erase heading not required.)

Instructions regarding War Diaries and Intelligence Summaries are contained in F. S. Regs., Part II. and the Staff Manual respectively. Title pages will be prepared in manuscript.

Place	Date	Hour	Summary of Events and Information	Remarks and references to Appendices

During the month casualties from shell fire etc have been less than usual. Balloon caused considerable trouble in trying to cut the telephone lines in front of the section. No major operations for duration of the month. Reinforcements amounting to 6 men arrived. Divisions exchange of personnel continues to run smoothly.

Gulbranson Major RE
OC 29 Division Sig Co [?]

WAR DIARY
INTELLIGENCE SUMMARY

Army Form C. 2118.

VI JUNE A

DATE	No. of ...	No. of Reg. sick...			DATE	...	...	Remarks
1	535	188			16	568	115	
2	687	170			17	524	192	
3	593	169			18	669	185	
4	525	140			19	737	146	
5	449	119			20	670	175	
6	570	105			21	729	126	Total Treated 14823
7	529	101			22	458	80	Reg. Sick Pkts 4158
8	434	112			23	410	97	
9	467	150			24	304	134	
10	571	163			25	221	80	
11	706	192			26	201	79	
12	562	182			27	199	122	
13	696	142			28	206	96	
14	562	188			29	207	89	
15	416	174			30	159	119	

CONFIDENTIAL

WAR DIARY.

of

29th Divisional Signal Co. R.E.

From 1/7/18 to 31/7/18

VOLUME No..........

29 Division Signal Coy Army Form C. 2118.
R.E.
July 1918.

WAR DIARY
INTELLIGENCE SUMMARY.
(Erase heading not required.)

Place	Date	Hour	Summary of Events and Information	Remarks and references to Appendices
WARDRECQUES	1st to 21st		During this period the Division was in reserve and the time was occupied in training and recreation. Mounted and dismounted linemen were instructed in cable wagon drill and elementary theoretical buried line work. Visual signallers were put through a refresher course and No. 5 section worked with them, gradually working up to long distance visual schemes. Attached Infantry for wireless duties were instructed both in theory and practice in the Loop Set, Trench Set, and Power Buzzer Amplifier.	
BAVINCHOVE	22nd		Division HQ moved to BAVINCHOVE with Infantry Brigades as follows:- 86th Bde close to NOORDPEENE 87th Bde at ST MARIE CAPPEL 88th Bde at CASSEL. The two latter were obtained through 2nd Army Advanced (Continued on page II)	

WAR DIARY 29 Division Signal Coy. RE

–of–

INTELLIGENCE SUMMARY. July 1918.

Army Form C. 2118.

(Erase heading not required.)

Place	Date	Hour	Summary of Events and Information	Remarks and references to Appendices
			(Continued).	
			Exchange at CASSEL and the former through 10th Corps Exchange at ZUYTPEENE.	
BAVINCHOVE	23rd to 31st		During this period the Division was in reserve to 10th Corps. The period was spent in normal training. All Officers carried out reconnaissances of the forward area of the right division, 10th Corps with a view to the possible employment of the Division in operations in this area. No other matter of special interest to report during this period. All lines used were maintained by 2nd Army or 10th Corps. Appendix A shows the number of messages and sealed packets dealt with each day.	

A Winton Major RE
OC, 29th Div Signal Coy RE

WAR DIARY July 1918 29 Division Signal Coy RE. Army Form C. 2118.
or
INTELLIGENCE SUMMARY. III Appendices A.

(Erase heading not required.)

Place	Date	Hour	No. of Messages	No. of Msgs Book Packets	Summary of Events and Information DATE	No. of Messages	No. of Postal Packets	Remarks and references to Appendices
	1		207	60	16	257	85	
	2		242	139	17	282	71	
	3		272	89	18	300	79	
	4		225	90	19	328	88	
	5		253	83	20	326	97	
	6		248	100	21	292	84	
	7		277	97	22	126	89	
	8		248	72	23	224	100	
	9		209	63	24	227	185	
	10		226	101	25	335	116	
	11		235	107	26	298	109	
	12		267	98	27	353	120	
	13		266	102	28	348	109	
	14		236	108	29	328	134	
	15		238	94	30	344	126	
					31	377	153	

Total of Messages = 8396
" " Packets = 3148

CONFIDENTIAL

WAR DIARY.

of

29th Divisional Signal Coy. R.E.

From 1st to 31st August 1918 (Inclusive)

VOLUME No.

WAR DIARY 29 Division Signal Co, RE

Army Form C. 2118.

INTELLIGENCE SUMMARY. August 1918.

(Erase heading not required.)

Place	Date	Hour	Summary of Events and Information	Remarks and references to Appendices
BAVINCHOVE	Aug 1st		Division still in reserve but preparing to take over from 1st Australian Division. Advance party of one NCO and four linemen sent forward to take over manned test points on buried route of cable in 1st Australian Div area.	
			88th and 86th Infy Brigades moved to LA KREULE area just north of HAZEBROUCK. Communication to them via 1st Aust. Div. through 15th Corps, breaking very far.	
	Aug 2nd		88th Infy Bde relieved 2nd Australian Brigade in the front line; 86th Infy Bde in immediate support with HQ at BORRE. Communication through 1st Aust. Div. Personnel and instruments to take over Signal Office and Lines of 1st Aust. Div. sent forward.	
			Wireless communication of 1st Aust. Div. also relieved as follows:-	
			One French det. to left Brigade; one French det to right Brigade	
			continued on Page II	

WAR DIARY
INTELLIGENCE SUMMARY

Army Form C. 2118.

29 Division Signal Coy. RE

August 1918.

Place	Date	Hour	Summary of Events and Information	Remarks and references to Appendices
ST SYLVESTRE CAPPEL	Aug 3rd		(continued) One Loop Set complete in the Forward Area and one Amplifier to carry out Policing duties. 1st Australian Division relieved and carried hassed to G.O.C. 29 Division at 10 a.m. at which hour communications of 1st Aust. Divn. were taken over. 87th Infy Bde took over from 2nd Aust. Infy Bde in reserve, with HQ north of HAZEBROUCK. 86th Infy Bde relieved 121st Infy Bde in the Right Brigade Sector of the Divisional front with one Battalion in the line. The Loop Set was installed between Battalion HQ and the line and Infy Bde HQ working satisfactorily at 4 h.p.m. Normal maintenance of lines, the majority of which were on the buried system. Arrangements made for change of Division HQ with 9th Division. HQ behind HONDEGHEM.	
	5th		Normal maintenance of lines. Nothing of special interest to report. continued on page III	

Army Form C. 2118.

WAR DIARY
INTELLIGENCE SUMMARY.
(Erase heading not required.)

August, 1918
29th Division Signal Co., RE

III

Place	Date	Hour	Summary of Events and Information	Remarks and references to Appendices
ST SYLVESTRE CAPPEL	5th to 16th		Normal maintenance of lines. Principal work carried out was salvage of existing lines in area. About 80 miles of cable was picked up in this period. Routes for continuation of forward buries were reconnoitred, but no labour was forthcoming to carry out this work.	
	17th		The Left Brigade moved to IONIC HOUSE W18 d.1.5 (their old Left Battalion H.Q.) preparatory to an operation. Battalion H.Q. situated at X.19 a.1.7 and E.5 b.7.3. A visual station was established at the south eastern end of HELF AVENUE, about 600 yards S.E. of NORDHELF. Communication to Brigade by buried line, Wireless and Visual. From Brigade Forward by Ground line, Wireless Loop Set and Visual.	
	18th		Attack on OUTTERSTEENE RIDGE commenced at 11 a.m. Communications to Brigade uninterrupted. From Brigade forward, some difficulty was experienced in keeping telephone lines through. The Wireless Loop Set was employed with	

Continued on page IV

WAR DIARY
INTELLIGENCE SUMMARY

29th Division Signal Co., Army Form C. 2118.

August, 1918.

IV

(Erase heading not required.)

Instructions regarding War Diaries and Intelligence Summaries are contained in F. S. Regs., Part II. and the Staff Manual respectively. Title pages will be prepared in manuscript.

Place	Date	Hour	Summary of Events and Information	Remarks and references to Appendices
ST. SYLVESTRE CAPPEL	18th		(continued). Success until a shell damaged the forward sending portion. Otherwise normal maintenance of lines.	
	19th to 23rd		The 88th Infantry Brigade relieved the 87th Infantry Brigade in the left sector on the night 20th/21st. Otherwise normal maintenance of lines.	
	24th		The 86th Infy Brigade moved forward to CURFEW HOUSE at E.3.C.0.9 and communication was obtained via Test Point at PC.13. (PRADELLES) by Ground Line along the road leading south to CURFEW HOUSE.	
	25th to 28th		Normal maintenance of lines during this period. Salvage work being particularly successful. About 40 miles altogether picked up since the 20th August. No trouble on any telephone lines.	
BORRE	29th		29th Divn Headquarters moved to BORRE at 10.30 a.m. Change over completed without any hitch and all communications continued on page V	

Army Form C. 2118.

WAR DIARY 29th Division Signal Co, R.E.
INTELLIGENCE SUMMARY.   August, 1918.

(Erase heading not required.)

Place	Date	Hour	Summary of Events and Information	Remarks and references to Appendices
BORRE	29th 30th		(continued) Satisfactory. The enemy commenced to withdraw opposite our front. BAILLEUL occupied and the line pushed forward to NOOTE BOOM. Brigade assisted by a supply of cable lines pushed forward to advanced Batn. H.Q., and each Battn. given sufficient cable to have one line to Company H.Q. in the front line.	
	31st		87th Infy Brigade H.Q. moved to S26c4.4, South of BAILLEUL. Lines to them erected:- I. Via the old H.Q. at IONIC HOUSE, and II. Direct from the end of the Bury at STRAZEELE via MERRIS and OUTTERSTEENE. Brigade H.Q. moved at 4 p.m., and good communication obtained by 6.30 p.m. Communication also obtained with them by wireless. The 86th Infy Brigade from the right sector moved into support, continued on page VI	

WAR DIARY 29th Division Signal Co, RE Army Form C. 2118.

INTELLIGENCE SUMMARY. August, 1918.

VI

Place	Date	Hour	Summary of Events and Information	Remarks and references to Appendices
BORRE	31st		(continued) The Divisional front being taken over by one Brigade. (87A) Light cable wagons pushed forward proved very valuable for the above construction. Appendix A shows the number of messages and Registered Sealed Packets dealt with each day.	

CMSimpson
Major R.E.
OC, 29th Divl Signal Co, RE

Appendix A.

WAR DIARY of 29th Division Signal Co. RE

INTELLIGENCE SUMMARY. August, 1918.

(Erase heading not required.)

Army Form C. 2118.

Place	Date	Hour	No. of messages	No. of Sealed Packets		Date	No. of messages	No. of Sealed Packets	Remarks and references to Appendices
	1		255	159		17	521	167	
	2		319	132		18	663	109	
	3		588	139		19	806	168	
	4		580	144		20	584	135	
	5		551	120		21	622	136	
	6		419	126		22	640	129	
	7		495	95		23	627	102	
	8		493	113		24	532	110	
	9		446	110		25	448	109	
	10		432	101		26	519	118	
	11		474	135		27	530	92	
	12		534	148		28	516	87	
	13		540	102		29	396	78	
	14		479	113		30	660	157	
	15		491	137		31	745	147	
	16		532	144		TOTAL for month	16,577	3862	

War Diary
of
29th Dv. Sig. Coy
for
September 1918,
is missing.

> the enemy . . . you should concentrate
> your forces and give up risky exped-
> itions . . . in East Africa, where
> we cannot reinforce you sufficiently
> to be sure of success".

After consultation, General Wapshare decided that the unhealthy climate of the Umba Valley, where the sick rate was rapidly increasing, made retention of the area undesirable. The force was to be withdrawn to the healthier area around Msambweni and Gazi.

Preliminary orders for the evacuation were issued by Br.-General Tighe on the 29th January, and during the next few days some of the units and stores together with the numerous hospital cases were gradually evacuated by sea to Mombasa, every precaution being taken for secrecy. The force intended to remain at Gazi and Msambweni - 4 companies 3/Kashmir Rifles, 4 companies 1/K.A.R. and 4 machine guns, under Captain E.F.D. Money - was detailed as the covering force and remained till the last, patrolling constantly up to the German outposts. By the 8th February all was ready, and that evening the other remaining troops embarked in the transport Barjora. By 7 p.m. the embarkation was complete, and Captain Money's force then marched off northwards. Camping that night by the Makwembi river

Vol 28.

CONFIDENTIAL

WAR DIARY.

of 29TH DIVISION SIGNAL COMPANY, R.E.

From 1st Oct. to 31st Oct, 1918.

VOLUME No.

Army Form C. 2118.

WAR DIARY
INTELLIGENCE SUMMARY.
(Erase heading not required.)

29th Division Signal Company, RE
October, 1918.

Place	Date	Hour	Summary of Events and Information	Remarks and references to Appendices
GHELUVELT	1st		Divl. H.Q. Advd moved to GHELUVELT. Brigade H.Q. in the neighbourhood of KOELBERG and KRUISEIK. Communication established by telephone and by wireless. Visual communication was established between Advanced Div. H.Q. and 87th and 88th Infantry Brigades at the above two places. The 86th Infantry Brigade H.Q. were about one mile North of KOELBERG, and were not in view from Advanced Division. Telephone lines ran along the main road towards MENIN, with loops round shelled cross-roads, etc., and with spurs off to Brigade H.Q.	
	2nd		The 88th Inf. Bde attacked GHELUWE during the morning, but did not advance much. Communication by telephone was maintained throughout the day. During the night 2nd/3rd, the 87th Inf Bde. took over the front from the 88th and 86th Inf Bdes, the latter withdrawing to positions quite close to Advanced Div. H.Q. (Continued on page 2).	

Army Form C. 2118.

WAR DIARY
INTELLIGENCE SUMMARY.

29th Division Signal Company RE

October 1918.

(Erase heading not required.)

Instructions regarding War Diaries and Intelligence Summaries are contained in F. S. Regs., Part II. and the Staff Manual respectively. Title pages will be prepared in manuscript.

2.

Place	Date	Hour	Summary of Events and Information	Remarks and references to Appendices
GHELUVELT.	3rd		(Continued from page 1). Nothing of special interest on this day, except that a new line was laid to the 87th Inf. Bde. H.Q. across country. In spite of increased hostile shell fire, telephone communication was maintained, but difficulty was experienced in communication to the rear H.Q. and to Corps. Additional trouble was also experienced on this day from traffic. On the night 3rd/4th, the 41st Division took over the front from the 29th Division.	
BRAKE CAMP.	4th		H.Q. moved from GHELUVELT to BRAKE CAMP, with 88th Inf. Bde. at BRAKE CAMP, 86th Inf. Bde. at RAMPARTS, YPRES, and 87th Inf. Bde. moving from the GHELUVELT area to the WESTHOEK area.	
	5th		On the night 5th/6th the 86th Inf. Bde. took over the front held by the Right Brigade of the 9th Division. Communication was established from the 9th Division and by Wireless. 86th Inf. Bde. H.Q. at STROOIBOOMHOEK.	

(Continued on page 3)

Army Form C. 2118.

WAR DIARY
or
INTELLIGENCE SUMMARY.
(Erase heading not required.)

29th Division Signal Company, R.E.

October, 1918.

3.

Place	Date	Hour	Summary of Events and Information	Remarks and references to Appendices
BRAKE CAMP.	6th		(Continued from page 2.) An Advanced Divisional Report Centre was established at MOELENHOEK just North of BECELAERE, and lines laid from this point to the 86th Inf. Bde. H.Q. Lines were also arranged from this place back to Corps H.Q. which were eventually put straight through to main Div. H.Q at BRAKE CAMP.	
	7th.		Considerable trouble was experienced on the line from Advd. Div. to Inf. Bde. from hostile shell fire which was also difficult between Div. H.Q and Advanced Division owing to the great length of this line, and the difficulty of construction and maintenance over the Crater zone.	
RAMPARTS, YPRES	8th-13th		Div. main H.Q moved to RAMPARTS, YPRES on the 8th. During this period, work was concentrated on communications from the Advd. Div. to Inf. Bdes., the lines being tested as far as possible and being altered to avoid places chiefly shelled. The Wilson Wireless set was also moved (Continued on page 4.)	

Army Form C. 2118.

WAR DIARY
INTELLIGENCE SUMMARY.
29th Division Signal Company, R.E.
October, 1918.

(Erase heading not required.)

Place	Date	Hour	Summary of Events and Information	Remarks and references to Appendices
RAMPARTS, YPRES	8-13th		(Continued from page 3) up to Advd. H.Q., use being made of the Corps set at the Ramparts for communication from the main Div. H.Q. The Exchange at BRAKE CAMP was closed down. On the 13th October the whole of General Staff and one Officer of "Q" Branch moved to the Advd. H.Q. and a Rwl. Advd. Exchange was established at the Inf. Bde. H.Q. On the night 13th/14th all three Inf. Bdes. moved into the forward area, being connected by telephone through the new Forward Exchange with Advd. H.Q. One Inf. Bde. (86th) established Forward H.Q. in the front line at LEDEGHEM STATION, and considerable trouble was experienced throughout the forward area on the night 13th/14th owing to hostile shell fire.	
	14th	At 5.30 a.m.	the Division attacked. Brigade H.Q. rapidly moved forward, and were kept in touch with the Forward Exchange by means of two detachments who laid single (Continued on page 5)	

Army Form C. 2118.

WAR DIARY
INTELLIGENCE SUMMARY.
29th Division Signal Company, R.E.
October 1918
(Erase heading not required.)

Place	Date	Hour	Summary of Events and Information	Remarks and references to Appendices
RAMPARTS, YPRES	14th		(Continued from page 4) D5 Cable. At 2 p.m. Adv. Div. H.Q. moved up to the position of the forward exchange just north of DADIZEELE. Brigade H.Q. at this time were about 2½ miles east of LEDEGHEM, in the neighbourhood of BARAKKEN. Considerable trouble was experienced on D5 single cable lines from traffic, especially from Batteries moving into positions. No trouble was experienced from hostile shell fire after zero plus two hours.	
BECELAERE	15th		On the 15th at 09.00 the 87th Inf. Bde. attacked on the Divisional front. Communications were improved by laying twisted cable, one detachment keeping with the 87th Inf. Bde. H.Q., the other detachment extending and completing the line from Adv. Div. to their H.Q. At the previous day. The whole rear Div. H.Q. moved up to BECELAERE, and communication was established with them on the original lines laid out before the commencement (Continued on page 6)	

Army Form C. 2118.

WAR DIARY
INTELLIGENCE SUMMARY.
(Erase heading not required.)

29th Division Signal Company, R.E.
October, 1918.

Place	Date	Hour	Summary of Events and Information	Remarks and references to Appendices
BEDELAERE	13th		(Continued from page 5)	
			Up the operations of the 14th. On the afternoon of the 14th Adv. Bde. H.Q. moved forward to POODLES FARM (about 2½ miles East of LEDEGHEM) where the 87th Inf. Bde. H.Q. were established at the commencement of the day. By this time the front line was across, and in front of the COURTRAI – ROULERS railway. Communication was established to the Corps from the new position via Corps Adv. Exchange, DADIZEELE, on the original lines laid by us on the 14th, and during the morning of the 15th.	
LEDEGHEM. STATION.	16th to 19th		Adv. Bde. H.Q. remained at POODLES FARM. On the 16th the 87th Inf. Bde. reached the line of the LYS CANAL, while Brigade H.Q. remained near SALINES, to which point two lines were laid and maintained. During the two days operations of the 14th and 15th Inf. Bdes. maintained communication with Inf. Battalions by laying (continued on page 7)	

WAR DIARY

INTELLIGENCE SUMMARY.

29th Division Signal Company RE
October, 1918

Army Form C. 2118.

Place	Date	Hour	Summary of Events and Information	Remarks and references to Appendices
LEDEGHEM STATION	16th to 19th		(Continued from page 6.) Single D2 cable, and establishing forward report centres from which lines were laid to Battalions when they halted. Communication was also maintained by runners, flags, and wireless. On the 16th the whole of Rear Div. H.Q. moved up to LEDEGHEM STATION. On the 18th October, the 88th Inf. Bde. took over the line from the 87th Inf. Bde. and moved their H.Q. in front of the COURTRAI - ROULERS railway, the two lines laid to SALINES were extended to this line, and communication was maintained without difficulty.	
	20th		The Division attacked and the line was advanced about 4 miles. The 88th Inf. Bde. attacked, and the 86th Inf. Bde. followed through them to the objective. As on previous occasions, communication was maintained by two cable detachments with Advd. Bde. H.Q., but on this occasion (Continued on page 8)	

Army Form C. 2118.

WAR DIARY
INTELLIGENCE SUMMARY.
(Erase heading not required.)

29th Brigade Signal Company RE
October 1918.

8.

Place	Date	Hour	Summary of Events and Information	Remarks and references to Appendices
LEDEGHEM STATION	20th		(Continued from page 7). They laid out twisted D.3 cable. Difficulty was experienced in crossing the LYS CANAL owing to the breakdown of the only available bridge. At 6.0 a.m. Div. Advd. H.Q. moved to the neighbourhood of SALINES, and in the afternoon moved forward to just north east of COURTRAI. Communication to Brigades was maintained and Brigade H.Q. being established in the neighbourhood ESSCHER, STEENBRUGGE and STACEGHEM. Difficulty was experienced with communication to Rear Div H.Q., and to Corps, owing to traffic, but one line was got through for telegraph through which was impossible until about 10.0 p.m. when the second line was put through.	
	21st		The positions of Brigade Hdqrs. remained, the danger 86th Inf Bde being in the line, 87th and 88th Inf Bdes in support and reserve. Communications to (Continued on page 9.)	

Army Form C. 2118.

WAR DIARY
INTELLIGENCE SUMMARY.
(Erase heading not required.)

29th Division Signal Company R.E.

October 1918

Instructions regarding War Diaries and Intelligence Summaries are contained in F. S. Regs., Part II. and the Staff Manual respectively. Title pages will be prepared in manuscript.

Place	Date	Hour	Summary of Events and Information	Remarks and references to Appendices
LEDEGHEM STATION	21st		(Continued from page 8) Corps were improved by a connection to a permanent wire which they had pushed forward to a point about one mile north West of GUERNE, the second line to Corps remaining via the old position of H.Q. at SALINES and POODLES FARM. A new Wilson Wireless Set was received from Corps, and now worked satisfactorily. Great trouble was experienced on the 20th of bringing to the motor of the old Set, breaking down.	
COURTRAI	22nd		The 87th Inf. Bde. having relieved the 86th Inf. Bde. in the line, attached at 09.00. One cable detachment was attached to 87th Inf. Bde. H.Q. and laid a line to their forward Battle H.Q., which became later on in the day their main H.Q. The second cable detachment was held in readiness, and was despatched at 14.00 to return to 86th Inf. Bde. which moved during the (Continued on page 10.)	

Army Form C. 2118.

WAR DIARY
INTELLIGENCE SUMMARY.
(Erase heading not required.)

29th Division Signal Company
October, 1918

Place	Date	Hour	Summary of Events and Information	Remarks and references to Appendices
COURTRAI	22nd		(Continued from page 9). Afternoon No 10 to a point one mile South East of ESSCHER. The two Brigade Hdqrs. (86th and 87th) were then about 600 yards apart and were connected by a lateral line. During the day the front line advanced about 2,000 yards. The only difficulties experienced in communication were due to shell fire.	
	23rd		87th Inf. Bde. H.Q. were shelled at 06.00, and the 87th Inf. Bde. Signal Section suffered seven casualties. On the night 23rd/24th the Brigade was relieved by the 124th Bde. of the 41st Division.	
	24th		The 41st Division took over the command of the 29th Divl. Sector at 06.00. 86th Inf. Bde. established H.Q. in a Chateau on the western outskirts of CUERNE. 87th and 88th Inf. Bdes. remained in the neighbourhood of STACEGHEM. The Division was in reserve.	
	25th–26th		These two days were spent in cleaning up and re-organising. (Continued on page 11).	

WAR DIARY
INTELLIGENCE SUMMARY.
(Erase heading not required.)

29th Division Signal Company R.E.
Oct 30th 1918.

Army Form C. 2118.

Place	Date	Hour	Summary of Events and Information	Remarks and references to Appendices
COURTRAI	25th 26th 27th		(Continued from page 10) On the 25th the 86th Inf Bde. moved to RONCQ, north-west of TOURCOING. On the 26th, 88th Inf. Bde moved to the area west of MOUSCRON. Communication to these Brigades was by Motorcyclist Despatch Rider only, except that the 86th Inf Bde. arranged a line which connected them to the Army Exchange at RONCQ. On the 26th, 86th Inf Bde. moved from RONCQ to BONDUES.	
MOUVEAUX	27th		Division H.Q. closed at COURTRAI, 31st Division H.Q. moving in. A.Q. re-opened at MOUVEAUX at 10.00. 88th Inf. Bde moved to CROIX, and 87th Inf. Bde. moved from the COURTRAI area to the area west of MOUSCRON. Telephone communication was established with 86th Inf Bde. at BONDUES, and 88th Inf Bde. at CROIX, although the latter did not move into the HQ to which the telephone line was arranged.	

(Continued on page 12).

WAR DIARY
INTELLIGENCE SUMMARY.

Army Form C. 2118.

29th Division Signal Company, R.E.

October 1918.

Place	Date	Hour	Summary of Events and Information	Remarks and references to Appendices
MOUVEAUX	28th		(Continued from page 11) 87th Inf. Bde. moved to ST. ANDRÉ, where telephone communication was established from Bde. H.Q. The 29th Machine Gun Battalion which had moved from the COURTRAI area with the 87th Bde group, established their H.Q. at MARCQ and were primarily connected via the 88th Bde. Exchange.	
	29th		The Machine Gun line to 88th Inf. Bde. was reeled up and connection established by a shorter route on one of the lines leading towards WAMBRECHIES. Normal maintenance of telephone lines was carried out, and the remainder of the time spent in routine work, re-organization, re-fitting and cleaning up.	
	29th 30th 31st		General note :- Owing to the everchanging position of H.Q., and daily alterations in telephone lines, diagrams (Continued on page 13).	

WAR DIARY

INTELLIGENCE SUMMARY.
(Erase heading not required.)

Army Form C. 2118.

29th Division Signal Company R.E.

October 1918

For the period were not kept up, but the principle of communication throughout was to keep touch primarily by telephone lines, utilising cable wagons to their fullest possible extent, and by having recourse to the alternative means of communication when telephone lines failed, but making these alternative means purely subsidiary.

For Messages and Registered Packets dealt with - see Appendix A.

AW Simpson Major R.E.
O.C. 29th Division Signal Company, R.E.

Army Form C. 2118.

WAR DIARY
or
INTELLIGENCE SUMMARY.
(Erase heading not required.)

29th Division Signal Company R.E.
October 1918

Place	Date	Hour	Messages	Registered Sealed Packets	Summary of Events and Information — Messages	Registered Sealed Packets	Remarks and references to Appendices
Ahsenha A	1		825	278	Brought Forward 9465	2895	
	2		730	253	17 746	254	
	3		667	261	18 630	211	
	4		729	230	19 745	178	
	5		563	180	20 638	184	
	6		525	193	21 720	117	
	7		224	213	22 683	92	
	8		456	98	23 542	93	
	9		606	106	24 391	78	
	10		687	123	25 369	81	
	11		895	146	26 458	93	
	12		832	137	27 430	67	
	13		867	133	28 373	74	
	14		751	198	29 398	119	
	15		670	216	30 360	126	
	16		735	230	31 309	147	
					TOTAL 18,857	4813	

Carried Forward 11,055

Army Form C. 2118.

WAR DIARY
or
INTELLIGENCE SUMMARY.
(Erase heading not required.)

29 Div Sig Co R.E.
November 1918

Instructions regarding War Diaries and Intelligence Summaries are contained in F. S. Regs., Part II. and the Staff Manual respectively. Title pages will be prepared in manuscript.

WO 29

Place	Date	Hour	Summary of Events and Information	Remarks and references to Appendices
MOUVEAUX	1918 Nov 1 to 7		DHQ at MOUVEAUX and Division still in reserve. This period was spent in usual routine.	
ROLLEGHEM	Nov 8		DHQ moved to ROLLEGHEM. The 88th Brigade in front line along R. Schedlt with HQ near ST GENOIS. 87th Inf Bde in support in area T.10, 11 & 12. 86th Inf Bde in reserve with HQ at MOUSCRON.	
	" 9		88th Inf Bde crossed R. Schedlt when the general advance ensued. Communication became very difficult because DHQ remained at ROLLEGHEM, and all Brigades were moved forward rapidly. In addition, the number of existing lines was totally inadequate, and considerable work on main lines had to be carried out, not only E. of R. Schedlt but also W of it towards evening 88th Inf Bde established HQ near the village of CELLES. The line was got through to them but went dis about 4.0am (10th). 87th Inf Bde established HQ at BOSSUYT Chateau and 86th Bde moved to area T.10, 11 & 12.	
BOSSUYT Chateau	" 10		DHQ moved to BOSSUYT Chateau at 9.0am. By this time Corps had very nearly completed a 4 wire route to this point, but until this	

Army Form C. 2118.

WAR DIARY
or
INTELLIGENCE SUMMARY.

(Erase heading not required.)

29 Div Sig Co RE

November 1918

Instructions regarding War Diaries and Intelligence Summaries are contained in F. S. Regs., Part II. and the Staff Manual respectively. Title pages will be prepared in manuscript.

Place	Date	Hour	Summary of Events and Information	Remarks and references to Appendices
BOSSUYT Chateau	1918 Nov 10		was completed, work back to Corps and rear Divns had to be carried on one pair of D8 cable as the other line was "dis". There was insufficient personnel to maintain the lines to the rear owing to the fact that Brigades in front were still advancing rapidly. 88th Bde moved about 10.0 am to ST SAUVEUR. At 6.30am the bridge over the RECHOLDT for wheeled traffic was through. One cable waggon was ordered to be ready to cross at 6.0am but broke a wheel with the result that it did not cross until 9.0am. Consequently the line to 88th Inf Bde at ST SAUVEUR was not completed until late in the afternoon.	
CELLES	"		At 4pm D.H.Q. "advanced" moved to a Chateau 1 Kilometre SE. of CELLES. By this time an extra pair of lines had been laid to the rear by Corps Signals but no results could be obtained on any lines either to the rear or forward. This trouble was soon found to be due to civilians cutting out large lengths of cable from all the lines. 87th Inf Bde moved to CELLES & 86th Bde to BOSSUYT Chateau	

Army Form C. 2118.

WAR DIARY
or
INTELLIGENCE SUMMARY.
(Erase heading not required.)

29 Air Lig Co R.E.
November 1918

Place	Date	Hour	Summary of Events and Information	Remarks and references to Appendices
	1918			
CELLES	Nov 11		Message received at 6.30am that hostilities would cease at 11.0am. Trouble from civilians cutting out lengths of line did not however cease and communication by telephone became totally impossible from this cause.	
ST SAUVEUR.	"		DHQ moved at 10.0am to ST SAUVEUR. About 12 noon an extra pair of lines had been laid to ST SAUVEUR and a single D5 line which was laid the previous day was also got through. These two lines held fairly well but the practice of cutting out lengths of cable by civilians continued and the services of the Belgian mission were requisitioned to put a stop to this and notices were placed in villages and hamlets pointing out the penalty which would be inflicted on anyone cutting out lengths of military cable. The results however were obtained in spite of this notice for 2 or 3 days. 86 & 87 Bdes located as in 10⁄. The 88th Inf Bde established HQ at LESSINES.	
	Nov 12&13&14		DHQ remained at ST SAUVEUR and the time was spent in re-organising the Company which had become scattered mainly owing to the absence	

Army Form C. 2118.

WAR DIARY
or
INTELLIGENCE SUMMARY.

(Erase heading not required.)

29 Div Sig Co R.E.

November 1918

Place	Date	Hour	Summary of Events and Information	Remarks and references to Appendices
	1918			
ST SAUVEUR	Nov 12		Of lorry bridge over the river, stores of all kinds having had	
	" 14		to be left with personnel in charge west of the river.	
	" 13		On the 13th 87th Brigade moved to ST SAUVER, 86th Bde to ARCANIER, 88th Brigade to GHOY and 29th Div Arty to rear CELLES.	
	" 14		On the 14th 87th Brigade moved to GHOY, 86th Bde to FLOBECQ, 88th Bde to LESSINES and 29th Div Arty to WODECQ.	
FLOBECQ	" 15		DHQ moved to FLOBECQ and all horse transport of the company marched to this place. Lorries however could not yet be brought over the river.	
	" 16		Lorries crossed the River Schildt and stores left at BOSSUYT were brought up to FLOBECQ and on the 17th these were sorted out and all stores not required or surplus to establishment were dumped at FLOBECQ preparatory to march into Germany.	
	" 18		87th Inf Bde moved to WANNEBECQ, otherwise locations unchanged	
ENGHIEN	" 19		DHQ and 88th Inf Bde moved to ENGHIEN. 86th Bde to SILLY, 87th Bde to BASILLY. Location 5 miles SE of ENGHIEN, and 29th Div Arty to BASILLY	

Army Form C. 2118.

29 Div Sig Co R.E.
November 1918

WAR DIARY
or
INTELLIGENCE SUMMARY.
(Erase heading not required.)

V

Place	Date	Hour	Summary of Events and Information				Remarks and references to Appendices
	1918						
ENGHIEN	Nov 19-20		Communication by wireless to Corps and Brigades, also by D.R.				
	" 21 to 30		Moves of units as shown below				
			D.H.Q.	86th Inf Bde	87th Inf Bde	88th Inf Bde	
			ENGHIEN to TUBIZE	To ITTRE	Location 5 mls SE of ENGHIEN	To Br. le Chateau	20th Div Only
TUBIZE	"21						
Brain l'Alleud	"23		To Brain l'Alleud	To GENAPPE	To GLABAIS	To St Lambert	To SAINTES Br. l'Alleud
OTTIGNIES	"24		To OTTIGNIES	To St Lambert	To Paul St Walhain		
Nil Abbesse	"25		To Nil Abbesse	unchanged		To OTTIGNIES	To Court St Etienne
	" 26		Location				
Gd ROSIERE	" 27		To Gd ROSIERE	To HARLUE	To FORVILLE	To St Lambert	To Gd LEEZ
HUY	" 28		To HUY	To WANZE	To STREE	To EGHEZEE	To FORVILLE
	" 29		To OUFFET	To OUFFET	To COMBLAIN	To WANZE	To STREE
ANTHISNES	" 30		To ANTHISNES	To AYWAILLE	To LA REID	To OUFFET	To COMBLAIN

General Notes. After the commencement of the Armistice until end of month very little line communication of any kind was used. C.W. W/T was in use for work to Corps, and SPARK W/T for work

Army Form C. 2118.

WAR DIARY
or
INTELLIGENCE SUMMARY.

29th Div Sig Co RE

November 1918

(Erase heading not required.)

Place	Date	Hour	Summary of Events and Information	Remarks and references to Appendices
			General Notes (continued).	
			to the Infantry Brigades whenever possible according to circumstances. Apart from this, all communication was carried out by motor cyclist DR's, who worked very hard especially as the state of the roads during most of the period was most difficult for motor cycling. The repair and upkeep of machines, which is at all times most difficult, proved very satisfactory.	

A.H. Simpson
Major R.E.
O.C. 29th Div'l Sig Co R.E.

2a Div Signal Co YB 30

Decr. 1918

Army Form C. 2118.

WAR DIARY
or
INTELLIGENCE SUMMARY.
(Erase heading not required.)

29th Div Sig Co R.E.

December 1918

Place	Date	Hour	Summary of Events and Information	Remarks and references to Appendices
SPRIMONT	1918 Dec 1		AHQ moved from ANTHISNES to SPRIMONT.	
	" 1 to 31		Moves of units as shown in tabular statement on sheet No.	
NINEZE	Dec 1 to 3		Communication solely by DR.	
MALMEDY	" 4		Telephone communication was obtained with 87th Inf Bde, and DR communication only with other groups.	
"KALTERHERBERG"	" 5		Telephone communication was obtained with Corps, 86, 87 & 88 Bdes but not with the 2nd Arty Group	
KESTERNICH	" 6		Telephone communication was obtained all round through local exchange	
ZULPICH	" 7 & 8		Telephone communication was obtained to the 86 and 87 Bdes but not to the 88th Bde or 29th Div Arty, as the line was out of order and DR's had to be used to the last two mentioned.	
HERMULHEIM	" 9		Telephone communication was established with 86, 87 and 88 Brigade groups only.	
SULZ	" 10 to 12		Whilst at SULZ the communication was arranged by working through COLOGNE Exchange where all the lines required for military use were switched over to Second Army military Exchange in the	

Army Form C. 2118.

WAR DIARY
or
INTELLIGENCE SUMMARY.
(Erase heading not required.)

29 Aux Sig Co RE

December 1918

Place	Date	Hour	Summary of Events and Information	Remarks and references to Appendices
SULZ	1918 Dec 10 to 12		Work exchange. A direct line was obtained and bridged in the COLOGNE Office. Prior to the lines being switched over to the military board considerable confusion arose as everyone tried to work through the Civil exchange where the difficulty of language proved a great obstacle.	
BENSBERG	Dec 13 to 20.		On arrival at BENSBERG the same principle was adopted. A direct line was however found to the 87th Inf Bde at BERG GLADBACH and Recorder working was established.	
SAND	Dec 21		Orders issued with regard to Telephone and Telegraph &c in Bridgehead area. All local circuits, Telephone or Telegraph, that crossed the Perimeter to be disconnected at the nearest Office or Exchange. All L. & I traffic to be stopped or to be taken over by British Military Authority.	
	" 22		Instructions re dismantling Local Telegraph and Telephone	

Army Form C. 2118.

WAR DIARY
or
INTELLIGENCE SUMMARY.
(Erase heading not required.)

29th Divl Signal Co R.E.

December 1918.

Place	Date	Hour	Summary of Events and Information	Remarks and references to Appendices
SAND	Dec 27		Majority of these however are already taken over for our own use. Division Area sub-divided for purposes of control into Brigade Areas, and each Brigade Office made responsible for his own Area. This includes completion of records and diagrams and keeping them up to date. Detailed instructions for disconnecting routes crossing the frontier issued to 88th Brigade. All circuits due to be disconnected were dealt with except the circuits to REMSCHEID which were mostly locals and involved a considerable amount of work.	III
SAND	Dec 26			
	Dec 1 to 31 st		For Locations of Brigade Groups during the month see sheet No	IV

J J Spence Lt RE
for Captain
OC 29 Divl Sig Co R.E.

Army Form C. 2118.

WAR DIARY
or
INTELLIGENCE SUMMARY.
29 Div Hg 60 RR

(Erase heading not required.)

December 1918.

Place	Date	Hour	Summary of Events and Information					Remarks and references to Appendices
			D.H.Q.	86 Inf Bde	87 Inf Bde	88 Inf Bde	29 Div Arty 29 Div M.G.C	
	Dec 1 /18		Moves of Units :-					
	Dec 1		From ANTHISNES to SPRIMONT	From AYWAILLE to LA REID	From LA REID to STAVELOT	From BOFFET to AYWAILLE	Located at COMBLAIN à.c.m. 30/11	
	,, 2		To NIVEZE					
	,, 4		To MALMEDY	To STAVELOT	To ELSENBORN MONTJOIE NIDEGGAN	To LA REID MALMEDY MONTJOIE	To NIVEZE STAVELOT KALTERHERBERG	
	,, 5		To KALTERHERBERG	To ELSENBORN SIMMERATH	To NIDEGGAN	To MONTJOIE	To KALTERHERBERG	
	,, 6		To KESTERNICH	To SIMMERATH	To LECHENICH	To EMBKEN	To SCHMIDT	
	,, 7		To ZÜLPICH	To KLEITENBERG	To KRIEL	To ERFECHEN	To HURTH KNAPSACK	
	,, 9		To HERMÜLHEIM	To RENSBERG	To BERG GLADBACH	To MULHEIM (South)	To BERG GLADBACH	
	,, 13		To BENSBERG	,,	To BURSCHEID EHRINGHAUSEN	To BERG GLADBACH	To NEUFRUCK	
	,, 15							
	,, 17			,,	,,	To WERMEL KIRCHEN	,,	
	,, 18		To SAND	,,	,,	,,	,,	
	,, 21		,,	,,	BURSCHEID	,,	BERG GLADBACH TO DABRING-HAUSEN	
	,, 30		,,	,,	,,	,,	,,	
	,, 31							

**RHINE ARMY
SOUTHERN DIVISION
LATE 29TH DIVISION**

DIVL SIGNAL COY R.E.

JAN - AUG 1919

2066 & 2084

RHINE ARMY
SOUTHERN DIVISION
LATE 29TH DIVISION

CONFIDENTIAL

WAR DIARY.

of

29th Divn Signal Coy R.E.

From 1/1/19 to 31/1/19

VOLUME No. 5

29th Divisional Signal Coy
Army Form C. 2118.

29TH DIVISION
SIGNAL COMPANY
R.E.

WAR DIARY
or
INTELLIGENCE SUMMARY.
(Erase heading not required.)

January 1919

Place	Date	Hour	Summary of Events and Information	Remarks and references to Appendices
SAND	1 to 31 Jan. 1919		No event of especial interest occurred during the month. All communications worked satisfactorily, though congestion on existing routes necessitated laying extra lines, cable, as follows:- (1) 3 pairs from ODENTHAL to ALTENBERG. (2) 6 pairs from SAND to BERG-GLADBACH. These were laid between 14-20 Jan. On 26th Jan. work commenced by German personnel to replace above cables by open wire lines with a view to saving cable. Attitude of German Post Office personnel was very obedient and willing. Conversations of German Civilian 'Phone Subscribers frequently intercepted. One case of gross irregularity discovered and reported to 29th Divn. Gen. Staff. After this Conversations kept strictly to business. No attempt was made by German personnel to disobey security orders or interfere with either Military lines, or lines disconnected across the Brimeter. On Jan. 25th the G.O.C. 29th Division inspected Headquarters, Wireless and No 1 Section of the Divisional Signal Coy and presented medal ribbons. Appendix "A" attached	

Allinson Major R.E.
O/C 29th Divl Sig Coy R.E.

WAR DIARY

Army Form C. 2118.

29th Div. Sig. Co. R.E.

Appendix A

JANUARY

Place	Date	Hour	Date	No of Messages	No of Reed Sealed Pkts	Date	No of Messages	No of Reed Sealed Pkts	Remarks
SAND	1919 31 Jan		1	217	11	16	400	19	
			2	321	8	17	415	35	
			3	532	22	18	418	39	
			4	356	13	19	204	20	Total Messages 10,801
			5	181	9	20	355	19	Regd. Sld Pkts 727
			6	434	20	21	438	31	
			7	309	19	22	228	24	
			8	257	23	23	338	45	
			9	399	9	24	357	34	
			10	313	28	25	296	31	
			11	299	24	26	222	36	
			12	325	19	27	360	20	
			13	400	12	28	344	19	
			14	362	28	29	355	21	
			15	415	24	30	340	28	
						31	410	37	

CONFIDENTIAL

WAR DIARY.

of

29th Div Signal Co RE

From 1/7/19 to 28/7/19

VOLUME No.............

Army Form C. 2118.

WAR DIARY
or
INTELLIGENCE SUMMARY.

29 Divisional Sig Co RE

(Erase heading not required)

FEBRUARY 1919

Instructions regarding War Diaries and Intelligence Summaries are contained in F.S. Regs., Part II. and the Staff Manual respectively. Title pages will be prepared in manuscript.

Place	Date	Hour	Summary of Events and Information	Remarks and references to Appendices
SAND	1919 1 to 28 Feb		Nothing of special interest to report. The time was spent in normal routine work. Appendix "A" attached showing volume of Telegraph & D.R.L. traffic	

[signature]
Major RE
OC 29 Divl Sig Coy RE

20TH DIVISION
SIGNAL COMPANY.
R.E.
7. 3. 19

Army Form C. 2118.

WAR DIARY
or
INTELLIGENCE SUMMARY.

(Erase heading not required.)

29 Div. Sig. Co. R.E.

Appendix "A"

February 19

Instructions regarding War Diaries and Intelligence Summaries are contained in F. S. Regs., Part II. and the Staff Manual respectively. Title pages will be prepared in manuscript.

Place	Date	Hour	Summary of Events and Information					Remarks and references to Appendices
			Date	No. of Messages Sent via R.E.	No. of Rgs Sent via R.E.	Date	No. of Messages Sent via R.E.	No. of Rgs Sent via R.E.
SAND	1/2/19		1	362	25	15	273	25
	28/2/19		2	305	21	16	150	20
			3	330	19	17	321	18
			4	365	14	18	325	21
			5	442	23	19	307	25
			6	415	16	20	326	11
			7	270	33	21	341	20
			8	302	21	22	450	26
			9	139	24	23	242	21
			10	349	34	24	330	15
			11	329	24	25	267	20
			12	342	23	26	431	19
			13	335	20	27	353	18
			14	343	24	28	352	23
						Totals Feb.	9150	603

CONFIDENTIAL

WAR DIARY.

of

Southern D. Signal Coy RE

From 1/5/19 to 31/5/19

VOLUME No.

Army Form C. 2118.

WAR DIARY
or
INTELLIGENCE SUMMARY.
(Erase heading not required.)

Southern Divisional Signal Co R.E.

MAY 1919

Place	Date	Hour	Summary of Events and Information	Remarks and references to Appendices
SAND	1919 1st to 31st May		Taking of Leave interest to report. A funeral interment by men attached to the Company for executive Branston, joined on 22nd inst. has attracted a heavy volume of regret and DR LS traffic dealt with during the month.	

A. Watson
Major RE
Cmdg Signal Co RE, Southern Div

Return of Messages, Registered and Special Packets dealt with at Sand Signal Office during the Month of May 1919

Date	Messages	Packets
1	480	27
2	390	35
3	395	20
4	281	13
5	448	29
6	424	46
7	411	45
8	384	25
9	377	47
10	412	31
11	197	2
12	358	26
13	425	42
14	380	37
15	377	20
16	370	48
17	351	28
18	218	9
19	312	40
20	488	36
21	445	27
22	451	42
23	496	26
24	344	30
25	199	17
26	469	39
27	448	34
28	464	26
29	597	36
30	487	46
31	380	44
Totals	12258 { Daily Average 395.41 }	966

WAR DIARY
or
INTELLIGENCE SUMMARY.

(Erase heading not required.)

Army Form C. 2118.

Southern Div Signal Coy RE

June 1919

Place	Date	Hour	Summary of Events and Information	Remarks and references to Appendices
SAND	1st to 19th		The training of attached Infantry etc (being transfer to RE) continued very actively.	
	20th		Preparations for a move forward were carried out and an advanced Divisional Signal Office was opened at Mermelskirchen. Telegraphic communication was established between Divisional HQ. Brigade headquarters at Burscheid (1st So. Inf. Brigade), Solingen (2nd Bde) + Burg (3rd Bde).	
			Attached "A" attached Above the volume of telegraph + DR.LS traffic dealt with during the month.	

R Hyman
Capt RE
OC Signal Coy RE Southern Division

WAR DIARY Southern Div Signals CRE
INTELLIGENCE SUMMARY.
Appendix "D"

Army Form C. 2118.

(Erase heading not required.)

Place	Date	Hour	Date	No. of Outgoing messages	To of Kingdom Visual / PUL	Date	Summary of Events and Information – No. of Incoming Messages	No. of Reg. Phils
SAND	1/6/19 –30/6/19		1	291	5	16	274	34
			2	475	20	17	753	37
			3	404	27	18	692	56
			4	393	21	19	514	31
			5	329	14	20	356	80
			6	281	49	21	465	6
			7	322	29	22	268	38
			8	196	2	23	497	30
			9	357	20	24	358	53
			10	357	58	25	396	16
			11	366	29	26	381	21
			12	348	26	27	375	24
			13	346	39	28	409	4
			14	345	21	29	323	—
			15	214	38	30	433	21
				Total June		June	11,508	849

Army Form C. 2118.

WAR DIARY
or
INTELLIGENCE SUMMARY. Southern Div Signal Co RE

(Erase heading not required.)

July 1919

Place	Date	Hour	Summary of Events and Information	Remarks and references to Appendices
SAND	1st		After the signature of Peace units returned to their old positions. Prior to the 20th June out-station communications were restored. Advanced Divisional Signal Office at Wormelhuile was closed.	
	21st		Capt D.F. Fector MC RE assumed command of the Company vice Major Gr. Lawson MC RE who proceeded to England on 30-6-19	
			Appendix "A" attached shows the volume of Telegraph and D.R.L.S. traffic dealt with during the month	

D. Mullin
Major RE
O.C. Signal Co RE, Southern Div

SIGNAL COMPANY,
R.E.,
SOUTHERN DIVISIONAL
No. 2
Date 2 AUG 1919

Army Form C. 2118.

WAR DIARY
or
INTELLIGENCE SUMMARY.

(Erase heading not required.)

Place: SAND

Date	No. of Kumagos	No. of Reg Patrols	Date	No. of Kumagos	No. of Reg Patrols
1	370	27	17	278	16
2	491	34	18	336	21
3	466	18	19	175	21
4	99	7	20	178	7
5	427	8	21	243	25
6	243	2	22	266	21
7	347	16	23	395	14
8	389	38	24	361	20
9	364	23	25	364	20
10	315	19	26	234	9
11	365	20	27	115	4
12	330	18	28	284	16
13	173	32	29	269	15
14	337	24	30	247	24
15	321	20	31	280	23
16	322	21	Total	9377	573

WAR DIARY
INTELLIGENCE SUMMARY. Southern Div Signal Co RE

August 1919

Place	Date	Hour	Summary of Events and Information	Remarks and references to Appendices
SAND	1st/31st		Training of Officers & men. Training in attacks & Bn. training proceeded satisfactorily. The storage of 130 men from Infantry were completed.	
	20		Sent R.M.S. Jax (KOYLI) proceeded to H.K. for demobilisation	
	23		Lieut J.S. Stinnell was posted to "C" Corps Signal Co	
			Attached "A" detailed shews the volume of telegraph and DRLS traffic dealt with during the month.	

from [signature]
for Capt RE
OC Signal Co RE, Southern Div

SIGNAL COMPANY
R.E.
SOUTHERN DIVISION
2 SEP 1919

WAR DIARY or INTELLIGENCE SUMMARY

Signal Office Souther Div

Army Form C. 2118.

APPENDIX A

Place	Date	No of Hom Regd Msgs	Regd Msgs	Date	No of Msgs	Regd Msgs	Summary of Events and Information	Remarks and references to Appendices
SAND?	1	278	15	16	267	5		
	2	297	26	17	170	21		
	3	171	7	18	282	25		
	4	246	24	19	322	13		
	5	268	18	20	261	14		
	6	245	28	21	272	12		
	7	186	20	22	220	28		
	8	276	10	23	157	15		
	9	307	25	24	150	15		
	10	157	25	25	227	17		
	11	150	41	26	240	12		
	12	347	16	27	222	11		
	13	314	17	28	171	9		
	14	323	17	29	263	6		
	15	320	18	30	252	19		
				31	143	17		
					7849	550		

Army Form C. 2118.

WAR DIARY
or
INTELLIGENCE SUMMARY.
(Erase heading not required.)

Place	Date	Hour	Summary of Events and Information	Remarks and references to Appendices
Sand	1 to 30		Nothing of special interest to report. Training Classification of Battalion Signallers proceeded with very satisfactory results. The transfers of 55 men from Artillery were completed of whom about 50% had already been demobilised.	
	7		2 Lt. T.L. Dawson. R.E. Posted to 9 Corps Signal Co. 7/9/19	
			Appendix "A" shews the volume of Telegraph and D.R.L.S. traffic dealt with during the month.	

S.T. Julian
Major R.E.
Commanding Signal Co. R.E. Southern Division

Appendix 'A'

WAR DIARY
or
INTELLIGENCE SUMMARY. Signal Co. R.E. Southern Division

Army Form C. 2118.

(Erase heading not required.)

Instructions regarding War Diaries and Intelligence Summaries are contained in F. S. Regs., Part II. and the Staff Manual respectively. Title pages will be prepared in manuscript.

Place	Date	Hour	No of messages	No of Register Packets	Date	Summary of Events and Information No of messages	No of register Packets	Remarks and references to Appendices
Sand	1		203	20	19	44, 39	2, 12	
	2		215	13	20	244	12	
	3		257	27	21	165	22	
	4		323	15	22	65	22	
	5		258	7	23	279	28	
	6		188	21	24	376	15	
	7		134	6	25	280	26	
	8		314	24	26	233	18	
	9		263	21	27	210	18	
	10		277	18	28	207	9	
	11		290	17	29	37	13	
	12		258	17	30	134	34	
	13		253	42		191		
	14		67					
	15		320	26		6860	541	
	16		223	18				
	17		270	14				
	18		326	18				
			4439	324